"Listening for the Sound of the Genuine"

"Listening for the Sound of the Genuine:"

Race, Religion and Renewal in the Life of Rev. Dr. Paul Smith.

By Hildi Hendrickson

Gilquist Press
New York, New York

Contact the author at:
hildihendrickson@gmail.com

This edition was prepared for publication by
Ghost River Images
5350 East Fourth Street
Tucson, Arizona 85711
www.ghostriverimages.com

Title taken from Thurman, Howard, 1980. "The Sound of the Genuine" Baccalaureate Address, Spelman College. Jo Moore Stewart, ed. *The Spelman Messenger* Summer Vol. 96 (4): 14-15.

Cover design by
Hildi Hendrickson

Edited by
Matthew Daddona and Meredith Tennant

ISBN 978-0-9995680-0-2

Library of Congress Control Number: 2017916710

Printed in the United States of America
November 2017

Table of Contents

Acknowledgements

I extend my heartfelt thanks to:

Paul Smith for being who he is and for inspiring me to undertake this project; Fran Smith for her incisive wisdom, patience, and hospitality; The Smith family for their willingness to share important details in the story;

Necole Brown, Marc Burt, Sue Carlson, Pam Champion, Marvin Chandler, Portia Chandler, Krista Smith Clapp, Charles Clayman, Fred Davie, Nathan Dudley, Paula Francis, Ed Goldberg, Howie Hodges II, Brian Johnson, Jim Johnson, Marsha Larner, David Lewicki, Sam Murumba, Amy Neuner, Joanne Nurss, Ellen Oler, Kathleen Smith Randolph, Paula Francis, Frances Smith, Jeffrey Smith, Leonard Smith, Luther Smith, Jr., Marcia Smith, Bernard Streets, Dennis Suskind, Marlene Smith Wright, Mike Trautman, John Utendahl, Mercia Weyand, Leonard Wilkens, and the other friends, colleagues, and parishioners of Rev. Smith who shared their insights and experiences with me;

Ambassador Andrew Young and Rev. Marvin Chandler for their contributions;

Sue Carlson, Marcie Chanin, Beverly D'Angelo, Leslie Emmons, Bob Fuhlrodt, Helen Heinrich, Ray Heinrich, Andrew Hendrickson, Holly Hendrickson, Kibra Johannes, Yusuf Juwayeyi, Marilyn Kleinberg, Ginny Lanoil, Jessie Lanoil Edelman, Rebecca Harris Lee, Karen Lucic, Judy McKee, Linda McKee, Max McKee, Rick McKee, Eugenia Morrison, Mark Pires, Harriet Power, Gustavo Rodriguez, Louis Raveson, Mark Uriu, Jill Wilson, and others for thoughtful comments and conversation about various iterations of the manuscript;

Howie Hodges II, George Kennedy and Hyacinth Reneau for their assistance with publication details, Matthew Daddona and Meredith Tennant for editing and copyediting, and Michael White and Ghost River Images for production and printing;

LIU Brooklyn for travel funds in Spring 2015 and sabbatical leave in Spring 2016;

My husband, Andrew McKee, for his daily, weekly, monthly and yearly support and enthusiasm. Thank you for your belief, perseverance, patience, and good judgment as we have traveled along this path.

(Any errors, omissions or other problems that may be discovered in the text are my own and not a reflection on the contributions of any of these supporters.)

Author's Note

This is the life story of a man who has learned to confront and subdue the anger and sorrow he feels over the ongoing tragedy of our country's racial politics. Schooled in the ethics and techniques of the civil rights era, Rev. Dr. Paul Smith is a translator between estranged people, a courageous healer of hatred, a man of God whose ministry knows no bounds. His story can teach us how to be the kind of people we need to be in order to live in a better world.

After the fashion of his mentor, the visionary theologian Rev. Dr. Howard Thurman, Rev. Smith has created vital, multiracial congregations in four different cities over the course of a 56-year career. Laying bare his thoughts, experiences, and emotions, this energetic orator has engendered conversations about race, class, and culture that have stretched across much of the country east of the Mississippi. He literally introduced Dr. Martin Luther King, Jr. and Ambassador Andrew Young to each other in the late 1950s and went on to march with them in the 1960s.

But unlike many of his more famous friends from "the movement," Rev. Smith has continued that work in the pulpit and in the community, Sunday after Sunday, month after month, year after year. Dr. Paul, as he is often called, knows how to create the communal human experiences through which bigotry can be defused. For him, the front lines have often been in the congregation, the neighborhood, the police precinct, the boardroom, and the hospital. He has baptized, married, and eulogized people from all walks of life with equal concern and enthusiasm. Dr. Paul has overcome every type of boundary that might have separated him from his fellows. He has become a master mediator, and he can teach us something about how we can live together in understanding, equanimity, and grace.

As an anthropologist, I find in Dr. Paul someone who is like-minded in thought and deed, someone who believes as much as I do in the power of sustained human contact as the antidote to bigotry and ignorance. As capably as anyone in my profession, Dr. Paul practices the radical humility, deep listening, and agile translation that create understanding between peoples who know little of each other. The irony is that his work goes on between Americans who have many values and beliefs in common yet live in spheres so separate that they treat each other like strangers from other nations. Dr. Paul works in what anthropologist Victor Turner called the "liminal" spaces—the zones of transition and transformation between the well-worn social identities we settle into and defend. He knows, as I do, that these are places of risk, discovery, and joy. They are spiritual places where we need to spend time to fully appreciate our common humanity.

I first met Dr. Paul at a fund-raising dinner in 2001 at the university where I teach and where he was a trustee. After collaborating on projects like bringing Ambassador Andrew Young to campus to speak to students, I invited Rev. Smith to join me in teaching a senior seminar on nonviolence. Our rapport was such that we team-taught that course four times over the next several years. It was while teaching with him that I saw the impact his stories have on people. A well-practiced minister, he sees both the humor and the pain in the human experience and knows how to tell a good tale. Though I am a Buddhist myself, I attended his church in Brooklyn Heights on occasion and was invariably moved by being there. His openness to others' beliefs is one of the powerful qualities that first impressed me. His many other gifts include being a deep and ardent listener, a compassionate and loyal friend, a born collaborator, and a searcher after God. Over the years we have known each other, I have had occasion to feel the effects of his pastoring firsthand, both in times of joy and in grief.

In this book, I seek to preserve and share a quintessentially American story. Dr. Paul has given me access to an extraordinary collection of writing, photographs, and memorabilia. I draw from more than 70 personal journals in which he has recorded his thoughts since 1957. As much as possible, this narrative is built around transcribed interviews with Rev. Smith, his family, friends, students, colleagues, and parishioners. It is my hope that this book will carry his wisdom to all who seek strength to continue fighting for justice and equality.

Introduction

If race lives on today, it does not live on because we have inherited it from our forebears of the seventeenth century or the eighteenth or nineteenth, but because we continue to create it today ... Nothing handed down from the past could keep race alive if we did not constantly reinvent and re-ritualize it to fit our own terrain.

Karen Fields and Barbara Fields, 2012[1]

On March 9, 1965 when he boarded a plane bound for Selma, Alabama, Paul Smith knew he was headed for a direct confrontation with hatred. Like most people in the country, he had heard that nonviolent protesters attempting to march from Selma to the state capital in Montgomery had been subjected to brutal violence. National television programming two days earlier had been interrupted by news footage showing well-dressed, pious marchers being beaten to the ground and tear-gassed by baton-wielding state and local law enforcement officers. The raw brutality directed at disciplined and resolute citizens shocked Americans from Main Street to Washington, DC. Yet Smith did not hesitate when Rev. Dr. Martin Luther King, Jr. sent telegrams on Monday asking clergy to join him in the march to Montgomery. The 30-year-old black minister with an active congregation, a wife, and two young children knew he had to answer Dr. King's call.

Typically for him, Smith did not go alone. He was leading a group of white midwestern ministers, most of whom had never before taken so public a political stand. His colleague, Carl Dudley, was the exception. Two years earlier, Rev. Dudley had invited Smith to move to St. Louis to co-pastor a historically black Presbyterian church downtown. The two men were accustomed to attracting attention; their collaboration confounded racist expectations every day. They were in the habit of fighting for their political beliefs.

This time, however, they were walking onto a battlefield where forces defending the legacy of slavery in America were in head-to-head confrontation with forces demanding change. On the fringes of the thousands who had come to march for justice that day were furious white vigilantes looking for a fight. The fact that racist violence had been so blatantly perpetrated in Selma two days earlier apparently emboldened others to do the same. The mere sight of black and white companions walking side by side inflamed a mob that started to close ranks around them. The next few minutes changed Paul Smith's life, and when the march to Montgomery finally reached its destination days later, it changed American history.

Since 1965, we have learned a great deal about some of the leaders of those transformative events. Historians like Taylor Branch have written dozens of volumes and tens of thousands of pages about the rise of Dr. King and his movement for change. Among King's lieutenants, Congressmen John Lewis, Ambassador Andrew Young, and singer/activist Harry Belafonte have written vivid accounts of their experiences at Selma and their political lives before and after that time.

What is less well known, however, is the part ordinary people played—what brought them to the firing line, what happened to them, and how their lives were changed thereafter. Presidents and legislators, journalists and judges cannot create social transformation on their own. Without millions of unassuming foot soldiers willing to put their beliefs on the line over and over again, there can be no movement for the famous generals to lead. The same kind of idealism, tenacity, and commitment is needed today. Events like the marching of defiant white nationalists in Charlottesville, Virginia in August 2017 make plain that racial bigotry is still alive and well in America.

What makes some ideas powerful and convincing enough to change society as a whole? How and when do some values come to be shared and acted upon by millions of people unknown to each other and far from the halls of government? How does the torch of justice get carried across the decades between the events when history is most consciously being made?

This book is about one of the many who never gave up working for political and social change. It explores the ways that one man's family, church, education, and community helped him become capable of deeply inspiring those around him who need help to fully believe in justice, truth, and democracy.

This is a minister's story, but it could be the story of a teacher, a social worker, a lawyer, or a police officer. It is one story among countless others that need to be told and retold, now more than ever, as the best of America's shared values are under overt, public attack. The moment is ripe for discovering and rediscovering how to use protest to create change, to be emotionally resilient over the long haul, to use introspection to change ourselves, and to bring new generations together in a common struggle. This narrative reminds and educates us that it is the deep-down, principled honesty—"the sound of the genuine"[2]—that all of us must seek in ourselves and in others. Following Paul Smith's example, we can learn how to cultivate the genuine in ourselves, to recognize it in others, and to have the courage to follow wherever it leads.

1

The new black man refuses to speak of love without justice and power.

James Cone, 1969[3]

Answering Dr. King's Call

As Director of Race and Religion for the Presbytery of St. Louis, Rev. Smith led the St. Louis delegation to Selma on March 9, 1965. Most of the men traveling in Rev. Smith's group were white ministers from places like Ferguson, Missouri, a suburb that has recently become synonymous with renewed racial strife. Typically for Smith but atypically for his companions, they were flouting authority in making the trip. The governing boards of their congregations had told them they could lose their jobs if they went to join Dr. King at the protests. Though King was gaining national prominence, his refusal to stop staging public protests was causing major consternation at the highest levels of government.

Smith had met Dr. King and thoroughly understood the righteousness of his cause. As has so often happened in his life, his certainty and enthusiasm carried others forward. Even some who did not go on the journey showed they knew what kind of support the travellers would need. As Smith recalls:

I remember our going to Ferguson the night before we were to fly to Selma. At the end of dinner our host, who was one of the families of Ferguson Presbyterian Church participating in our exchange program, said to us: "We unfortunately will not be able to join you and our minister on the trip to Selma. However, we want you to know you have our spiritual, financial and prayerful support should you need us. Do what you believe is right for everyone and know that we have lawyers primed to come to Alabama should you be arrested."

Dr. King's telegram, which had gone out through the National Council of Churches network across the country, constituted a direct appeal to clergy. He made a powerful case:

No American is without responsibility. All are involved in the sorrow that rises from Selma to contaminate every crevice of our national life ... I call, therefore, on clergy of all faiths, representatives of every part of the country, to join me for a ministers' march to Montgomery on Tuesday morning, March 9th. In this way, all America will testify to the fact that the struggle in Selma is for the survival of democracy everywhere in our land.[4]

Having decided to answer Dr. King's call, Rev. Smith and his colleagues quickly learned there were no seats on the regularly scheduled flights to Selma that day. Roughly 800 clergy from 22 states were rushing to Alabama to put themselves on the line for justice.[5] Fortunately, Archbishop Joseph Ritter of St. Louis Catholic Church called August Anheuser Busch, Jr., a scion of the local beer company, and asked for help. In a matter of hours, Paul and his colleagues were bound for Alabama in "Auggie" Busch's DC-9. All told, some 40 ministers were aboard. Everyone knew they were on a collision course with the fury of the white South.

What transpired that March at Selma is now seen to have been a watershed for the whole nation. Though people could not know it at the time, the complex, long-term, and multistranded reality of the "movement" was reaching a crescendo. The efforts and sacrifice of countless volunteers over many years had finally won the full attention of the nation, the White House, and the press. What everyone witnessed thanks to the media was that the contrast between the resolute marchers and furious club-swinging law enforcement personnel was undeniable under the floodlights of countrywide and international public attention. Ordinary people and Congressional legislators, governors and police officers, black people and white—everyone who cared about freedom and justice—could see that change could no longer wait.

The political activity at Selma was built upon the outcomes of decades of organized resistance, sacrifice, failure, and triumph. Twenty years earlier, groups like the Congress of Racial Equality (CORE), made up of black and white, women and men, had formed to undertake nonviolent protest in the name of equality. The earthshaking 1954 Brown v. Board of Education Supreme Court decision became the legal foundation for making the "separate but equal" approach to public education illegal.

In 1955, 14-year-old Chicagoan Emmett Till, on summer vacation in Money, Mississippi, was killed for whistling at a white woman. Years later, the woman said he had not deserved his fate. The boy was taken from his relatives' home during the night and beaten until he died. His body was strapped to a piece of mechanical equipment and thrown into a river. The horrible condition of the boy's face as he lay in his open casket caused national revulsion. Not long afterward, Rosa Parks and others refused to give up their seats on city buses in Montgomery, Alabama. The successful Montgomery Bus Boycott was accomplished by working women in particular who were willing to walk to work through a long, cold winter.

In 1957 after the Boycott, Dr. King and others founded the Southern Christian Leadership Council (SCLC), one of many influential activist organizations. In 1960, younger leadership with their own ideas about nonviolent resistance formed the Students Non-violent Coordinating Committee (SNCC). Sometimes together and at other times at odds, these groups planned increasingly organized campaigns of civil disobedience and nonviolence around the South, creating legal challenges to discriminatory laws. In 1961, CORE launched the Freedom Riders campaign to force the integration of the interstate transportation system. At bus stations in cities across the South, outright murderous violence awaited those attempting to integrate national bus lines. Some of the worst violence occurred in Birmingham, Alabama, which Dr. King characterized as "probably the most segregated city in America." In the late 1950s and early '60s, the bombing of black homes and churches had become such regular events that some called the city "Bombingham." Eugene "Bull" Connor, the city's Public Safety Commissioner, became legendary in the region for his brutal treatment of local and national activists.

After a young John F. Kennedy was elected in 1960 to succeed President Dwight Eisenhower, free access to the vote became a par-ticularly active battlefront in the struggle for equal rights. Systematic efforts by activists to register black voters in cities and small towns all over the South resulted in even more terrible violence. One of the worst cases occurred when CORE workers Michael Schwerner and James Chaney, along with summer volunteer Andrew Goodman, went missing while assisting the voter registration campaign in Mississippi, a state notorious for its segregation and the subjugation of black citi-zens. When the young men's buried bodies were found days later, the fact that they had been murdered for their earnest and lawful political work horrified the nation.

A partial accounting of events in 1963 alone shows how one event after another relentlessly shocked the national conscience. The year opened with newly elected Governor Wallace of Alabama declaring in a public address his belief in "segregation now, segregation tomor-row, segregation forever." That spring, the Birmingham Campaign of daily demonstrations against segregation got underway, organized by Rev. Fred Shuttlesworth and the SCLC. In April, after Dr. King was arrested and jailed at one protest, he wrote and published his famous "Letter From a Birmingham Jail," articulating the movement's intention to not comply with unjust laws and decrying the absence of support for the justice movement from white clergy. In May, Bull Connor's decision to use attack dogs and fire hoses against peacefully protesting teenaged girls in bobby socks made the international news and caused a national uproar. On June 11, Governor Wallace barred the doors of the University of Alabama in a failed attempt to keep black students from enrolling.

The very next day, World War II veteran and NAACP voting rights organizer Medgar Evers was gunned down in front of his family by a white supremacist in the driveway of his Mississippi home. (It took 30 years for his killer to be brought to justice.) In August, the nonviolent and intensely hopeful March on Washington for Jobs and Freedom brought masses of people and impassioned speakers to the Reflecting Pool between the Washington Monument and the Lincoln Memorial. A few weeks later, President Kennedy still had to use the National Guard to enforce the integration of Birmingham city schools. On September 15, four little girls were killed in a bombing at the 16th Street Baptist Church in Birmingham. Then in November, Kennedy himself was shot and killed.

All this was part of the lead-up to Selma a little over a year later. After the 16th Street Baptist Church bombing, voters' rights campaigns and demonstrations intensified in Alabama. Selma was chosen as a point of concentration for protest, though activists had seen it as a hopeless cause.[6] In 1964 and early 1965, local activists like Amelia Boynton Robinson helped to organize thousands around Selma who were arrested at nonviolent demonstrations and jailed. Workshops helped train activists how to endure taunting, intimidation, physical violence, and jailing. Ordinary people learned to take a toothbrush to demonstrations, knowing they were headed to jail, sometimes for days before they could be bailed out. Though incarceration was an especially frightening prospect for law-abiding people of color, prayer and rousing song helped keep their fear at bay.

It was the particularly wrenching death of one of these big-hearted protesters that set the first attempt to march from Selma to Mont-

Downtown Selma looking toward the Edmund Pettus Bridge. (Photo by author)

gomery in motion. On the evening of February 18, 1965, Jimmie Lee Jackson, a local church deacon in his mid-twenties, walked out of a church with his family to demonstrate for voter's rights in nearby Marion, Alabama. In what was clearly a staged attack, a mass of state troopers and auxiliary police told the marchers to turn back and then set upon them as the streetlights suddenly went dark. An angry white crowd looked on as dozens of people were seriously beaten. When the violence fell on his 82-year-old grandfather, Jackson attempted to pull his family to safety in a nearby café. Pursued inside by state troopers, Jackson's mother was attacked as she tried to defend her father. When Jackson stepped up to shield his mother, two troopers set upon him, one of whom shot him twice in the stomach. Jackson's beating continued as he lay on the ground outside after he tried to escape the café. The local and national press spread news of the wanton brutality the next morning.

When Jackson died in a local hospital eight days later, complications from the gunshot wounds were given as the official cause of death. However, in 1979, one of the black doctors at the hospital, Dr. William Dinkins, revealed to researchers for the "Eyes on the Prize" television documentary that Jackson had been recovering well when two white doctors took him back into surgery.[7] He protested but the other doctors insisted. In surgery, Dr. Dinkins noticed that Jackson appeared to be getting too much anesthetic and told the anesthesiologist to give him more oxygen. The other doctor defiantly declared that Jackson needed more anesthetic, and a few minutes later, Jackson stopped breathing.

Even without knowing about the final insults to which Jackson had been subjected, activists in the region were stunned and infuriated by the nature and extent of the violence in Marion. Only a few days later, after large funeral ceremonies had been held for Jackson in Marion and Selma, James Bevel of the SCLC, among others, called for marchers to take their outrage directly to Gov. Wallace in Montgomery. Bevel, John Lewis, and local minister Hosea Williams were among those chosen to lead the marchers to the capital. Local Sheriff Jim Clark and Major John Cloud of the state troopers led the forces that awaited them on the other side of the bridge.

Today, it is chilling to walk from the foot of the Edmund Pettus Bridge up toward the unknown. Named for a Confederate general, like so many features in the Southern landscape, the steeply arching iron bridge soars over the Alabama River dozens of feet below. You can see nothing of what is on the other side until you reach the very crest of the bridge, at which point you are completely exposed. On March 7, 1965, when about six hundred marchers first attempted to cross, what came into view was a veritable army of state troopers with billy clubs, whips, and gas masks backed up by sheriff's deputies, many of them on horseback. The protesters sang and prayed before quietly refusing to disperse. Fatefully, Major Cloud and Sheriff Clark ordered their men to advance. Their forces fell en masse upon the unresisting protesters in a clamor of swinging whips and charging horses. Witnesses say that protesters screamed and dodged blows, while a white crowd behind the troopers cheered as the beatings rained down.

John Lewis, then Chairman of SNCC, was the first to go down under vicious blows to the head. Middle-aged Amelia Boynton, the first black woman to run for office in the state, was knocked unconscious to the sidewalk. Men, women, and children scrambled to get out of the way of the fists, clubs, and horses until tear gas enveloped them all. The marchers retreated and were chased all the way back to Brown Chapel AME (African Methodist Episcopal) Church and other places of refuge. After the melee was over, more than 90 people needed treatment at nearby medical facilities.[8] Images of what came to be known as "Bloody Sunday" were broadcast and published around the country and around the world.

Preparing for the second attempt to cross the bridge on Tuesday, March 9, everyone had seen the kind of physical punishment that almost certainly awaited. Still, several thousand willing volunteers, black people now joined by many more whites, lined up two-by-two behind Dr. King who had been on his way back to Selma when the first march commenced. Resolutely, the ranks mounted the bridge again to face a greatly expanded sea of law enforcers as well as dozens more reporters. It was about 3:00 in the afternoon. This time, though, as the marchers paused near the far end of the bridge, law enforcement was told to draw back. King had been made acutely aware that by setting off down the highway he would be for the first time violating a federal order, not a local one, and so he had been convinced not to cross the bridge. Surprising everyone, he abruptly told the marchers to turn back and return to the church. Witnesses say that the masses of protesters at the front of the line met those farther back like opposing walls of water.

—⁂—

This was the confusion into which Rev. Smith and his St. Louis fellow clergy plunged. Due to the large number of flights trying to get to Selma that day, their plane had been diverted to a small airfield outside of town. It appears that the group arrived in the early afternoon, just about the time that King was leading the "turnaround" on the bridge; historian Taylor Branch mentions "two new planeloads of clergy from the Midwest"[9] arriving at that point. Smith remembers lining up to march but not being able to get near the bridge due to the crush and confusion. So his group went to Brown Chapel, about ten blocks away. The chapel, like so many other churches in the South, had become

Brown Chapel AME (African Methodist Episcopal) Church, Selma, Alabama. (Photo by author)

a central meeting place for those gathering around Selma to mobilize for social action. Smith remembers King speaking, the masses of people there, and the sense of danger in the air. "Everyone went straight to the church. It was packed, hot; there was no A/C. You were wondering whether somebody might throw a bomb in there. There was no security sweep of the church or the areas downtown."

Inside, King was attempting to shore up his forces and mollify SNCC leaders in particular who felt betrayed by the aborted march. Some were angry that it was only with more white people in their ranks that violence appeared to have been averted. Others expressed gratitude for the renewed forces and the outside support. Andrew Young of the SCLC told the group that there hadn't been much choice. After the morning's court order was issued prohibiting them from carrying on the march, "if we had run into that police line, they would have beaten us up with court approval."[10] As was usual for these gatherings, the afternoon wound down with more speakers and attempts to buoy the group with song.

There was more mayhem to come in Selma that evening, however. Smith and Dudley were headed to their own trial by fire as they walked out to find their plane. As colleagues and friends, the two men were used to working and socializing together. But on a day crackling with racial tension, there were some who didn't like seeing a black man and a white man walking together, for any reason. Smith and Dudley soon became aware that a hostile crowd was gathering around them.

> We were about 150 yards from the church. Carl and I looked up and we were being surrounded by about 50 or more angry white people, mostly men, who began shouting at us and calling us names. They referred to Carl as an "N" lover as they got closer and closer to us. There was some minor pushing and shoving, but Carl and I had had nonviolence training, which was a prerequisite for clergy like us who were directly involved in the movement. I was not terribly frightened at first, but as they got closer to us, it became clear that Carl and I could be harmed.

Frustrated that they could not get a rise out of their victims, the tension in the crowd rose. Finally, one man's hatred boiled over, and he spat in Paul's face. For Rev. Smith, it was a life-changing moment. He was furious.

> For one moment Carl froze because he knew I had been violated. As well as we knew each other, he had no idea how I would respond to [that]. And in a nanosecond I

thought to myself, "I am going to die or get hurt badly because I am going to knock this guy in the mouth!"

In the next millisecond, Smith saw his wife and children's faces before him and realized he couldn't give in to his anger. His second daughter had been born on February 22, just a few weeks before. Heeding their training, the ministers knew they could not fight back. Smith says they looked at each other, turned, and ran. The laughter of the thugs followed them; someone said, "Look at those niggers run."

Dudley later wrote, "Like soldiers surviving combat, this encounter with hatred and possible harm has sealed our friendship as brothers for the rest of our lives."[12]

It is fortunate that the two did not try to stand their ground, because that very night, a white Unitarian minister from Boston felt the full force of white Southern bigotry on the same back streets of Selma. Like the St. Louis group, Rev. James Reeb and more than fifty other Unitarians had arrived too late to join the attempt at the bridge. Reeb and others decided to stay the night and were soon welcomed into a black restaurant nearby. It was when they re-emerged after dark that they were accosted by several white men armed with clubs. While two colleagues were kicked and punched in the face, Reeb was clubbed in the head so violently that the injuries killed him several days later. That evening, Dr. King spoke to a crowd at Brown Chapel, thanking the remaining out-of-town clergy for their efforts and asking for prayers for Rev. Reeb and his fellows.[13] By the next morning, President Johnson and the nation had heard that a white minister had been savaged in Selma at the hands of white thugs, and another wave of shock and outrage swept across the land.

Meanwhile, Smith had made his way back to the airfield to discover the pilots had a new concern. There were rumors that there might have been attempts to sabotage the airplanes by putting sand in the gas tanks. While Smith waited for the pilot to look over the Busch plane, the sky blackened with what looked like a severe thunderstorm. They managed to take off but were quickly ground in Birmingham by the weather. Smith then found three lawyers from a Presbyterian church in Alton, Illinois, just across the Mississippi from St. Louis, who had to be in court the next morning. Together, they rented a car, intending to drive the 600 miles back home.

With lawless rage thick in the air, however, just being black and white men together in a car was dangerous. As they drove through the dark rural landscape that night, they heard on the radio about the attack on James Reeb and the other Unitarian ministers. Smith admits that "it was the only time I think I was literally afraid of being in the South because the KKK was on the loose and showing up in strange ways trying to intimidate us. En route to St. Louis, we were not protected by the National Guard who [were later] sent to Selma by the President."

As it neared midnight, Paul asked his companions to drop him off at the home of a family he knew in Athens, Alabama, near the Alabama-Tennessee border. It is quite possible that that decision spared them all confrontation, injury, and even death. They knew that they were completely alone on the road in hostile territory where anyone might be looking for an opportunity to let loose their murderous feelings. As Paul walked up to the darkened house his companions were anxious, wondering who would open the door when there was so much to fear in the dark. But the residents quickly recognized Rev. Paul and drew him in to safety. All of the men eventually made their way home unscathed.

Smith learned that day that hand-to-hand combat on the front lines of the racial struggle was too dangerous a place for him as a husband and father. He had felt the full force of his anger and knew he could not afford to test it again. Smith said later, "I told them they were going to have to get me a desk job!" But he had no regrets. In his journal the next day, he wrote: "3/10/65 No man is an outsider in this world because we all belong here. In comment to being called "outside" agitators in the racial strife in Selma, Alabama. Outside agitators are necessary to stir the consciences of the people."

That momentum played out. The third and successful attempt to cross the Pettus Bridge and march to Montgomery came 13 days later on March 21. By that time, court battles and high-tension political maneuvering by King, President Lyndon Johnson, and other government officials had resolved in the marchers' favor. Critical to this was the speech given by Johnson on the evening of March 15 to a joint session of Congress. In the wake of the appalling events at Selma, Johnson made the case for voting rights legislation before a huge national TV audience, saying,

> ... about this there can and should be no argument. Every American citizen must have an equal right to vote ... What happened in Selma is part of a far larger movement which reaches into every section and State of America. It is the effort of American Negroes to secure for themselves the full blessings of American life. Their cause must be our cause too. Because it is not just Negroes, but really it is all of us, who must overcome the crippling legacy of bigotry and injustice.[14]

Everyone was stunned when Johnson ended his address by saying, "And we *shall* overcome."

The marchers set out for the third and final time from Selma about a week later, with federal troops and the National Guard in place to ensure that the march could proceed without violence. The activists crossed the bridge successfully and endured a rainy and uncomfortable four-day trek to Montgomery, where they were joined by thousands of others. In front of the imposing state capital building and former capital of the Confederacy at the crest of a hill, Dr. King spoke, famously asking how long people of color would have to wait to freely exercise their right to vote and participate in the political process. Black entertainers including Harry Belafonte, Sidney Poitier, and Dick Gregory roused the crowd to heights of joy and hope. However, even the euphoria of that day was marred by news of violence. That night, Ku Klux Klan members killed a middle-aged Michigan woman named Viola Liuzzo who was at the wheel of her car on the Jefferson Davis highway. Her crime had been helping to ferry back to Selma some of the stalwart marchers who had finally made it to Montgomery.

While pieces of civil rights legislation had been passed in 1957, 1960, 1963, and 1964, the most explicit and powerful piece of voting legislation of all—the Voting Rights Act—was passed by Congress in August following these events in Selma. The Act prohibited state and local entities from devising discriminatory obstacles to registration and voting. It also laid out a process of government oversight in parts of the country where such methods had been the norm. Thereafter, people in designated states and cities began to register and vote, many for the first time in their lives.

Remarkably, Rev. Paul Smith, representing the Presbytery of St. Louis, was in the room at the White House the day President Johnson signed this most consequential bill into law. Statesman John Lewis, who was also present that day, has written that it "represented a high point in modern America, probably the nation's finest hour in terms of civil rights … It was certainly the last act for the movement as I knew it. Something was born in Selma during the course of that year, but something died there too. The road of nonviolence had essentially run out. Selma was the last act."[15]

Only a few short days later, the largest-scale rioting ever seen in this country broke out in the Watts neighborhood of LA. Thirty-four died, hundreds were injured, and thousands arrested. In 1965, Lewis saw this coming because so many deep problems remained. "The lack of concern on the part of the American public and the lack of concern and courage of the federal government breed bitterness and frustration … Where lack of jobs, intolerable housing, police brutality and other frustrating conditions exist, it is possible that violence and massive street demonstrations may develop … "[16]

Though there have been monumental breakthroughs, like having a black President in the White House, many of the same deep, structural problems continue to plague us. Levels of economic inequality have ballooned to new heights. Ordinary Americans are still fighting to find affordable housing and decent jobs. After the death of Michael Brown in Ferguson, Missouri, in 2014, protesters were back in the streets bringing media attention to the unending stream of black deaths at the hands of law enforcement. The election of President Trump has emboldened new generations of racist and xenophobic extremists to publicly proclaim their views. John Lewis, now a senior Congressman from Georgia, surely sees the terrible irony that his exact same statement could be made today, more than fifty years later.

Even the principles enshrined in the Voting Rights Act are being debated anew. In 2013, a conservative Supreme Court greatly weakened the Act by removing the federal oversight requirement for voting districts that had historically discriminated against some of their citizens. In the Shelby County v. Holder decision, Chief Justice John Roberts wrote for the majority that the extraordinary measures enacted to address the "insidious and pervasive evil" of racial discrimination in voting were unnecessary, since "the conditions that originally justified these measures no longer characterize voting in the covered jurisdictions."[17]

Sadly, he has already been proven wrong. Since that key Supreme Court decision, lawmakers have unabashedly created obstacles to exercising political power in Texas, North Carolina, Alabama, and other states.[18] Stricter voter ID laws have been enacted; days, times, and methods for voting have been diminished rather than expanded; new maps drawn with almost mathematical precision to disempower some while benefiting others have eclipsed the gerrymandering of voting districts, which both parties have been guilty of. Meanwhile, the Trump administration has taken steps to curtail illegal voting, a scourge that has never been proven to exist. As was recently observed, "it would appear that the lessons of Selma have yet to be learned."[19]

2

There was something wonderful and magical about the way Granny listened. The people she listened to always seemed restored and refreshed. Little did I realize at the time that this would be her wonderful legacy to me ...

Paul Smith, 1998[20]

On Granny's Porch

The roots of Rev. Paul Smith's confidence and compassion run wide and deep. He counts his grandmother, his parents, and early ministers among those who helped set him on a successful path. Dedicated teachers, both black and white, took an interest in him at college. From then on, he was guided by some of the most celebrated of the country's African American minister-scholars. He remains a member of two of the oldest and most deeply rooted of black men's fraternities. He has attracted brilliant colleagues throughout his professional career with whom he has enthusiastically collaborated. His two closest mentors and colleagues have been men of prodigious intelligence and professional reach—Rev. Dr. Howard Thurman and statesman Andrew Young. He turns to the Bible as a profound source of ideas and inspiration and is married to a woman of wide experience and incisive wisdom.

Smith knows what his strengths are and sees them as gifts from God. These include his ability to listen deeply, to speak publicly from his heart, and to connect with people across hostile territory. He is a sure and enthusiastic leader, yet he allows others to shine. His brand of ministry is open and inclusive; he is not dogmatic and does not proselytize. Lifelong habits of prayer, meditation, and writing have allowed him to develop uncommon self-awareness and humility.

Smith's family has multicultural roots like so many of those whose ancestors were brought here in slavery. In our country's particular history of racial classification, this makes him "black." He was raised within the African American world. But in his professional life he has taken more opportunities than most to cross perceived racial boundaries. He has made it his business to talk about race and to talk to white people in particular about race. In the end, he has had profound experiences and deep relationships that transcend the illusions of racial difference.

Odie Wingo Overby, South Bend, Indiana, 1940.

Smith sees his mother's mother, Mrs. Odie Wingo Overby or "Granny," as the lodestar in his early life. Everyone old enough to have known Odie remembers her as a forceful personality, a life-long churchgoer, an independent and hardworking woman, and an attentive mother and grandmother. Born in 1883, she lived into her nineties, survived three husbands, raised two daughters, and was an active force in the daily lives of nine grandchildren and sixteen great-grandchildren.

Two of Smith's cousins have been able to trace Odie's family back to the Civil War period in the extreme southwest corner of Kentucky. Odie Ballard Wingo was born in the small town of Cuba in Graves County, Kentucky. In 1851, when the mighty Illinois Central Railroad began connecting Chicago to the South, the rails bypassed Cuba[21] while bringing prosperity to other towns in the region. Nearby Wingo appears to have been founded around 1854 by a man named Jerman Wingo who allowed the railroad to run its tracks across his land.[22] Wingo began selling goods there and the town that coalesced eventually took his name.

The fact that Odie's family shared that name is not an accident. The best available evidence suggests that Odie's father Ferdinand (Paw Paw) was named Wingo because Jerman was his father.[23] The family has located public records that show an enslaved woman named Maria (or Mirah) was the mother of Ferdinand and his older brother George. While Jerman was married to a white woman with whom he had eleven other children, it appears that he took responsibility for Ferdinand and his brother.

Great-grandson Bernard Streets relates that Odie's mother Nancy Wingo, known as Mammy, talked about this.

> Mammy Wingo told me Paw Paw's father was his owner and that his father always looked out after him and his siblings as best he could. She said Paw Paw is a "true Wingo" and that his surname was taken because he was his white father's son and not simply because he was the slave, [a] piece of property and just tacked on the owner's name. Mammy often stated that Paw Paw

was "blood kin" of the Wingos.

Graves County oral history provides some corroboration. "As Kentucky came into the Union as a slaveholding state, Mr. and Mrs. [Jerman] Wingo could own slaves and had several. Many of them took his name and were willed land when he died. Even after they were freed, many of them refused to leave Mr. Wingo."

Received family wisdom supports the view that there was a surprising level of mutual respect and sociability among at least some of Smith's forbears. Streets recalls Mammy saying that every summer, the entire Wingo clan, "white, colored, Indian, and all mixtures would gather for a kinfolks' picnic." Mammy and Odie further asserted that Ferdinand was directly related to a Cherokee chief named Wingo—this may have been none other than Jerman Wingo himself. Rev. Smith says he knew his granny was part Cherokee but does not remember her ever going into the details of her ancestry.

When Odie was growing up, her parents ran a boarding house somewhere in the environs of Cuba and Wingo, perhaps on land inherited from Jerman Wingo. Eventually, the family moved to the popular Kentucky spa town of Dawson Springs where their successful "Wingo House" launched the family into the middle class. The inn attracted wealthy people of color who came to enjoy the salubrious effects of the local hot springs. Bernard Streets was told that business was good.

> Our great-grandparents had a small staff of housekeepers, yardmen, kitchen helpers, and a wagon driver who would go to the railroad station there and collect the guests and transport them to the guesthouse. Paw Paw Ferd was a gourmet chef, known widely for his tasty cuisine creations ...
> Mammy was the business manager and supervisor of staff, as well as the bookkeeper. She taught herself accounting and obviously was good at it, because other establishments hired her to officially audit their books. She told me that the other business owners trusted her

work and paid her well. She said to me, "Bernard, these quality white folks never called me by my first name. They always addressed me as, 'Mrs. Wingo.'"

Remarkably, a diary written by Odie when she was 18 years old has survived for more than a century. It constitutes a unique window into the life of Rev. Smith's most influential ancestor. Some of the first entries written in December 1901 give a sense of her preoccupations and her buoyant spirit: [24, 25]

… arose 15 to 7 o'clock dressed & cleaned up the house ate breakfast & left for school thinking this was examination day left my book at home to my surprise Miss Lou made Carrie & I go back home & get them. *Mailed Ed Holland letter Willie gave me a tablet for examination Oh; Diary he is the most adorable fellow Diary I am as happy as a lark & Pearl says she is as happy as a jay.*
    B. Wingo

Dec 5 *Diary my mind is wandering Odie says it is all about Mr. Lockhart though it isn't true Diary just wait until school is out then I will break the news to you* we are going up to Odie's to practice when I come home I will be ready for C.M. I will see you again
    B.

Dec 6 weather cloudy
arose & dressed for school & Carrie was so long about coming I had to go after her on our way to school met Mr. Duke had a few words with *him wonder why Burnett doesn't write? How glad I am to see this snow I have been playing snowball isn't it fine sport Pearl? I dreamed I was making love with Mr. Mallery will it ever come true? No never; well I don't know*
    B.

The three most common subjects mentioned in the diary are letter writing, "going to town," and meeting the railroad trains. Presumably, much of this hustle and bustle revolved around guests in her parents' house. Odie writes of exchanging letters, visits, gifts, and photographs with over 100 people in the course of the six-month diary. She writes most often about her parents, aunts and uncles, and her grandmother, but fifty-eight other people are mentioned by name multiple times. Another sixty individuals are mentioned once. Sixteen different ministers are named in the entries. She mentions twelve girls who must have been relatives or friends.

Odie mentions towns like Hopkinsville, Paducah, Madisonville, Mayfield, and Cadiz, which are within an eighty-mile radius of where she was born and raised. However, she also writes about more distant places including Louisville, Chicago, Atlanta, and Denver. This suggests that Odie had awareness of and/or communication with people across a broad expanse of the American Midwest.

In addition to household chores, Odie's responsibilities included helping her mother with sewing, washing, and ironing. It is likely that at least some of this work was for the boarders who were staying at the house. She also apparently worked for wages at a local hotel. She attended school and church and had a busy social life including regular "prayer," "literary," "society," and "watch" meetings.

The young Miss Wingo also had time for leisure. Among the pastimes Odie mentions are reading; singing and playing music; playing checkers, dominoes, and croquet; looking at magazines; and going walking with friends and family. Twice, she writes about having her fortune told. Odie and her friends sat for at least two photographic portraits. She mentions two popular novels by name—*Thelma* and *Two Orphans*. She was particularly excited by the railroad; she mentions trains or train personnel more than a dozen times in a few short months. Odie slips easily into a distinctive argot when she talks about the dashing young men who worked on the rails. She calls them "the kids," and "the Dining Car boys." She obviously gets a thrill out of "cutting a dash with the R.R. boys."

Odie Wingo (seated at left), Dawson Springs, Kentucky, 1899.

Most people in western Kentucky during the later nineteenth century were farmers with small-scale holdings. Whites outnumbered blacks by about six to one in 1870.[26] The center of Kentucky's slave economy at that point was far to the east in the farmlands between Lexington and Louisville. Kentuckians fought on both sides of the Civil War, with many black soldiers serving on the Union side. Yet after the war, many whites sharply disagreed about the federal government's power to abolish slavery altogether. Due to resistance from slaveholders in the state, the 13th Amendment was not ratified in Kentucky, and slavery continued to be legal for decades. This left the legal status of formerly enslaved people undefined for many years.[27] In fact, rather stunningly, the 13th, 14th, and 15th Amendments were not formally ratified in Kentucky until 1976.[28]

Despite this, people of color in Kentucky began to claim their voting rights and to secure positions in business and government after the war. Black people began to sit on juries, to become doctors and lawyers in small but significant numbers, and to hold public office. There was a black city councilman in Hopkinsville between 1895 and 1907, and "others ... served as deputy sheriff, county coroner, and county physician."[29] Whites and blacks attended school together at Berea College, sat together in church, worked side by side in the coalmines, and lived in the same neighborhoods in Louisville.

However, this season of moderation was short-lived. As black people moved out of the South, the proportion of black to white in the state population declined to 13 percent in 1900.[30] From that point on, four out of five families, black and white, lived in rural rather than urban areas. "An intense provincialism" is said to have prevailed in Kentucky at the end of the nineteenth century. Coupled with this was a rise in lawlessness and vigilante-style violence against people of color, Jews, foreigners, and whites with conflicting political views.[31]

There is some evidence of overtly racist violence in places close to Odie's home. An article published in the *New York Times* reported in 1896, "All Mayfield Under Arms: Excitement over the Kentucky Race War."[32] A black resident had been lynched, provoking several hundred black people from surrounding towns to take up arms and began to converge on Mayfield just before Christmas. Wingo is mentioned as one of the places where "the negroes had massed ... 250 in number, and ... every one had some sort of weapon." As the news of these armed gatherings spread, the white population responded by barricading their homes and passing out weapons. A special train was organized to bring white reinforcements from Fulton to Mayfield.

The *Times* reported the next day that three people had been killed and several houses burned down. But to call what occurred a "race war" seems overblown. One of the dead was a black man who, sadly, had simply stumbled into the conflict. In the end, it seems it was possible for cooler heads, both black and white, to prevail.

> Mayfield, KY. December 24. Fears of further race troubles are rapidly passing away. At a mass meeting last night the petition, signed by over 100 Negroes, asking for peace, was read. The excitement was appeased and many of the armed citizens and volunteers from surrounding towns returned to their homes ...
> Will Suett, the negro killed yesterday morning at the railroad station, had just returned from St. Louis to spend Christmas at home. His death was declared unprovoked, and the white citizens are now raising a fund to support his aged mother.[33]

Though Kentucky became increasingly known for its violence after the turn of the century, Odie says virtually nothing to suggest how racial conflict affected her and her family. In one entry, she mentions a friend who has to leave "because she can't stay with the white folks any longer." In two others, she repeats two aphorisms in jest.

> Dec 25 weather mixed
> This is Xmas day I have been feeling good all day Carrie & I have had the whiskey Oh; well Xmas comes but once a yr even a Negro must have his share

2–22 weather clear

This has been a lovely day Carrie & I went to see Cora stop by Pearl's told fortune said that I was going to marry [an] old man Oh well it is better to be an old man's Darling & a young man's slave to[o] true to be a joke.

While it is possible that a girl of eighteen might not have known much about the grim politics of the day or might not have chosen to write about them, the diary as a whole suggests Paul Smith's grandmother was raised in a comfortable home and felt secure in her community, despite its sharpening racial politics.

As an adult, though, Odie weathered more than her fair share of devastating events. Her married life seems to have started out happily. Her first husband was "Johnny Boy" Johnson, who had been born in Cadiz, KY in 1879. By the time they married, Odie was twenty-five and John close to thirty. Her wedding photo from 1908 shows a group of well-dressed women and men of color seated against a huge tree and a rocky background, enjoying a day outdoors. The couple must have ridden the train when they moved to Chicago, and in 1909, they had a daughter, Evangeline. Bernard Streets says that Granny told him that Johnson surprised her at one point with the deed to some land where they could some day build a house.

They were unable to fulfill this dream. Instead, they faced a life crisis—the death of their first child. As reconstructed from census information and a death record, Evangeline died in March 1911, at the age of two and a half. The records do not say what caused her death, but she died in Chicago and was buried in Dawson Springs. The same death record gives John Johnson's occupation as Post Office clerk. So it was with some measure of security that the couple went on to have more children. Daughter Josephine (Paul Smith's mother) was born February 1, 1912, and Odie's namesake Odie Mae was born November 1, 1913.

Then while still a young man, John Johnson became one of the millions who died during the devastating flu pandemic of 1918. It is remarkable that Odie herself survived one of the deadliest flus known in history. Still, Johnson's death left her alone at thirty-five with two daughters under the age of six. Probably shortly thereafter, Odie and her children returned to Dawson Springs. It is a testament to Odie's courage and determination that she went on to attend Western Kentucky Industrial College for Negroes, in Paducah, as a widowed mother.

Odie also married again. Over the course of a long life, she had two other husbands: Winstead Overby and Claybron Merriweather. The family has an old photographic portrait of Overby that shows him to be a handsome man of means. It appears that they lived in Dawson Springs and then moved to South Bend, Indiana, sometime around 1924. Bernard Streets relates that Granny wanted his mother Odie Mae and her sister Josephine to call Overby "Daddy." However, Streets was told that the girls could never bring themselves to comply. How Overby felt about being a stepfather is not known.

Just as the family was settling into its first few years together, another shattering event struck. Streets has located a notice from a South Bend newspaper in November of 1927[34] giving the details.

NEGRO KILLED BY FREIGHT TRAIN
Run Over also By Yard Engine Which Follows
Winstead S. Overby Dies in Police Ambulance on
Way To St. Joseph's Hospital

Winstead S. Overby, age 62, coloured, 134 North Birdsell St. died at 5:22 o'clock this morning as a result of injuries sustained when he was struck a few minutes before by a New York Central (Illinois division) freight train at the Arnold Street crossing and run over subsequently by a yard engine which was following the train. Mangled, he still showed signs of life when the police ambulance reached the scene, but died on his way to the St. Joseph's Hospital. It was sleeting at the time and it is believed that he did not see the train. He was on his way to

work at the time of the accident. Surviving are
his widow ... and two children ...

A receipt in the possession of the family shows that Odie paid a
mortician $250 in full for her husband's funeral two days later.

Another marriage record from 1937 shows that Odie married
a Claybron Merriweather. Very little is known about this marriage.
Family history has it that Merriweather was much older than Odie
and had been her teacher. It is not certain when he died, but Odie
clearly outlived him too. The fact that she went back to using Overby's
name after Merriweather's death suggests her heart lay with her former
husband.

For at least some of her later years, Odie's mother Mammy lived
with Odie in South Bend. Odie devoted her later years to caring for
her mother, daughters, and grandchildren, including the one she kept
a special eye out for—grandson Paul. When Mammy died in 1958,
she was ninety-three and had outlived Ferd by twenty years. Odie
Ballard Wingo Johnson Overby Merriweather herself died in 1975 at
age ninety-one.[35]

In contrast to—and perhaps because of—the loss and upheaval experienced by his grandmother and his mother, Rev. Smith's own childhood
was quiet and tranquil. When he was born in South Bend on Sept. 20,
1935, Odie was in her fifties and had been in the city about a dozen
years. She and Overby had bought a rather large rambling house on
the western side of the city where she rented rooms to boarders, as had
her parents before her. Sited on a triangular piece of land bounded
by Birdsell St., Orange St., and West Colfax Ave., the house was only
about a block and a half from the center of the African American
business district. The neighborhood included a mix of larger homes,
an undertaker's business, and a pool hall. The family's church, Greater
St. John Missionary Baptist Church, was at North Adams and Liston
Streets, two blocks from Odie's home.

Paul's parents' house on North Carlisle Street was about ten blocks west across a flat expanse of modest but widely spaced homes. Together, Josephine Wingo Smith and her husband, Leonard, raised five children there: Joan, Marlene, Leonard, Paul, and William. As the two oldest, Joan and Mimi formed a natural unit. They were followed by another duo, Lennie and Paul. Then came Willie, the youngest. He was doted on by older sister Marlene. Their bond was such that the two were not allowed to sit together in the back of the car, because they would "carry on" so much.

Odie Overby and her Sunday school class, (Paul Smith, center front). South Bend, Indiana, Easter 1941.

Odie's house was the center of her family's life. As Paul recalls, "Granny was the matriarch of the family and all the family gatherings were at her house because it was so large and could handle all of us. Granny was my Sunday school teacher and the pastor at the church respected her very much … She tutored all of us."

Smith remembers that as a child, whenever he visited the house his grandmother made sure the children went to visit Mammy's room to say hello. Their great-grandmother was generous with them, often giving them some coins from her purse. Being the oldest boys, Lennie and Paul spent extra time at their granny's house. They looked after the yard, the chickens, and the coal furnace. The boys had to stop by each morning to clean out the ashes and load in new coal. Every evening, they "banked" the coals for the night. Granny regularly sent the boys out to buy her "spark plugs"—chewing tobacco. That was the only time they were allowed to go into the pool hall.

Both Granny's mettle and the community's feelings about her are clear in another story about Granny's house. "Somebody tried to get her to buy a furnace one time, a charlatan. When she found out she was being cheated, she confronted the guy and he beat her up. Well, when the guys at the pool hall heard about it, they went out and found the guy and kicked the daylights out of him!"

Odie was listed in the 1930 census as "White" and other years as "Negro." Her light skin helped her get a job at Sears. Paul remembers, "Granny was well respected by whites who I am sure thought she too was white. But never in my memory did I know her to pass for being white. My mother and her sister looked white because they were light-skinned." Paul's wife Fran recalls Odie saying that nobody at the job asked her "what she was" and she just didn't say. The fact that she walked to work from her home in the black neighborhood never came up.

One year, she took grandson Paul to Sears to pick out a bike. He says, "They didn't know she was black. They asked if she wanted it on account. She said, 'What's that?' Black people didn't have credit! She paid cash in full for the bike."

Today, Indiana University at South Bend runs a Civil Rights Heritage Center a few blocks from where Granny lived. Built in the shell of what was formerly the indoor swimming "Natatorium," the Heritage Center's goal is to chronicle the story of civil rights advances in South Bend. There are some who objected to locating the museum in a facility that was explicitly segregated from when it opened in 1922 until 1950. The fight to desegregate the Natatorium had involved many of the prominent black leaders in the city including a husband-and-wife team of lawyers named J. Chester and Elizabeth Fletcher Allen.[36] To Paul and Lennie, what mattered was being the first black kids in that pool.

Starting around the time of the First World War, South Bend became an industrial city attracting immigrants and southern blacks alike. As a local historian has written,

> When white immigration declined after 1914, scores of black laborers from the South arrived to take their places in the factories of Studebaker, Singer, and Westinghouse. Census numbers grew from 604 in 1910 to more than 1219 by 1920, but the latter figures undoubtedly should've been higher, given the makeshift and uncertain housing available.[37]

Despite the Depression, there were jobs in South Bend in the 1930s. Among the sprawling manufacturing facilities were Bendix Brakes, the Oliver Chilled Plow Company, and Birdsell, which produced farm implements. These businesses attracted immigrants and locals alike, creating what seemed to Smith in his youth to be a relatively open, multicultural, and multiracial community.

> [South Bend] was integrated in a sense in the factories; blacks and whites worked together. Black men worked in the foundries; they did the most dangerous jobs. If there was a job stamping papers, say, a white person would get that job. If you were black, you looked for a job at Studebaker's or Bendix (you couldn't get one at Singer). But everyone lived in the same community. [It] was as mixed as any place I have ever lived. There were immigrants from Yugoslavia, Poland, all over ... South Bend had Europeans, immigrants ... their mentality permeated the place for me and my classmates. They didn't have college degrees but they sure paid for their kids, cousins, to have access to the Dream.

Others have testified to the fact that the laborers' neighborhoods were populated by immigrant whites and southern blacks who got along well since "they were all newcomers."[38] Former residents remember a safe neighborhood where black and white families taught each other their special recipes and sent their kids to the same local grammar school and high school. Though not all jobs were open to black people, the availability of work produced rising prosperity for the transplanted families.

The people who moved to cities like South Bend for the jobs had few options for housing, however. The federal government was building housing for workers necessary to the war effort, but the construction was meant to be temporary. With the influx of more and more Great Migration immigrants from the South, 5600 in the year 1940 alone, slum-like conditions quickly developed in the black housing districts in the industrial center of South Bend.[39]

This made rooming houses like the one Granny ran, essential places of respite. Paul's sister Marlene remembers that the place on Birdsell Street had two bedrooms upstairs, one downstairs and two apartments attached out back. Odie successfully made a living there for many years. Paul's worldview first took shape on the porch of that home.

> Granny sat in a rocking chair ... There was a little chair right next to her on the porch of the rooming house. On one side of the street was a beautiful big home. On the other side was a funeral home. Next to that was the pool hall.
>
> I was very mischievous as a youngster and always in trouble ... I don't care what I had done bad or wrong, if I got to my grandmother, she would say 'leave that boy alone!' My parents could never ever discipline me if she was around. She saw something in me I couldn't see in myself until much later.

Odie's influence in the community was magnified by the fact

that everyone walked to work. From the point of view of a child, the world came to her.

> Everyone knew Mrs. Overby. So when people were coming home from work, they would stop and say hello. Doctors, lawyers, people from [the] pool hall ... She'd say to people going by, "Come up and talk to me. How's your family?" Everyone knew her. Guys would tip their hat to Mrs. Overby ... it made no difference what station a person had in life. You knew if she wanted to speak to you, you should do it. Granny was the go-to person. She talked to everybody. And I sat next to my grandmother, listening to these stories.

When Paul expressed an interest in being baptized, it was Odie who arranged it. In the Baptist Church, of course, this requires immersion.

> I was not baptized in my home church. We didn't have a baptistery, a pool. I was baptized at the church down the street. The minister there lived at Granny's until he had a house. You know, you have to confess that you believe in Jesus. I was about eleven, twelve ... If you didn't have a baptistery, you were baptized in the St. Joe River.
>
> So I was baptized at Pilgrim Baptist church. My parents didn't know it until Granny told them. Granny was there, my whole family. Granny told my parents it was going to happen. Granny set it up. She said, "This is my grandson and he *will* be baptized." Just like Thurman's grandmother.

Paul's parents were people of modest means, but the city was prospering, and the family lived well. The presence of Notre Dame made South Bend a university town. Its students ran the Ku Klux Klan out of town when the KKK attempted to hold a rally in downtown South Bend.[40] Paul remembers it as a racially fluid community.

> My classmates were more white than black probably. The church was all black. A couple of white people joined our church—they were teachers. They had a lot to do with my going to college. One of them, Mrs. Bolden, became good friends with my parents and my aunts. She'd say, "Keep your eye on this kid." She would come check in with my parents about how I was doing in school.
>
> The black community there was middle class. I don't remember any kids from the ghetto. They were in school, but they were not among my friends. Even our high school basketball team was as integrated as any today. I never felt like an outsider racially. We had white people in our homes; we were in theirs ... We were not afraid of white people or intimidated. When we were in the rich neighborhoods at lunchtime, we went inside and sat at the table with everybody else. [In South Bend], we were all there together, immigrants, white and blacks ...

Paul's father Leonard was too short to be hired for factory work. Instead, he became a master cleaner in the Holmes' Silver Crystal China Shop, another place where white and black interacted easily. Paul says, "Our store was where white families registered their daughters who were getting married. We all worked there at one time or other. Mr. Holmes had two children of his own. His wife kept everything in order. They both loved my dad. He helped my dad get a car—went down to the car dealership with him to make sure he didn't get mistreated."

In addition to their regular jobs, "Smitty" and his wife catered parties in the big houses and fancy neighborhoods across the river on the east side of town. They were on familiar terms with everyone including the wealthy families, white and black.

My dad had had very little formal education. Twyck-enham Drive was the rich part of town where it was all white people. We went to those homes and made good money working for those families.

Now that I think about it, class-wise there was no reason for my daddy to be there with those people. But everyone knew my parents, respected them, trusted them—Knute Rockne and the corporate people. In fact, [my parents] helped recruit the other people who worked [in those homes]. The crème de la crème—my mother and father knew them and were known by them.

My father was the only male child with six sisters so you know he was spoiled. My dad did all the cooking— maybe he learned it growing up with those six sisters. He [cooked what he called] "Smitty burgers"—my classmates always wanted [those]!

Leonard did not have the elite education his sons would one day receive, but like his mother-in-law Odie, he played a central role in the community.

When the black community wanted to make changes, my father was one of the organizers. They met in the doctor's offices upstairs every Saturday. I asked my dad, why are all these black men gathering? My father said because we're talking about making changes.

This was about 1945. I went with my father and brothers to these meetings. You knew something important was going on. Think about it. It was serious. It was spirited. My father had the least amount of education. But it was his job to tell the Knute Rocknes that [the local men] had met, and [the corporate folks] needed to come talk with that group … We had a lot of hand-me-down clothing, but everyone respected my dad.

There was a significant and powerful group of African American leaders in South Bend at the time that helped change things for their fellow citizens. Between 1950 and 1954, the Allens and others joined together to confront the housing shortage head-on. After forming a corporation in secret, buying land, and arranging to have houses built for African Americans who could afford to buy in, the group helped create a truly successful, middle-class black housing development in the center of South Bend that came to be called "Better Homes of South Bend."[41] A whole generation of kids benefited from growing up in the district, and most of the houses are still occupied.

Once in school, he was discovered to be a gifted athlete and recognized for his musical talent. A "Pupil's Report" from the General Arts Studio gives the 12-year old high marks for various musical skills. It reads: "Paul is one of our best pupils. Encourage him all you can for he has a good future in music."[42]

Most importantly though, he displayed such a gift for preaching that he was offered his own church at sixteen. Like John Lewis who preached and held funerals for the family chickens as a young boy,[43] Paul's parents said he pretended to be preaching from the time he was about eight years old. He was quickly recognized for his abilities and supported in his ambitions, not just by his parents, but also the other adults around him. He recalls,

> I would walk into the barbershop with my dad and two brothers, and people would say, "Smitty, have your son say something to us." And I would.
>
> I was often asked to recite poetry, read scripture, and give a message early on in my life. Remember, the black church and community was a place of nurture and opportunity for all of us. If you even *thought* you wanted to be something, the community was there to encourage you on. I do not remember much about my early topics except they always had to do with inspiring people to reach their potential; they were messages of hope in the midst of despair and I often used the

Psalms and the Gospels for my texts.

His sister Marlene remembers that after the family went to Sunday service, Paul often disappeared to preach elsewhere. Rev. Bernard L. White, the new minister at St. John's when Paul was growing up, took it upon himself to mentor young men like Paul who showed promise with Christian oratory. He allowed the boys into the pulpit to "try it out." Rev. White was young and energetic, and St. John's thrived under his leadership. Paul recalls that the reverend's ministry "addressed the racial and political issues of the day, including challenging the white political structure." NAACP meetings were held at St. John's and national-level civil rights leaders visited to speak.

Within a few years, Paul was being wooed by other black Baptist churches that had things to offer that were impressive to the young man.

> It was almost like recruiting. When I would speak, the recruiters would be there. And the people would say, "That kid is going somewhere! We better get that kid now!"
> They'd say, "Why go to college? You don't need to go to college. We'll take care of you. We got it. What do you need? A car? We'll give you a car. Money? We have money. What else do you need?" And Granny said, "You need an education!"

Paul was thrilled with the way he was treated when invited to speak in Cassopolis, just over the state line in Michigan. But this was not what Odie and Josephine had in mind for him.

> I was *not* going to be a Jack Leg preacher! That is a term for black ministers who had little or no formal education but were charismatic and great speakers. My parents and my grandmother would hear none of that. I had a gift, but it needed to be honed.

Granny [and] my parents, were saying, "Yeah, this is okay, but that's not for you." And it was almost saying, "You're better than that." They couldn't say it, but that's what they [meant]. You need to want more. You can't settle [for] being some boy wonder …

The traditional black Baptist church had for generations been an arena within which men of color could gain an education, status and a steady income. Yet Smith's family and community pushed him into a wider world. Rev. Smith believes that the South Bend lawyers, the Allens, were instrumental in helping him get to Talladega College. Elizabeth Allen's father had been a builder for the American Missionary Association, and both he and his daughter had graduated from Talladega. With their encouragement, Smith won an academic scholarship that made it possible for him to their alma mater.

Ever caring and pragmatic, Smith's granny wanted to be the last to speak to the young man before he got on the train to go south to college. Paul recalls, "I'm sixteen. She was the grandmother who doted on me, my Sunday school teacher. My mother and father are on the train getting my seat, and Granny said, 'Leonard, Josephine, why don't you go? I'd like to talk to my grandson.' They got off the train."

Odie had three parting contributions to make. First, she gave her grandson $25. The fact that tuition at Talladega for the year was $350 suggests just how sizeable this gift was. Then she asked him, without warning and in rather blunt language, if he knew about sex. He says, "I almost fainted. I said, 'Well no,' because I didn't really know. I almost fainted!"

Granny made sure he understood—if you don't know what you're doing, don't blunder into anything you will regret. She then imparted a final piece of wisdom that revealed she was not as nonchalant about race as she had appeared to her grandson. She said, "Don't get involved with anyone darker than you!"

3

I have indeed broadened my knowledge, and have become more aware of my Christian call to the ministry. I realize how important it is to know what you stand for, lest you fall for anything.
Paul Smith, 1957[44]

Riding the Hummingbird into the Fire

In September 1952, just before his seventeenth birthday, Paul Smith left South Bend to attend Talladega College in Alabama. Like his grandmother before him, he boarded the Illinois Central Railroad bound for new places. However, while Odie Overby had ridden the train north toward the promise of Chicago, Smith was riding "The Hummingbird" south from the same city, bound for the heartland of Jim Crow. He was on a beeline toward a challenging educational institution, a first meeting with Martin Luther King, and the start of lifelong friendships with men, like Andrew Young, who went on to become some of America's most influential leaders.

He was also headed toward some of the most virulent racial bigotry he would ever encounter. After the Civil War, northern abolitionist church associations had helped to build and staff new colleges in the South, intended to give former slaves and their descendants a level of education most had never before been provided. However, for the Great Migration parents who wanted their children and grandchildren to attend these prestigious institutions, it meant sending their loved ones back to the regions they had worked so hard to leave behind. The older people were aware of the ironies involved and anxious about the teenagers' safety. By Paul's account, his mother and father were "terrified."

He, however, was not. Like other young men on those journeys, Smith jumped feet first into the adventure. His focus was on new challenges, new surroundings, and pretty girls. He had not thought much about the fact that interstate transportation was still segregated.

> I got on the Hummingbird in Chicago; I went by my-self. And what's important about the Hummingbird is that on that train there were kids from Illinois, Indiana … The train went south to Jacksonville, Florida. We would get on the train, all these black kids. We had our own cars. The porters looked out for us. We got on with forty or fifty kids going to Tennessee State, Fisk, Alabama A and M, and all those southern schools … I didn't know enough to be scared. I was falling in love—I'd never *seen* so many pretty girls! The idea was to get a seat next to one of them. We used to say [you'd] fall in love in Chicago, then you'd get to Indianapolis and see somebody finer than the first one—and fall in love again. And then you'd get to Nashville, and you'd be in love again!

Sleeping in their seats because black people were not permitted to ride in sleeper cars, the students arrived at the train station in Birmingham the next morning. They had two immediate obstacles to overcome. First, they needed to negotiate the several miles between the train station and the Trailways bus depot. That part of the journey had even Paul concerned. Though it would be several years before the Freedom Riders would meet savage violence at that bus station, Birmingham was already known as a racist hornet's nest. Going through the station, Paul saw his first "Whites Only" signs and noted that the facilities for people of color were particularly foul.[45] From there, students had to ride the segregated bus fifty-four more miles to the college. With typical insouciance, Paul made a friend who could help—Claudette Beck, who was already a sophomore at Talladega.

> The [bus] station was for whites only. It was my first experience with segregation, being in that Trailways station. Claudette guided me through the station with my big footlocker with all my worldly goods ... You were taking your life in your hands to ride those buses, you know. That bus was invariably 90 percent black. If there were white people on the bus, they were all the way up front. Probably scared of us. There were too many of us ...
> But I had enough sense that I didn't do anything to bring attention to [myself]. I was thinking, *This is one fine sister! She can help me anytime she wants to ...*

The parents of these college-bound students had good reason to be afraid. It was only three years later that Emmett Till was murdered in central Mississippi, two hundred miles to the west. A Chicago kid on summer vacation with relatives in the south, Till might one day have ridden the Hummingbird to college himself. Instead, he was tortured and died at age fourteen. The mutilated boy in the open casket made it impossible for the country to ignore what racist violence had done to a young black teenager. After that, it may only have been the protection provided by A. Phillip Randolph's unionized train porters that made it possible for black parents to put their sons and daughters on a train going south.

From the perspective of Paul and his year-older brother, though, the trains were the link to a thrilling and much wider world. Paul remembers that what seemed important to them about the 1954 Brown v Board of Education decision was that it outlawed segregation on the national railroads. This meant that the two young men could ride in the observation car for the first time, and they took full advantage of the new freedom. The deeper significance of the Supreme Court decision, of course, soon became clearer to the young men.

Talladega College has a long history and a powerful origin story. Only a few months after the Civil War ended, two former slaves, William Savery and Thomas Tarrant, proposed to build a school for people of color in Talladega, their hometown. The American Missionary Association and a former Union general who had been appointed head of Alabama's Freedman's Bureau helped the community acquire land and a building previously owned by a white Baptist institution. Ironically, Savery and Tarrant had themselves helped to build the structure before the war. "Thus a building constructed with slave labor for white students became the home of the state's first private, liberal arts college dedicated to servicing the educational needs of blacks."[46] The school first enrolled students in 1867. By the end of the century, dozens of other historically black colleges and universities (HBCUs) were educating students.

Today, the college website notes that "the campus is a quiet place—away from the distractions and fast pace of urban living." But when Paul Smith arrived in 1952, it was a small, steadfast oasis in the chaotic social and physical landscape of the Jim Crow South. The wood frame–and–brick campus buildings are well spaced around the crossroads of West Battle Street and what is now called Martin Luther King Jr. Drive. West Battle, the main road through the campus, runs east-west and slopes down to the east as it leaves the campus gates to join the main road leading to the town of Talladega. Outside those gates in Smith's day, there was a little roadhouse called "High Pockets" that students frequented when they wanted to eat something other than cafeteria food—though as Paul notes, they "had to enter through the back door, of course." Down that road, one might also encounter hostile white locals or see their cars driving conspicuously by outside the campus.

Despite its liberalism, Talladega had its own brand of bigotry. Paul relates that he had to include a photograph with his application to the college and says, "If I had been blacker, I might not have gotten in." He says that the phrase "light, bright, and damn near white," was used to describe those who some considered the elites within the black community. It is unclear how much or how often darker-skinned students were actually discriminated against. However, he says the use of the phrase was commonplace.

Inside the gates, Talladega was thriving in 1952. It had just hired its first African American president, an Alabamian and an alumnus of the college. Dr. Arthur D. Gray had earned his PhD at Chicago Theological Seminary in 1934.[47] This deeply impressed Smith.

> Going to Talladega—that was really a cultural shock. The college was the black intelligentsia. I was shocked to see so many white teachers there at this small black college. The student body was all black—there may have been a white student or two there. But it was a historically black college … The president of the college was black … He was a Congregational minister, had served in Chicago before becoming President of Talladega … those black ministers were not like the black minister I grew up with. [Gray was] very sophisticated, very well spoken, no shouting, no theatrics in his preaching—very grounded.

Talladega's faculty were highly educated blacks and whites who felt it was their Christian duty to ensure that black students in the South had access to a sound education.

> I had never had any instruction in high school, from anybody black, never, in South Bend, Indiana. All my teachers were white … So now I get to Talladega, sixteen years of age and here are all these black PhDs who are my professors. The president of the college is a black Congregational minister. And now the white professors, who were in the predominance, clearly had my best interests at heart. I had not seen that before. You know, the teachers in my high school—there were

maybe seventy, eighty people in a class. I was a number.

Several professors recognized Paul as a gifted student and went to extra lengths to teach him. Peg Montgomery was a professor of English who worked with him closely. Ma Gibson, a teacher of classics, met with Paul once a week at her cottage on campus. Paul read aloud to her so that he could learn to speak well. Those teachers sacrificed more than just their time; for them, the Deep South was hostile territory too. Rev. Smith says the white teachers who lived on campus with their families were at times no safer outside the campus gates than the black students they served.

Most important in Paul's development was Dr. John Bross, a white professor of Psychology and Religion. Bross was raising a family on campus, and Paul joined them for dinner nearly every Friday night. Bross took Paul to lectures and conferences, introducing him to a wider academic, religious, and political world. Their connection was clear when Bross preached the ordination sermon years later at Paul's first pastorate in Buffalo.

But not all the teachers were so impressed with Smith.

> ... the Biology teacher [was] a PhD, single, very attractive. And you did not play around her class, you hear me? You did *not* play around in her class. She was saying, "I am a PhD; this is how I got to where I am. And you have to get to where I am, and I am going to help you get there. You are in *my* class. You will study, you will learn, you will do x, y and z."
> I had never had a black professor say that to us. And she was not just speaking to me. She was speaking to everybody who was in that class. By God, you're here, your parents are footing this money—you damn well better come in here serious. You better not be playing any games or think I'm going to play any games with you. I want you to succeed. And if you want to succeed, I will help you do that. But if you don't, don't

waste my time.
[She'd say] … very nicely, "Mr. Smith, Mr. Epps. So you didn't do your homework today? Can you tell me why?" [He'd answer] "I was at basketball practice." [She'd say] "What will basketball practice do for you?" And you have to answer! … They knew the key to our success was to go the path they had gone on. Even the white professors had my best interests at heart. I wasn't used to that from anyone in South Bend.

Despite his abilities and the support he received, Smith's first year at Talladega was difficult. He was very young to be plunging into college life. A letter typed to his father sometime that first semester reveals how much his thoughts were still of home.

Paul Smith
Talladega College
Stone Hall, Rm. 206

Dear Daddy,
How is everything? Today we are having the entrance exams, and we have to have them for three days. My typewriter came today but my trunk has not come yet. I'm still very lonesome and I hope that I'll get over it soon. The check is to be written for $182. Tell Leonard and them to please write me and tell mother to tell Willy to take the library books to Catherine's house. In a half hour our exams will begin. Tell Willy to get me Julius Mason address, and some of the other kids too. The upperclassmen were in our dorm trying to paddle us, but our Counselors wouldn't let them. Last night we had a freshman get together with all the teachers there, and we had to introduce ourselves and show some kind of a talent, and it was real swell. I met two girls on the train that were going to same place that I

was, and they are real cute. After the get together, the upperclassman ran us all the way home. They told us that we will have to put up with all this until Thursday [sic]. I haven't much more to say so I guess I'll close now with all my love. Don't forget to tell them to write me. Bye now. They have a chapel here for the students to attend.

Your loving son,
Paul Smith

Rev. Smith can say now what he surely could not then—that it was the social side of college that was troublesome. Even though he was a tall, athletic northerner who made friends easily, he was in some ways still innocent. "I wasn't ready for girls! I thought I was. But at college, I'd see these girls every day. We went to the movies on campus since they were segregated in town. It was freshman year, [I was] with a girl at the movies. And suddenly she put her hand on my leg. No high school girl had ever done that! It was exciting but I was scared."

So during the academic year 1953–54, Smith stayed home and worked. It was one of the very few detours on his road to adult life. He took some classes at the South Bend campus of Indiana University "to stay sharp." And it helped. He says, "I found my groove that year I was out. When I got back, I was ready." Meanwhile, his stories of college life had convinced Lennie that he was missing out. In the late summer of 1954, both boys got on the train in Chicago and roared off to become "Dega" men.

—⁂—

Talladega College is located in the wooded heart of Alabama, close to Montgomery, Birmingham and other small cities that were becoming battlegrounds in the struggle for social justice. In 1952, the year Paul first enrolled at college, Arthurine Lucy was housed and educated at Talladega while the fight went on in court to make her the first black person admitted to the University of Alabama at Tuscaloosa. One of her lawyers, Arthur D. Shores, was Chairman of the Board at Talladega, and he made sure she kept up with her studies while the case dragged on. He told the other students, "this is a safe haven for her. Be nice to her." Paul remembers seeing her in the dining hall.

But fellow students were not the only ones alert to her presence. Paul recalls that Arthurine "stayed at the President's house. That's when the Klan came. They gathered down the hill … we saw them there getting ready to do something about Arthurine being on campus … The Klan couldn't get at her in Tuscaloosa so they wanted to try while she was at Talladega." IIn the end, Talladega students, like those at Notre Dame, banded together near the campus gates to show they were not going to let anyone dangerous into their midst. Arthurine was safe, at least for the time being.

Off campus, the landscape was claimed and defined by whites who felt no need to disguise their hostility and often seemed to relish confrontation. Paul had come to Talladega on an academic scholarship but was welcomed onto the basketball team. This meant traveling to other black colleges to compete. Packed together into a car, black students and their coach had to negotiate a veritable minefield between safe havens. Meals were not a problem, as the coach took them to the homes of alumni or black church folk in the region. But they couldn't avoid taking breaks and stopping for gas:

> When we had to use the bathrooms, we could not of course use the one inside the gas station because it was reserved for whites. Outhouses were always in the back of the station, and they were reserved for black folks. On one occasion, we had to go through the gas station to get to the back door [and] the outhouse. As we waited our turn, we [looked] over the candy, nuts, and sodas—which we could not purchase—over the counter. [Then] I realized the men who were sitting outside of the gas station had come inside to check on us. They were basically speaking nasty words to us and as they were walking towards us, I realized we would

be surrounded by them in a few moments. A sudden panic rose in all of us, and within seconds we headed towards the back door and eventually found our way to the waiting car being filled with gasoline. Whoever was filling up our car was apparently in charge and did not want to miss the sale.

Were it not for him I don't know what would have happened to us. My brother and I will never forget that experience and the fear which quickly engulfed us. We were targeted because we were black college students hopefully on our way to becoming successful—and they were not.

Attorney Shores came to the rescue in another near miss with violence during Smith's college years. The team was traveling to Birmingham to play against Miles College, another HBCU. The distance was less than sixty miles, but the interstate highway system had not yet been built, so the trip took several hours. Despite driving carefully to avoid trouble in the city of notorious Bull Connor, the team's car slid into the rear of a car ahead of them that had stopped abruptly.

The white person in the car ... jumped out with fire in his eyes, calling us the "n" name and threatening to beat us all to death. As we began getting out of the car ... he realized we outnumbered him, and he began to be a bit more conciliatory ... [Then] a bus pulled up beside the accident and opened the door and the bus driver said to the white driver, "I saw what happened and it was those niggers' fault." The bus and passengers remained until the police arrived.

Now I was really frightened, but the coach kept his cool ... [He] invoked the name of the civil rights attorney from Birmingham who had gained national attention through the movement of Dr. King and who had represented many prominent black folks in

Birmingham—this gained us some respect. [Soon] Mr. Arthur Shores showed up at the scene ... and within a few minutes we were back in our cars on our way to Miles College. I can see the faces ... and I can still hear the shouting of the white man. I realize how fortunate I am to still be here today ...

Smith did not go home at Christmas in his senior year, because Dr. Bross arranged for he and two other black students to attend a conference at all-white Davidson College in North Carolina.

We three—two black guys and one black girl—drove with Bross to the conference. When we got there, they had the area cordoned off with police cars. People shouted nasty names at us. They split us up [for sleeping arrangements]. I was in a room with someone who had never, *ever* been that close to a black person. He was not happy at first ...
That was one of the first interracial conferences for black and white students. We ate together, lived together. That was 1957. The objective was to put black and white students together from a religious perspective so we could all get used to each other.

Dr. Bross and other faculty knew that history was being made all around them, and they wanted their students to know as much about it as they could. In the spring of 1957, Talladega professors took students to Montgomery every Friday to hear the speakers that Rev. Martin Luther King, Jr. was inviting to Dexter Avenue Baptist Church. At the time, the young minister was serving in his only full-time pastorate in the little brick church a mere block from the massive white pillars of the Alabama State House. Smith heard speakers including Rev. King, Vernon Johns, Adam Clayton Powell, and Ralph Abernathy a stone's throw from where the Selma marchers would make their stand a few years later. Smith says the eloquence and power of those speakers spurred him to work even harder on his own oratorical style. The visitors from Talladega did not go unnoticed, however; one Friday, their car was splashed with acid while the students were in the church.

Smith's contact with Rev. King became even more personal one day in May, 1957. As Paul remembers it, his fraternity had asked King to visit Talladega to speak and spend a few days. Andrew Young had come to the campus because he wanted to meet King. Young's own account adds some details. "The Alpha Phi Alpha fraternity chapter at Talladega College in Alabama provided my first opportunity to meet Martin Luther King. Alpha Phi Alpha was my fraternity at Howard University, and the president of Talladega, Arthur Grey, was an Alpha and a Congregational minister. I accepted Grey's invitation in the spring of 1957 to speak for the Alpha Phi Alpha's annual program at Talladega ... When I arrived I discovered I was one of two speakers. Martin King was the other. I looked forward to hearing him speak and to meeting him with great anticipation."[48]

A popular, multitalented and ambitious young man, Paul himself pledged Alpha Phi Alpha in 1955. Smith remembers that the chapter met in the basement of Silsby, a brick science building at the center of the campus. Initiations in those days were watched over by older members of the chapter to make sure no one got hurt.

That May, the students gathered to hear King and Young speak. Paul recalls, "We were in the brand new gym—there must have been five hundred people. This old, old man lifted his hand and there was a hush. He said, 'I just want to say something to you.' Everybody was patient with him. He said, 'I don't want you to move too fast and I don't want you to move too slow.' And King listened! He listened to all the questions."

Smith was one of the Alphas who got to escort the speakers around campus that weekend. In the course of fulfilling his duties, Paul says, and Young concurs, that it was he who actually introduced Young and King to each other. The partnership of the two men, of course, changed America.

It is not surprising that a fraternity brought the three together. Founded by African Americans at Cornell in 1906, Alpha Phi Alpha

Talladega College, 1957. From left: Richard English, Frank Harris, Martin Luther King, Jr., Charles Haynes, Paul Smith, John Bross. (Photographer unknown)

is the oldest and perhaps the best-known fraternity for men of color in the country. While there are many other highly respected black fraternities and sororities, the history and membership list of Alpha Phi Alpha are unmatched. As articulated on their website, the organization's goals are "scholarship, fellowship, good character, and the uplifting of humanity."[49] Smith's case demonstrates the way these values have informed members' lives.

The impact of these voluntary organizations on the life of Paul Smith and many others in the black community over the past century cannot be overstated. Going far beyond what their white counterparts have historically aspired to, black fraternities and sororities have long created "a lasting identity, a circle of lifetime friends, a base for future political and civic activism … a forum, post college, through which some of the best-educated blacks in America can discuss an agenda to fight racism and improve conditions for other less-advantaged blacks."[50]

Writer, lawyer, and black elite insider Lawrence Otis Graham contextualizes the rise of these organizations. Shut out of white fraternities and sororities for decades, black students at both the HBCUs and at the best white colleges have joined together in social, intellectual, and political powerhouse networks for decades . Alpha Phi Alpha became part of what are called "the Divine Nine"—major fraternities mostly founded in the first quarter of the century. While Graham notes that the groups have been criticized for creating class divisions within the black community, he points out that fraternity brothers united with nonmembers in the crucial protests that brought the civil rights movement into the public eye.[51]

The Talladega meeting of the three young Alphas is a perfect example of the powerful potential inherent in these elite fraternal societies. Invitations extended to rising stars of public life like King and Young helped circulate ideas and information. The speaker circuits linked the HBCUs to each other and to other academic institutions. It was through this system that Paul repeatedly heard his most crucial intellectual and teacher, Rev. Dr. Howard Thurman.

Paul remembers those few days with King as transformational. Young, on the other hand, was very disappointed.[52] He had traveled to Talladega from rural Thomasville, Georgia where he was managing two churches and a voter registration drive. Having heard a great deal already about King, Young had hoped they could talk politics, theology, and philosophy. It turned out that King needed a break from the spotlight and wanted to talk mainly about his newborn child. For his part, King was using venues like Talladega to fine-tune the speeches he would later deliver in far more pressured circumstances. In May 1957, King was polishing the speech he delivered a few days later at an important early march, the Prayer Pilgrimage, in Washington.[53]

As a senior, Smith was elected to lead a new chapter of the NAACP on campus. Smith says that this happened because he asked the most questions in the planning meetings. Nonetheless, he was certainly being recognized for his speaking abilities and leadership potential. He recalls,

> We kept up with the activities of other campus chapters. There were conferences to go to—we'd get on a bus and go to Atlanta. It kept us abreast of what was happening nationally in Washington, New York, Chi-

cago ... [with] the fight to grant us our rights. It was the premier African American organization ... In those early days, the NAACP had corporate partners ... There were corporate people making sure that whatever the NAACP needed would happen.

College drew Paul and Lennie into powerful social networks that continue to be important in their lives today. Along with classmates, professors, fraternity brothers, and future professional colleagues, both men met their future wives at Talladega. Paul met Frances Pitts in June 1956, as he was about to begin his senior year. Both her father and mother, along with two uncles on her father's side, had graduated from Talladega. Fran's mother was visiting the campus that summer to attend her class reunion, and Fran was going to enroll as a freshman that fall. Paul had a coveted job waiting tables in the private dining room for President Grey, the faculty, and administration. It was there that he first caught a glimpse of Fran when he waited on her and her mother.

Frances must have been memorable to most of the young men she encountered. Born in Soperton, Georgia, she was the smart, beautiful, eldest child in a successful middle class family. Fran had grown up on the grounds of Fort Valley State College, an HBCU southeast of Atlanta where her father had been a math teacher. Her family shared basic values with Paul's but also came with a different set of expectations. Hers was an educated household where opera and theater were appreciated. As she puts it, "I was used to a university atmosphere."[54]

Located outside the white town, the Fort Valley campus was a safe haven in hostile territory. However, the black neighborhood did not receive the same services as the areas where white people lived. The roads near the college were not paved, and they often became muddy and dangerous. Fran says, "one time our car slid off the road into a ditch. My father decided he had had enough. So he went to the meeting of the [town leadership]; they knew who he was. They said he wasn't supposed to be there and asked him what he wanted. And he said, 'I pay taxes in this town. I want my goddamn street paved!' So they paved the street but just as far as our house." The paving stopped

Deforest Chapel, Talladega College. (Photo by author)

about a foot past a tree at the corner of their property.

Paul got to know Fran during that school year and fell deeply in love. Already a well-known senior, he had begun preaching in the churches on campus, including the formidable Deforest Chapel. As he recollects, "I was the man!" He had many friends on campus, some of whom he is in touch with to this day. But he had made his choice. One evening in April of 1957, Paul enlisted the aid of his fraternity brothers to jump from behind the bushes in front of Silsby Hall and sing Fran a love song. When he presented her with the Alpha Phi Alpha pin he had paid $35 to buy, Fran did not refuse it. In those days, that meant marriage was likely to be ahead. As Fran recalls,

> My parents were in the Congregationalist Church and Talladega was a Congregational school. So it was all familiar. They went to Talladega as well as my father's brothers. So it was in my background to marry clergy; it was acceptable and appropriate. Education and

profession mattered in terms of who you would marry. I'm an old-fashioned girl. People of my generation, when you got married, you were supposed to support your husband in whatever he did. That's what you did. The same with getting married right out of college—it was the day after graduation for us! I was barely twenty-one when I got married.[55]

Early in the relationship, an opportunity arose for Paul to show his mettle. Fran's former boyfriend from Fort Collins arrived on campus to play basketball against Paul's team. He says the students were gossiping about what would happen between the two young men, how they would interact on and off the court, and whom Fran would spend time with after the game. It did not appear to be a match-up that would favor Paul, and he says he succumbed to a moment of malice. "Everyone was buzzing about [it]. He was huge, six-three or four. He made about thirty points in the first half alone, and my friends were laughing because I was guarding him! He shot my eyes out. One of the only bad things I did was at one point, I pushed him over toward the bleachers; I should have gotten ejected from the game."

Yet after his team was soundly beaten, Paul's instinct led him in a direction that surprised everyone—he went to talk with the fellow. "I told him, 'I know you used to know Fran well. Why don't you and she take some time to talk?' Everyone was real impressed with the way that reduced all the tension." Stepping closer to a source of challenge or hostility, not to fight but to mediate, soon became one of Smith's special strengths.

In his final year at Talladega, Smith wrote a senior thesis that allowed his intellectual voice to be heard for the first time. The eighty-page document provides an early look at his ideas about God, faith, denominationalism, church practice, and doctrine. Entitled, "A Comparison of the Baptist and Congregationalist Denominations," the paper is articulate, thoughtful, and well written. It clearly reveals both Smith's personal struggle with his denominational affiliation and his growing certainty about ministry as his professional path. In it, he asserts that "there is a great need for such a study as this, for the reason that [it] enables us to know why we are what we are."[56]

Despite all the support and training he received before he went to college, Smith describes himself on the first page of the thesis as having been uncertain about his future profession.

> Before coming to college, I had no idea of becoming a minister. I wasn't too sure that I would come to college. At this state in life a young person is at the "brim of confusion," however I tried to unravel my confusion by coming to college.
> Both my parents are Baptists, and so the rest of us in the family followed suit, and became Baptists. Its [sic] interesting to know that out of seven members of our family, there are only three Baptists left.

In the text, Smith reviews the history of the Baptist and the Congregationalist denominations and identifies key differences between them, including their views on covenants, baptism, communion, the literal interpretation of the Bible, and whether God's Word is living or immutable. While recognizing positive aspects of Baptist beliefs and practices, Smith makes clear that he has journeyed away from the Baptist church of his family and feels closer to Congregationalism.

Among the distinctive characteristics of the Congregationalism that Smith cites approvingly are a concern for church unity vs. a divided Protestantism, the fact that congregants are not asked to renounce the teachings of other churches, the tradition of allowing ministers from other denominations to serve as pastors in Congregational churches, and an emphasis on the liberty of the Christian person. He writes that the mergers that have occurred in Congregationalist history have "truly been representative of the Christian spirit."[57] He also appreciates the weight given to education by Congregationalism and its critical nineteenth-century role in founding colleges like Talladega.

At age twenty-two, Smith straightforwardly declares that he is not a literalist in his interpretation of the Bible—that he believes the Word of God is a living entity, and that he finds individual freedom and choice in matters of church doctrine to be of central importance. He asserts that the "narrowness" of Baptist ideas on baptism in particular, "is one of my major reasons for rejecting the Baptists."[58] Rather than insisting on the necessity of full immersion as the Baptists do, Smith writes that he prefers the Congregationalists' freedom to choose between forms of baptism and their recognition of baptism performed in other denominations.[59]

Smith finds that Baptist and Congregationalist views of Salvation through Jesus are quite in accord. But evincing the iconoclastic views and the prescience that Smith became known for, he writes,

> I would question … references to "heaven" where Jesus Christ is supposed to be now. I believe that Christ is somewhere in the universe, but to call this place heaven isn't exactly what I had in mind. I don't believe in a heaven or a hell in the sense that Heaven is the place for the good and Hell a place for the evil. I think that we as human beings make our heavens or hells here on earth.[60]

Perhaps most revealing is a viewpoint he articulates twice in his paper: "It makes no difference whether you're a Baptist, a Methodist, or a Congregationalist, we are all one under God. As long as God is the ultimate of any religion, I feel that this religion is good."[61] This kind of willingness to look beyond issues of sectarianism has animated his life ever since.

In concluding, Smith declares that his thesis has done its job: "As a result of this project, I know now why I am a Congregationalist, and not a Baptist, anymore. I am also aware of the fact that there is a great need for more people to look into the history of their denominations, to see if their group is doing God's will. This is important in our world today, if we are to ever become united … "

In May of 1957, the Smith family gathered at Talladega to celebrate Paul's graduation with a B.A. in Psychology and Religion. Later, as a reward for his hard work, Leonard Smith gave his son $100 and the keys to the car. Paul was to enroll at Hartford Seminary that fall, and he had planned a celebratory road trip with his friend Richard English. Though his new friend Andrew Young had suggested he come take non-violence training, Paul had made his plans and promised only that he would pray about it. In high spirits, he and English hit the highway, headed for Detroit.

Once there, though, Paul made a decision that would change his life. Shortly after arriving in in the city, a marquee outside a church caught his eye. It read: "Dr. Benjamin Elijah Mays -- Everywhere I Turn, I Find Jesus." The chance to hear the President of Morehouse College and one of the most respected scholar-theologians of the day was irresistible to the young minister-to-be. Smith attended the sermon and says it "penetrated my heart and soul."

Afterwards, he was on fire with determination to devote his life to God and service. He didn't need to joyride any longer. Smith turned back to South Bend to return the car and the remaining $75 to his father. It was Paul Smith's first truly adult decision, one that marked him indelibly. He says it was also the only time he ever saw his father cry. With that sweet send-off, Paul headed back to the South to begin his professional life.

4

The road to professional education is not an easy one. I would say that it is the most lonely road that a man can take, if he is serious about really doing something.

Raymond Pitts, 1958[62]

First Rites

In the spring of 1957, someone at a Methodist church in Anniston, Alabama, contacted Talladega College looking for a temporary pastor. While not yet finished with his senior year, Smith did not see why his relative youth and inexperience should keep him from taking the job: "I was a student, but I was available and I had something to say." Every Sunday for four months, he boarded a regional bus in Talladega and traveled twenty-seven miles northeast up Rte. 21 to the church.

While the infamous, near-fatal attack outside Anniston on a bus full of Freedom Riders was still four years off,[63] getting on the segregated bus for a ride of an hour or more made Smith "not afraid, but nervous." As has so often been the case, though, he quickly acquired an advocate and protector. Another black minister who was riding the same bus each Sunday began to sit with him. "He looked out for me. We'd talk about what I was going to say at church that day. We were probably the only two blacks on the bus. It cost 25¢ each way. The church paid that and gave me $10 [weekly]."

Drawing on his friend's guidance and his own long experience of preaching, Smith was able to meet the demands of that first professional job. He moved on quickly, however, to much weightier responsibilities. After his graduation, Smith was hired as a "summer supply" minister. This time, he was to serve at a Congregational church in Athens, Alabama, about ninety-five miles north of Birmingham. Smith was on a visit home to South Bend when he received word that a highly respected member of the Athens community had just died—Mr. Allen, the local mortician. Ending his visit early, Smith scrambled to catch a bus back to Alabama to assume his position as leader of the church. He knew that as the new pastor, he would be expected to lead the funerary rituals.

When he arrived in Athens, Smith and the man who came to pick him up were a bit surprised to see each other.

> There was a gay undertaker, embalmer, and hairdresser there named Jesse. He did everything. Everyone knew him and trusted him …
>
> The bus was late. All they knew was that the minister was coming on the bus. Jesse was designated to pick me up. I got there in the middle of the night. And there was Jesse. He said, "You're mighty young—are you sure?" He was the decision-maker for the black community in Athens. And he could sing!

Smith assured Jesse that he was the man they were waiting for, and they drove through the dark to Athens. The new pastor discovered the next day that he had one important ally in the crisis; the deceased man's wife had gone to Talladega, "so she had confidence in me." But the deacons of the church were skeptical when they met him. They grumbled, saying, "That kid doesn't know how to do a funeral!" Moving quickly to prove them wrong, Smith created a bulletin for the service that gave him structure during the ceremony. He enlisted the elders' aid in reading the Old Testament scripture. By the time it came to the committal of the body to the ground in the cemetery outside town—the part of the ritual Smith was most unsure of—Smith had the old hands on his side, and they helped him conclude the rites. Thus, Smith started learning how to lead others through the pressure, emotion, and politics of a small town funeral. These skills would grow and deepen with time.

There were sharper lessons to come in Athens. While living with a host family, the Higginses, Smith became aware for the first time that on the radio in the South, black people were spoken of using only their first names, never "Mr." or "Mrs." Being from the North and the city where that indignity, at least, was not the norm, Smith decided to take some action. He wrote to the station manager and soon received a letter in return. In it, Smith was told that he was in the South now, and the rules were different. He was to "remember his place" and told that they had "people who would take care of me if I didn't follow the rules."

Despite the threat inherent in that response, Mr. Higgins did not tell Smith to back down. Instead, Higgins told the young man he was proud of him and then shared stories about how the older man and his family had "survived the cruelties of southern living and segregation." Smith later realized that the support of such stalwart families had made a huge contribution to the political efforts of the day. They may never have marched in a protest, but they housed, fed, and encouraged the young firebrands in their midst. It was in fact the Higgins household that welcomed Smith in when he was looking for a safe haven in the middle of the night on the way home from Selma in 1965.

—∞—

Proving that his ministerial skills could earn him a living was critical in 1957, because Smith wanted to move forward in his courtship of Frances Pitts. At Christmas that year, he visited Fran's family in California and proposed to her. As Smith tells it, he was riding high when he arrived, fresh off his first airplane trip and carrying Granny's ring in his pocket. He had finished his first semester at Hartford Theological Seminary and was on his way to the career in ministry he had always envisioned. He enjoyed a wonderful visit with the family he expected to call in-laws and went back to seminary feeling confident there was nothing to keep his plans from unfolding. However, in early February 1958, he received a letter.

Fran's father was a warm but formidable intellectual who wrote to voice some strong objections to Fran and Paul marrying that year—or the next. Dr. Raymond J. Pitts, Sr. had long before set himself a series of goals that he fulfilled on his way out of Fort Valley, Georgia, and the Deep South. He too was a member of Alpha Phi Alpha. While working and raising a family, Dr. Pitts became determined to earn his PhD in Mathematics at the University of Michigan. As Paul tells the story, Pitts was told by one of the math professors when he arrived for classes, "We've never given a black man a PhD in Math. What makes you think we'll give you one?" And Pitts said, "You watch me!" Over several years, he successfully completed the course of study. However, the degree was only awarded to him after the bigot and chair of the department died many years later. Meanwhile, Pitts had moved his family to Pasadena in 1956.

Dr. Pitts's three-page, single-spaced, typed letter laid out his objections to Paul's marriage plans. He was welcoming but serious.

> I want to take up the matter of your and Fran's marriage at some length and suggest some changes in plans which I hope will be acceptable to you.

Dr. Pitts relayed the hopes of he and his wife that all their children would receive "the best education possible that would make of them the best Americans they could be." He explained the family's move to California as motivated by that desire.

> Frances has the chance to enter Pomona College, possibly on a scholarship. Pomona is a Liberal Arts College of the highest caliber and operated by the Congregational Church. Two years of study [after two years at Talladega] with the freedom from home responsibilities and with time to develop on her own initiative would

make her the kind of person who could be a real asset
as a minister's wife.

Raymond Pitts was speaking from experience: " ... my girl too had
my engagement ring and I could not even get back south for nearly
two years." But he believed Smith's hard work at seminary toward his
future goals would be sustaining during such a separation. He advised
Smith to "strive to be the top man at the Seminary," to use his time to
study, travel, and make contacts that marriage would otherwise make
difficult. With patience and logic, he explained all the advantages for
both Paul and Fran if they both completed their education before they
married. He described his own trajectory.

> I believed then that I could become one of the top
> flight mathematics teachers in this country; that from
> this could be made possible a good sound home and
> family life for my girl and the five children; that good
> sound education and travel would be the accepted way
> of life for us; that we would own a home, yes, and in
> this home each person would grow happily into the
> best possible person he could be; and above all that our
> family could be contributors to our American culture
> and not just consumers and victims of it as we are
> sometimes forced to be.

The soundness of the argument and the gentleness of its delivery
proved impossible to deny. The marriage was put on hold, and Smith
went to Hartford on his own.

—∿—

Hartford Theological Seminary in Connecticut was and is a progressive
institution.[64] Associated with the United Church of Christ (UCC),
it offers degrees and certificates in such fields as Interfaith Dialogue,
Islamic Chaplaincy, International Peacemaking, Transformational
Leadership, and Spirituality. Hartford has had a Black Ministries

Leadership Certificate since 1982 and offers newer certificates in Hispanic and Women's Leadership. Its Christian-Muslim relations program has existed for a century. What was in Smith's day called the Kennedy School of Missions sent students all over the world to evangelize.[65] Foreign students from all over the world also came to Hartford to study.

Smith chose the institution for those qualities, knowing too that his friend Andrew Young had graduated from Hartford a few years ahead of him. Smith asserts that after the interracial conference at Davidson College the previous Christmas, "I knew integration was possible." He went to Hartford anticipating the challenge of competing among the best, whomever they might be. As has happened over and over again in his life, Smith was breaking down racial barriers by simply enrolling there. "I was one of only three black students. It was me, Ralph Logan Carson, and a black woman [Julia McClain]. Guess who I was assigned to as a roommate? Ralph. The first day of class at orientation, they all looked at me and said, 'Where's Ralph? You have to meet him,' they said. 'He's going to be your roommate.'"

Ralph was also blind. This might have been an obstacle for a less accepting person than Paul, but a mutually agreeable arrangement was quickly organized. The school proposed that if Paul would read Ralph his lessons and help him get acclimated, he would be paid $50 a month. To the scholarship student who had worked his way through Talladega, "that was good money." Soon, Ralph had nicknamed Paul "Mr. Smooth" and was attending basketball games to support his friend. Ralph went on to become Distinguished Professor of Christian Theology at Southeastern Baptist Theological Seminary, just one of the many formidable intellects who have surrounded Smith since his college days.

In 1957, everything about Hartford looked grand to the twenty-two year old there on scholarship. Smith felt that his world was expanding exponentially. Hartford Seminary "was like heaven." He says, "students from all over the world went to the Kennedy School and went from there to India and all over ... So I was not only going to a 95 percent white environment on this campus, but my orientation went way [beyond Hartford] … " [On a seminary trip] "I remember being in a room with a fireplace. Fall was absolutely beautiful. I had never been in a hotel like that … It was everything I had seen pictures of in books … "

He was impressed that the "big, white UCC churches" invited Hartford students to be on staff as student pastors, assistants, and youth group leaders. When Smith returned to Athens, Alabama to work during the summer of 1958, they were amazed by how much he had learned in just one year.

In his final year at Hartford, Smith sent a newspaper clipping and a note about the seminary students' fieldwork to his parents. The article[66] mentions the name, home country or state, and service assignment of about fifty Hartford students at various stages of their studies. Smith himself had been assigned as a student assistant at Union Baptist, a "huge black church" in downtown Hartford. With self-awareness and pride, Smith underlines for his parents his name and the names of the other three black students, noting that only two of the four were working in black churches. He also noted the name of his roommate that year, who was white. Without braggadocio, he suggests to his parents that some of the people at their church in South Bend might want to see the article. In closing, he sends "Mother and Daddy," "the Howards," and "the neighbors" his love.

—៣—

While at Hartford, Smith began to use journaling as a regular form of reflection. Smith's use of the tool he calls "my therapy" became very consistent in the early 1980s. Over 60 years he has produced more than 70 journals. The two earliest journals bear entries starting in 1957. Recurrent subjects include racial injustice, knowing one's self and knowing God, and developing an understanding of death. In his writing, Smith is direct and honest about moments of inspiration and awe, feelings of anger and sadness, and his own shortcomings.

On the inside cover of the small maroon and black notebook with some of the oldest entries, Smith inscribed his intentions:

Existential Realizations – in an attempt to capture the thoughts of my moods from time to time; an attempt to acquaint myself better with myself. Most of us are moody from time to time; it is my hope that I can understand myself, my reactions, and my thoughts as I encounter myself through the various phases and aspects of the world. Paul Smith 11/16/59.

The earliest entry is a rhyming love poem that Smith believes was authored by someone else. On March 21, 1957, the young man who copied it into his journal was surely thinking of Frances Pitts, who received Smith's Alpha Phi Alpha pin a few weeks later. Two other poems by Smith follow under the titles "The Lord Will Make A Way Somehow," and "Don't Quit." On later dates, Smith writes paragraphs entitled: "You Give Yourself Away," "No Faith," "Love." Among the entries in this journal are aphorisms including:

- A man should know himself, accept himself.
- Don't make a career of religion just to change your own soul.

Subsequent entries suggest that the notebooks quickly began functioning as a place to work through sermon ideas. One long passage on how people discard their friends, associates, even their church and God in their pursuit of success, is labeled "Parts of a Sermon 'Void if Detached.'" Other topics are listed on a page entitled, "Sermon Points:"

- Who has the choice to live life on his own terms? Compromises must be made. We have to live creatively in a frame of reference.
- Job: Even though he slay me, yet I will trust him.
- Life is a miracle, Love is a miracle.
- "God is there too in the desperation. I do not know why God should strike but God is what is stricken also: Life is what despairs in death and desperate is life still." J.B.

In an early description of his meditative practice, Rev. Smith writes in 1961 about creating an island of silence before prayer.

I bring to my quiet time my concerns to examine them—to see them more clearly—and to know what God would have me do. My concern today is with the need for meaning, which is the condition of so many of us who come to the church. We need meaning to fill the empty places in our empty lives. I would therefore say to my church, say to me that which is significant so that I may have some directions as I seek to live with wholeness the brief days allotted to me.

Always alive to the politics of the day, Smith writes approvingly in June 1960.

[James] Lawson is accused of fomenting civil disobedience, but the Christian Church is grounded on 300 years of civil disobedience.

The last entry in this journal contains his commentary on his experiences at Selma.

3/10/65 No man is an outsider in this world because we all belong here. In comment to being called "outside" agitators in the racial strife in Selma, Alabama. Outside agitators are necessary to stir the consciences of the people.

The first nine entries in another early journal labeled "Supply Service Record Book" were written in October 1959 during Smith's last year at Hartford Seminary. The first entry, the subject that prompted him to start a new notebook, is the most desperate, angry outpouring to God about the struggles of black people that exists in all his voluminous writing. Entitled "A Psalm of Hatred," the passage is a furious entreaty occasioned by the murders of black men in three Mississippi: Money (where Emmett Till was killed in August 1955), Poplarville (where Mack Charles Parker was lynched in April 1959), and Clarksdale (where Booker T. Mixon was beaten and died of injuries officially described as the results of a hit-and-run accident in October 1959). From the dating of the journal, it appears that it was the news of Mixon's death that prompted Smith to express his outrage on paper.

> 1959—We call upon thee O God, as we lick the wounds from our recent defeats. Why is it O Lord, that thou cannot see us in all walks of life? Our black faces are smutty and filled with sweat from our battle. We remember too well our defeat at Money, Mississippi at your hands, the Great White Father; and yet you sent your wrath upon our brethren at Popularville [sic], ye on to Clarksdale, where the blood of the black man runs freely. Why O God has thou sent thy wrath upon our people? A people who lift their voices in deep, sensitive spirituals and songs to thee? Why hast thou sent down the angry ropes, the gnashing dogs and the evil demons, which whisk away our loved ones during the night? Why, O Lord, hast thou chosen a child, who was barely able to distinguish between good and evil? Have we been that evil? Have we violated too many of your laws! O God, we hate our persecutors, although you tell us to love; but thou knowest it is difficult for us to love when we can feel cold steel beating against our heads, blood running down our backs—our friends and loved ones being burned out of their homes. We hear convulsive sobs from our women and children as they run throughout our towns, burning and destroying. If thou lovest us as you say, why must we suffer so? Why does your wrath continue? Our hatred for thee grows stronger as our days come and go, because our prayers are not answered; our work is in vain and thou who are the great White God, continues to send down thy wrath upon us; we are dying, neglected, gaunt and desperate and thou dost not hear our plea. Is there no balm

in Gilead? Is there no peace in Mississippi? Hear us
and answer!

Throughout his life, Smith has struggled to absorb news of violence
perpetrated against innocent black people. The fact that he has never
again accused God of being the source of people's misery suggests
that these were the thoughts of a frightened and furious young man.
A critical part of Smith's spiritual journey since those days has been
finding other ways to make sense of these relentless and terrible events.

In quieter moments, Smith's early journal entries articulate a
willingness to engage in searching self-reflection that has become a
way of life for him.

Oct. 1959 Perhaps one of the tragedies of human society is that no public man is as good as his private self
might have been. The interior life is the vital part of a
man. Do we really know the interior of our lives? Obviously, yes, even though we fear the interior the most.
Calvin has said, "A man must know himself if he is to
know God; and man must know God if he is to know
himself." In Him we live and move and have our being.

12/2/59 One must have the courage to interview
himself.

In another entry from 1959, he voices a view of race that has held
firm through his life.

When you sincerely love God in your heart, and accept the love of God in Christ Jesus, you move from
the realm of color into the realm of oneness; people
become people[,] not kinds of. This is the case of one
losing his identity, knowing who he is in relation to
other people and God, and not according to his color
or the achievements that have been made.

In February 1960, Smith comments on what had long been an annual event in church circles—"Race Relations Sunday."[67] Harkening back to his senior thesis, he writes approvingly of black and white ministers exchanging pulpits, giving all of them "a chance to be Christians for a change." He goes on to make a strong statement against racism in the church.

> We have to stop fumbling along in the name of Christianity … All are our brothers or none is. Race Relations should be observed every day, not just at a special time of year. Our church doors should remain open to all, regardless of race, creed or color. God loves children and people, not races and colors.

Paul Smith became "Rev. Mr." Smith upon completing his studies at Hartford Seminary on May 23, 1960. The graduation program shows that his friends Ralph Logan Carson and Julia McClain graduated as well. Among the thirty-five others were eleven students from Connecticut, thirteen from other states in the US, and one student each from Egypt, Syria, Lebanon, and the Philippines. At Hartford, Smith's understanding of people and of himself had undergone enormous growth.

—⚉—

Still greater personal transformation was on the horizon that summer. On June 12, Paul Smith and Frances Pitts were married in Pasadena, California. Smith must have taken the Hartford journal with him on the trip because one entry mentions the awe-inspiring scenery he and his parents encountered on their drive across the country. When his father says of the magnificent scenery, "All this was made by God," Smith calls him "a natural theologian in his own way [who] caught the glimpse of the eternal." In the back of the book, he keeps a careful "expense" record of how much they spent on gas along the way.

The expansiveness of that trip seems to have carried over to his wedding day. On the day of the ceremony, Smith writes in his journal

Wedding photo of Frances Pitts and Paul Smith, Pasadena, California,
June 1960.

about marriage being "a wonderful estate to enter into, especially if
the two people are in love and happy." He states that in a marriage
with a foundation in Christian principles and in which the two people

have "given completely of themselves," there is much to look forward to. He asserts that he "believes very strongly that ours has been such a marriage."

In a journal note written decades later,[68] he provides some details about the wedding. He also articulates his view on the kind of ministry he felt he was "always destined" for.

> 6/12/13 Fifty years ago today I was in Pasadena, California to marry the person I love. Fran and I stood before her parents [sic] Episcopal Priest on a beautiful afternoon and repeated our vows. My parents and Fran's parents stood happily by our side as we joyfully committed ourselves to each other. Kathy, Fran's sister and Bill, my younger brother were maid of honor and best man. I remember hundreds of people, black and white, happily sitting in the church in support of us. Classmates from Hartford Seminary surprised me by showing up for the ceremony. I had no idea they would attend. The two classmates were white students who had earlier graduated from seminary with me. Looking back I realize I was always destined to be involved in ministry that would include people from all racial and ethnic backgrounds. The fact of my being ordained in a denomination with only a handful of black people is just another sign of what would become my life's work.

By today's standards, Paul and Fran had seen very little of each other in the two and a half years since their engagement. Paul notes in 2013 that he married "a beautiful and talented woman whom I had not seen but once since the announcement of our intention to marry." As Paul settled into his first semester in Connecticut, Fran had moved to California to spend her remaining college years closer to her parents and younger siblings. True to their vision, her parents supported her desire to spend half of her senior year in Europe. It was a transformative journey; Fran says she understood what freedom really felt like the moment she stepped off the plane in Copenhagen. She went on to graduate from Whittier College in California where she majored in Psychology and Sociology while securing her teaching credentials. That proved immediately useful, because Paul's first job offers were not what he had hoped they would be.

Later in their first summer together, though, Smith was struggling with the day-to-day reality of sharing his life. On August 5, 1960, he records another installment in a lifelong meditation on how to live with anger:

> What is the best way to channel one's hostility? Where does one go when he gets angry? When should one forgive when there has been a misunderstanding? I have found in these two months of marriage that it is extremely difficult for two people with different backgrounds to work out their differences. It's even more difficult if there is a difference in the range and degree of experience along life's road. While these problems do exist, they will remain unless the two can work these differences out together …

With delicacy and discretion, he muses about what to do if one person seems more secure than the other. He wonders whether one party should play the dominant role, making decisions knowing that unhappiness will result. Searching himself for fault and affirming his love for his wife, he concludes with a prayer.

> I am deeply troubled at this point because I don't quite know what the right thing to do happens to be. I think I know and this makes me feel that I'm being selfish. I do love my partner in marriage and will never stop loving her; however, the adjustment seems so pressing now. Can it be that our values are mixed? Have I put too much emphasis upon things rather than on the essence that makes life[?] Oh God, help me in the midst

of this crisis that together we might be brought to a clearer understanding of our roles and lives as we meet the cruelties and necessities of the day.

With the union of Paul and Frances still strong after more than fifty years, it is clear they found a way to navigate through the difficulties of early marriage. After the wedding, they packed as many wedding gifts as they could into Paul's father's new Chevy and set out on the road toward another new territory—the Northeast. By the fall of 1960, they had moved to a new city and started new jobs. They were learning what they had to offer as professionals and looking forward to having children. The partnership that would carry them into lives shared with the most humble and the most powerful of people had finally begun.

5

To Rev and Mrs. Paul Smith = 489 Atchison St. Pasadena Calif

Your many friends in Salem Church are thrilled and thinking of you both on the happiest day of your lives We pray that God may attend you with his richest blessings Please accept our sincerest congratulations and best wishes for a long and happy married life. We are looking forward to your return to Salem=

Members of Salem Church.
                    Western Union Telegram, June 11, 1960

Urban Alliances

The summer before his marriage, Paul Smith had gone northwest to Buffalo, New York, for an internship at what became Salem United Church of Christ. The German-speaking congregation liked Smith so much, they offered him a job starting immediately after his graduation from Hartford. They knew he might take a job elsewhere, but they were willing to wait for him. That was fortunate because, contrary to Smith's optimistic expectations, other job offers were scarce the follow-ing year. After his graduation from Talladega, the Baptists had opened their arms to him again. He had again resisted their overtures. He knew he wanted an urban ministry and one where his education would be put to good use. But despite his history of successfully crossing racial boundaries, he was still only being considered for certain positions. "It had to be a black church. We were just not being called for other churches," he says now.

A promising offer eventually came from a black UCC church in Detroit. The congregation was made up of middle-class and upper-middle-class African Americans. Smith responded quickly, acutely conscious that he was engaged to be married and "didn't have a place to go, didn't have a job, didn't have a place to live!" However, the Detroit church took too long to finalize the terms of its offer. Just after Smith signed on with Salem United, the minister in Detroit called to extend his church's offer. At a key turning point in his path, the young pastor chose to keep his word to the elderly parishioners in Buffalo.

> The guy I was supposed to work with, a white guy named Howard Fuller, [was] just a beautiful, beautiful human being. There was just no way. I said, "You know that church [in Buffalo] is going to be so disappointed. That church has waited for me, knowing that I was between a rock and a hard place." And not only did they offer me a job as assistant minister, they found an apartment for us. Howard Fuller knew I was getting married, that I was engaged. By that time, we had set a date …

The telegram sent by Salem Church just before Paul and Fran's wedding exemplifies the warmth and cordiality that the church was extending to the young couple. The elite black church in Detroit got no for an answer, and the Smiths started their work in Buffalo. As Assistant Minister, Smith was set to work alongside Rev. Fuller, with whom he had already formed a bond. However, the wisdom of Dr. Pitts's advice to finish their degrees before marrying immediately became apparent. With her degree and impeccable teaching credentials from California, Fran quickly secured a job in Buffalo "making ten times more money than I was going to make as a minister," Smith says. As her father had hoped, Fran proved to be a "valuable asset" to

Smith and his ministry right from the start.

Though it was in the Northeast, Buffalo had much the same character as the South Bend of Smith's early years. Polish, Irish, and Italian immigrants, drawn by the promise of jobs in Buffalo's factories, settled in neighborhoods on the east side of the city. African Americans from the South who came looking for a new life found themselves clustered in the southeastern sections of the city.[69] However, by 1960, Buffalo was beginning to deindustrialize. Thereafter, it endured steady population loss, increasing segregation, and the development of urban ghettos.

Salem United was located on Sherman Street, on the east side of the city where Germans and Poles had been concentrated. The Smiths moved into the top floor of a two-family house that the church had rented for them and went straight to work. Now that Smith had been "called" by a specific church, ordination and installation were to follow. The details of these ceremonies differ by denomination, but they are the most significant rites of passage in a young minister's career. Smith was ordained in the Congregationalist Church with which Salem United had just merged. Celebrated in the context of a service, his ordination entailed his making a statement of his faith. Then by the laying on of hands, trusted leaders of the church formally recognized his new status in the congregation and wider church polity.

Smith's community of origin rallied to support and honor him. The service was reported in a South Bend newspaper.[70] Dr. Bross made the trip to upstate New York from Alabama to preach the ordination sermon. Both Congregational and Baptist ministers from Buffalo participated in the ceremony. One of Smith's early supporters from South Bend, Rev. Grant, accompanied Smith's parents on the trip to Buffalo.

The elderly, German-speaking congregation at Salem United had already warmed to Smith and he to them. Their interactions somehow worked despite their differences. Paul says, "They spoke no English but they would take my hand. I would pray with them. They would talk with me even though I didn't understand what they were saying. But they were so interested and fascinated, that here was contact with an African American they were having toward the end of their lives ... "

In an article on his career published in 1980 by *Presbyterian Survey*,

Smith discussed with author Jim Auchmutey the techniques he used to reach the parishioners at Salem Church.

> Smith said he rarely felt racial pressure in Buffalo. He tried to associate himself in the parishioner's minds with church traditions. By performing an annual candlelight service, for instance, he gained a degree of acceptance even though, he conjectured, the congregation may have been lulled by pleasant memories and "may not have heard a single word I said."[71]

The article relates that in Buffalo as in Athens, Alabama, officiating after the death of a parishioner revealed some hidden truths.

> When one church leader died and the White pastor was out of town, Smith had to assume funeral duties. Reluctantly, the family decided to allow the Black man to perform the ceremony, then the undertaker talked them out of it. A White minister was brought in.

"When the rest of the congregation heard about that," Smith remembers, "they made sure that everyone knew that sort of thing would not be condoned anymore. From that day, they made sure I'd be there for funerals."[72]

Serving the dying, whoever they might be, and officiating after their deaths has become a great strength of Smith's pastorates. His experience with one Salem parishioner in particular led him to a deep insight about the kind of work he had been called to do. "I remember Christ Harlach. I saw him probably three weeks before he died. I can just hear his broken German with just a tinge of English, saying how much he appreciated my being there—that he could go home now to be with God. The circle was, for him, completed."

Smith is emphatic when he tells this story. "You can't have that experience in an all-white or all-black church. You can't. You *can't*. I can see him now with tears in his eyes, knowing he was dying, and still he managed to say that. I knew I could not be settled on just a totally African American congregation. You can't have that kind of an experience in a single-race church. You just can't. You can't. The beauty is in the diversity ... "

Anthropologists, journalists, teachers, and clergy know there is a special sweetness in finding commonality with people unlike you. It affirms one's humanity to make a bond across what are ordinarily seen as lines of difference. The rewards are huge—an enlarged sense of what is possible among human beings and the hope for humanity that comes with that. Paul Smith understood this a very long time ago.

Smith's confidence and his reputation strengthened during his years in Buffalo. From about 1961 on, he began to speak at other churches and appeared twice on television. In 1963, the African American weekly magazine *JET* published several pages on Smith, highlighting his multiracial congregation and the fact that he was using jazz to reach his parishioners. The young preacher told the writer he did not see any conflict between "my religion and my interest in jazz." Typically self-assured and upbeat, he notes, "I could always play drums, and I decided to use my God-given talent to help spread the good news of the gospel." One of four photos published with the article captures Paul and wife Fran, well dressed and smiling on a couch with six-month-old Kathleen in Paul's arms. It was the era of the Kennedys' White House, and the attractive Smith family appeared to be in a Camelot of their own.

Smith is quick to recognize senior pastor Rev. Fuller as an important factor in his success at Salem. "Howard was the first real pastor other than my home minister who actually taught me what ministry was about. He was really on it—a Renaissance man at Salem with these German parishioners. I went there in my senior year of seminary. He recruited me to work with him ... Howard let me into the inner circle of ministers."

This "inner circle" came to be called the Ministerial Alliance. About a dozen clergy began to meet once a week in the spring of 1961 for fellowship and discussion about the social and political issues of the day. They were mostly young men, newly married and just starting out as clergy. Three of them were black: Smith, William Hayes, and Porter Phillips. Smith recorded the minutes at what appears to have been a very early meeting of these men in one of his journals. The group was structured enough to have a Chairman of the Program Committee, a President, and a Constitution. Their concerns included a land development project, addressing segregation in area hospitals, and trying to combat the influence of organized crime in one part of the city.

> There was a little group of about twelve of us. We were kicking some butt! I mean, we were *out* there. A gangster owned everything and we took him on. We were too young to be afraid. The government was so corrupt in Buffalo the people took it over. Same as in Ferguson [Missouri].
>
> This gangster who controlled all of Buffalo—it was like Elliott Ness, really! And here we were, these young ministers making it tough for them. We were lucky we didn't get killed! But I think the gangster knew better. He knew we were insignificant, young innocent ministers trying to do the right thing. We were not a threat. Except that we were—we just didn't know it! Because what we were doing did make a difference.

One of their group in particular, George Leak of the African Methodist Episcopal Zion Church, had to hire bodyguards because he ran the drug activity out of his neighborhood.

Leak also played a key role in the ministers' contributions to the wider political struggle. Responding to calls for volunteers, Smith says the Alliance pulled straws to see who would represent them on a planned bus ride across the South. It fell to Leak to join what came to be called the "Freedom Rides" in 1961. Leak was one of those who almost died when white segregationists, furious that the bus riders were testing the new federal mandate to desegregate interstate travel, attacked the Riders' broken-down Greyhound bus near Anniston, Alabama. The mob battered the bus with axes and pipes and eventually set it on fire. If there had not been a government investigator onboard who pulled his gun, scaring off those outside who were trying to block the door, everyone in the bus would have died.[73]

Knowing how dangerous it was on the front lines of the struggle, Smith joined Andrew Young's nonviolence training program in Savannah, Georgia, during his first year out of seminary. Smith says that Young was delighted when he saw Smith getting off the bus to join the group at Dorchester Academy, formerly an American Missionary Association school. As Young remembers it, "what I saw in him was a new generation of ministers that were gonna have to carry on. Because ... Dr. King was very frank. We just needed to find something worth living for, because we probably wouldn't live long doing what we were doing. He said we'll all be lucky if we see 40."[74]

The Congregational Church had lent Young and other leaders the use of the Dorchester property as a place to hold workshops to prepare activists for the rigors of nonviolent protest. Volunteers came from all across the neighboring states. "We would charter a bus in Louisiana and it would drive across Mississippi, Alabama, and Georgia, and you know, bring people there on a Sunday afternoon. They'd get in Sunday night, we'd start Monday and we'd end up Saturday night and they'd start back."[75] Smith says it was the role-playing workshops and lectures in Savannah that helped him survive his later trip to Selma.

Back in Buffalo, Smith found other opportunities to make a difference. In 1963, he became Industrial Relations Director for the Buffalo Urban League. A League official told a South Bend newspaper reporter about the need for the job Smith had been given.

> About 18 different organizations for civil rights, housing and jobs have popped up here (in Buffalo) during the last year. Many of them are handled by ministers, so we want to see if we can get a correlated program with them. I believe Rev. Mr. Smith is just the man to work with them.[76]

The same article mentions changes in the congregation at Salem United. To the hometown readers interested in how one of their own was faring, Rev. Smith's church was described as "interracial." It was further noted that his "congregation has about a 60–40 per cent Negro-white composition." This suggests that the young minister was successfully attracting new worshippers to the UCC church.[77]

The Urban League is currently led by Marc Morial, the former mayor of New Orleans and a close friend of Smith's who has shared his pulpit. The mission of the organization, as articulated today, is "to enable African Americans to secure economic self-reliance, parity, power and civil rights."[78] Smith says, "It all had to do with fact that I, as an African American kid, could not get a job in a white corporate firm." In his role for the Buffalo Urban League, he talked with corporate administrators to place black workers and improve company relations with people of color. He also worked to get contributions from white businesses for Urban League programs.

Both of these roles were early forms of the "diversity" consulting that he continues to engage in today. Smith says, "I knew my gifts were more than just being a preacher, a minister. I had been exposed to more. I knew what possibilities were there." Evidence that he was having an impact comes at the end of the Supply Record journal where the names of four people are listed under the heading, "Jobs Secured."

Working to change the system from within was not the approach advocated by the strident black politicians of the day, and Smith occasionally took some heat for his beliefs. There came a day in Buffalo, for instance, when Smith accepted an invitation to attend a talk given by black nationalist Malcolm X. The fiery Muslim speaker invited the whole Ministers' Alliance to attend a monthly gathering at the Buffalo mosque where he was scheduled to speak. Smith believes that Malcolm knew about the efforts of the Alliance to combat the criminal influences in Buffalo and supported them. Smith was the only one to accept the challenge, however.

When Smith arrived and the event began, Malcolm was cordial. Later in discussion, though, Smith says, "I got stomped on." One can imagine that the young minister's idealism did not impress perhaps the most vocal proponent of black separatism at the time. Malcolm X "dominated the discussion, and made me look like I was out of my league," Smith says. Nonetheless, he relished the opportunity to interact with the man whose passion and intelligence had won him many admirers; "it was enlightening for me just to be in his presence and surrounded by such a devoted following of people." The two did not meet again, since Malcolm X was assassinated in New York City in 1965, a few weeks before the marches in Selma.

By the mid-1960s, urban unrest had become the ordinary tenor of the times. Violent street confrontations in Harlem in July 1964 were followed immediately by three days of "race riots" in Rochester, near Buffalo, in upstate New York. A few weeks later, rioting flared in Philadelphia. Violence and destruction as had never been seen before rocked the Watts section of Los Angeles in August 1965, Newark in July 1967, and Detroit in 1967. The parallels with present-day race politics in the US are striking—all these events were set off by confrontations between urban populations of color and over-zealous, heavy-handed police.

Against this backdrop, efforts to integrate churches like Salem United took on vital importance. Late in his four years in Buffalo, Smith gained the crucial assistance of another minister who became a lifelong friend. Like Smith, Marvin Chandler had been born in Indiana. He too had been courted by the Baptist church after receiving his undergraduate degree at Indiana University. Chandler's great intelligence and warmth, however, drew the attention of mentors who encouraged him to pursue a graduate degree. Chandler was accepted into the prestigious Colgate Rochester Divinity School where he studied from 1959–63. The Smiths were already in Buffalo when Chandler moved his family there, intending to commute to Rochester for his studies.[79] The two families quickly became close, and the Chandlers soon began to help out at Salem United.

Rev. Chandler's wife, Portia, says the two men were "like brothers, like two peas in a pod."[80] Both were dedicated, creative, high-energy people. Both had an interest in urban ministry and were comfortable with ecumenicalism. Both were talented musicians who began collaborating to bring jazz into joint services at area churches. When Smith was asked to preach at a church out of town, he often invited Chandler to join him, and the two played jazz as part of the service.

One of the techniques Chandler became known for starts with several members of an audience choosing one musical note each on the piano. From those notes, Chandler improvises a complete piece of music on the spot. The effect is literally to create harmony out of dissonance, thereby delivering at an almost subconscious level, the ministers' fundamental message about the human potential for unity. It is an unforgettable demonstration.

—◊◊◊—

Another transformative friendship that developed for Smith in Buffalo was with the Rev. Carl Dudley, his companion at Selma. Dudley was pastor at First Presbyterian Church of Buffalo from 1959–62[81] and a leading instigator of the crusading efforts of the Ministerial Alliance. Though they did not yet know each other well, Dudley reached out to Smith not long after being called in 1963 to lead an all-black church in downtown St. Louis.

Following his heart and his spirit, Smith answered the call to be Dudley's co-pastor. As LaClede Town, a brand new style of community development, arose around the old church, the two dynamic pastors set out to prove that church leadership could be shared interracially and that the church could help create lasting urban communities that brought people together from radically different backgrounds.

Leaving Buffalo meant disrupting the life the Smiths had been building. While Fran recalls that "that first job had a pretty decent salary," nothing was guaranteed in St. Louis. After marrying, Fran had expected that she would teach for a time and then have her first child before returning to work. She notes that this was not early feminism; it was practicality. Black wives and husbands both had to work to make enough money to support a family. Fran's mother had laid out the path for her. "The planning was [for children] two years apart. It was a prescribed thing. My mother said you were supposed to do all this, being the oldest. You did what your parents said to do."[82]

Unexpected events had already interfered with the plan. Fran relates that her first pregnancy resulted in a miscarriage. She was told that she should wait some months before trying again. When Fran became pregnant again, her doctor insisted that she stop working immediately. Though it was in the middle of the school year, Fran complied. She points out that one could not teach school while pregnant in those days, so she didn't have much choice. Happily, the pregnancy went well, and Kathleen, the first of the Smiths' three daughters, was born on September 7, 1962.

Smith also says that when Dudley called him to talk about joining forces in St. Louis, he and Fran had just fought for and purchased a home. Some of the neighbors in the segregated Williamsburg section of Buffalo were not happy to see a black family coming and had staged protests. In a turn of events that had lifelong consequences for Smith, "the minister of the all-white Presbyterian church stepped up in our support. He and members of the congregation came over the day we moved in and welcomed us and were present to offset the protesting neighbors. That is when I decided to join the Presbyterian denomination."

It happened that both Dudley and Berea in St. Louis were also affiliated with the Presbyterian Church. Taking note of these "clues," Smith put the Buffalo house back on the market, took the job, and committed himself to a new denomination. In four years, he had developed competence and experience as a preacher and a pastor and discovered the ease with which he could communicate across all kinds of social boundaries. He had begun a long and fruitful association with the Urban League and made strong bonds with professional colleagues. He had also begun to learn about being a husband and a father.

He did not know it, but St. Louis would be the site of his meeting with the great teacher whose work had inspired his own. The choice to leave Buffalo helped him fulfill his deepest aspirations.

.

6

I can give testimony of Paul's influence in St. Louis. [He and Carl working together] was a kind of emblem of what the faith could be. It had influence over people who had no intention of joining Berea. They [felt] that Berea was doing something that their congregations should be doing. By the time I left St. Louis, [Berea] had a very different meaning for the life of that community. The community itself changed dramatically.

Luther Smith, Jr., 2015[83]

Spirit in St. Louis

In 1964, when Rev. Smith, his wife, and daughter arrived in St. Louis from Buffalo, Rev. Carl Dudley had already been in the city for two years, working to make a new mixed-income housing development into a racially integrated neighborhood. The community that was rising up was like nothing anyone had seen before. Eventually encompassing 1400 apartments and townhouses, LaClede Town was explicitly designed to bring a mix of people and a mix of residences together as a whole. As a former resident puts it, it was "cool, hip, cheap and populated by people committed to making integration work."[84]

The development came to include a swimming pool, a Laundromat, a coffeehouse, and a pub. Artists contributed substantially to both LaClede Town's reputation and to its street life. The resident

Black Artists Group (BAG) became famous for its musical and theater performances.[85] A number of important jazz ensembles grew out this rich context. There were poetry readings, dance concerts, and softball games.

Rent was set according to the income of new residents. A concerted effort was made to house a group of families who were as heterogeneous as possible.

People from different nations, cultural groups, economic strata, and religious communities lived, intentionally, side-by-side.

> It brought together a community of people—black, white, brown, Jews, Christians, Muslims, atheists, lawyers, architects, sanitation workers, actors, athletes, draft dodgers, hookers, social workers, welfare recipients, musicians, reporters, waiters, politicians, doctors.[86]

Berea Presbyterian Church was central to the plan from the beginning. Located at 3010 Olive Street, in the run-down Millcreek section of St. Louis's Central West End, the church had had a strong black congregation since its founding in 1898. It also had a history of activism.[87] Nonetheless, it barely escaped being flattened by bulldozers when the city of St. Louis razed everything else in the neighborhood. It was only the negotiation of church leaders that allowed Berea to be saved.

By the time the Smiths arrived in 1964, Dudley was overseeing major renovations to the church. These included reversing the orientation of the structure so that the front doors opened north onto Olive Street and were more accessible to people in the new development. A new community room was added to the building that soon saw constant use. Rev. Dudley moved his family to the neighborhood so that they could live across the street from the church. The Smiths settled into a small apartment nearby. The two ministers quickly became the spiritual center of the community. As a former resident of LaClede Town wrote in 1997,

Carl Dudley and Paul Smith, two Presbyterian ministers—one white, one black—transformed a historically
black church with a dwindling congregation into an
ethnically diverse institution that was often standing
room only.[88]

Carl Dudley and Paul Smith, Berea Presbyterian Church, St. Louis,
Missouri, 1965.

For a time in the late '60s and early '70s, the community was
considered a national model for successful urban renewal and integration. Nathan Dudley notes that "it was unusual in that the people
considered it their social life as well as their place of residence."[89]
Smith says, "It was experimental—interracial, interfaith, believers and
nonbelievers, all together." He emphasizes that the experience caused
"a major, major shift in my thinking about what a church should be."
The church doors were open for all kinds of joint projects and activities, and events there drew people from other parts of St. Louis.[90] It
was a middle-class congregation, with successful black professionals
from all over the city coming to worship.[91] Nathan Dudley cites the
manager of the development, Jerry Berger, as describing Berea as "a
dynamite church, one that's alive and unafraid."[92]

There wasn't enough money to pay both Carl and Paul, so, building on his Urban League experience, a job as Director of Race and Religion was created for Paul and paid for by the area presbytery. As Smith remembers it, "they knew I could put people together of different races and religions." They aimed to create bridges between some of the white and black churches in St. Louis. Smith says,

> One of the signature programs we started involved white members of five suburban Presbyterian churches of which the Ferguson Church and its pastor were participants. With the blessings of the St. Louis Presbytery and the five congregations, we invited a minimum of two white families to become full members of Berea Presbyterian Church, which at that time was an old, historic African American congregation … Ferguson Presbyterian Church was one of the first congregations to send families to our program.

In 1965, when Paul Smith and Carl Dudley got off the plane in Selma to march with Dr. King, these were the white ministers who made the journey with them.

By joining Dudley at Berea Presbyterian and remaining in the denomination throughout his career, Rev. Smith's professional life has been shaped by a "presbyterian" model of church governance. This kind of church polity falls between the "episcopal" model, which concentrates power in the hands of a local bishop, and the "congregational" in which the local assembly self-governs. Presbyterian churches split decision-making power between a rotating group of "elders" elected from the congregation (the "session") and an area council assembly made up of representatives from the local congregations (the "presbytery.") The presbyteries in turn send representatives to the General Assembly.[93]

Lay leadership plays a major role in Presbyterian church decision-making and ritualizing. Session members serve three-year terms and are "ordained" by the laying on of hands, just like ministers. Ministers are called "teaching elders," while elected lay leaders are "ruling elders." While being given a unique role vis-à-vis the congregation, a Presbyterian minister is advisory to the Session and is subject to the regulation and supervision of the Presbytery.

Fortunately, collaborative leadership has come naturally to Smith from the beginning. Though Dudley was a few years older and more experienced than Smith, he never treated his new co-pastor as anything less than an equal. Dudley later encouraged Smith take the lead on the Selma trip. That kind of professional and spiritual generosity had a huge impact on Smith: "He celebrated my gifts like I celebrated his." In contrast to some of the autocratic ministers encountered in his youth, Smith has never hesitated to share power.

In changing his denominational affiliation, Smith knew that he would be one of a small proportion of Presbyterian ministers who were black. But this too was something he was unafraid of and even came to relish. The congregation at Berea was ready to help. One day early on, a parishioner told Smith he wanted Smith to pick him up and bring him by his house. The man, who worked as a chauffeur for a wealthy white executive, was known for his sharp appearance; Smith says, "Even when he was dying, he wore silk robes with his initials on them." Welcoming Smith to his home, the man presented Smith with a surprise from Rich's Department Store. "He said, 'I'm so glad you're here. You're young. I've made a purchase for you. I notice you don't have any white shirts. Presbyterians wear white shirts! I want you to be successful.' And he gave me four white shirts!"

A worship service program from Berea dated February 28, 1965, has survived among Smith's papers. Its cover bears a photo of Berea's stone façade with a crowd of well-dressed parishioners on the sidewalk in front. It is noted in the order of worship in the program that Reverends Dudley and Smith alternated in leading the service. Smith delivered "Void Where Detached," the sermon he had been working on since Hartford.

One of the innovations at LaClede Town was the Circle Coffee Shop and Bookstore. Long before the name "Starbucks" was first heard in Seattle, this venue and its performance space became the artistic

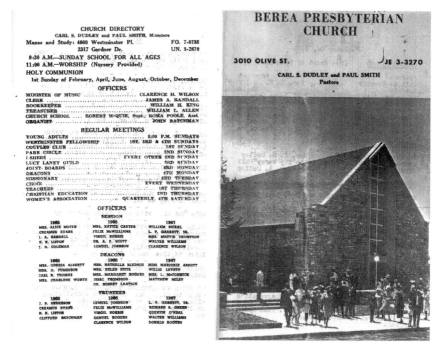

Worship service program, Berea Presbyterian Church, Feb. 28, 1965.

heart of the development.

> At LaClede Town, the Circle Coffee Shop, and Berea Church, opportunities for artistic experimentation and a cadre of young artists dissatisfied with the city's arts scene came together in a dynamic mixture. The nearby Berea Presbyterian Church [administered] the Circle for the LaClede Town Management … and the Circle's tiny stage hosted readings, dance, improvisational theater and music from the likes of Hamiet Bluiett, Julius Hemphill and Oliver Lake—all with a strong focus on audience participation.[94]

The community was politically active, even somewhat radical. In 1966, Carl Dudley and other ministers from St. Louis drove up to Chicago repeatedly to train with Saul Alinsky, the radical community organizer.[95] At a time when controversy over the Vietnam War was becoming strident, Nathan Dudley remembers that it was suggested that people invite the media to witness the burning of their draft cards in the sanctuary. When an elderly, long-time parishioner was asked what she thought of the plan, she said she thought that the sanctuary was "just the place for them to burn those cards."[96] While on the one hand running a summer day camp for kids, the church also occasionally allowed the Black Panthers and political activist groups to meet there.[97]

One of the many significant innovations that Smith and Dudley implemented at Berea was to open up conversations about funerals and death. This was important because their multiracial congregation brought differing expectations to such events. At Easter in 1965, the young ministers together with Berea's lay leadership produced a mimeographed booklet on the subject that was distributed to parishioners.[98] Smith and Dudley urged families to plan in advance for a loved one's death. The pastors' advice included never making funeral arrangements alone. They cautioned people to keep their financial limitations in mind and to remember "the simplicity of our faith." Those with material goods were advised to have a will.

Expectations about funerary arrangements differed between black and white parishioners. Smith knew that many members of Berea Church had grown up with the black Baptist traditions he had known in South Bend. In those churches, the central focus of the funeral service was the open casket positioned in the front of the church near the pulpit. Goodbyes were said directly to the deceased person in the casket by mourners and preachers alike, after the service was over. Emotions tended to run high. Sometimes after the funeral service, the casket was driven through the deceased person's hometown or neighborhood, "one more time." Cremation was not considered an option. Smith has heard many a black Baptist minister exclaim, "You can't preach a funeral without a body!" Meanwhile, some white members wanted a closed casket or cremation and a memorial service.

The Berea leadership suggested that everyone did not have to approach these issues the same way. IIIIn the case of a funeral, it was suggested that the casket be covered until the end of the burial services with a simple cloth belonging to the parish. Smith says now that this made it easier for people of modest means to choose a plain casket rather than feeling obliged to buy something more costly. Also unusual for some were the possibilities of autopsy, organ donation and donation of the body for scientific study. Dudley and Smith stated that these too were "fully consistent with our Christian faith."

The confluence of people, traditions, and personalities at Berea made the work difficult at times. Smith was paying close attention to the ways his flock interacted, as one journal entry shows.

> A few days ago a group of citizens in St. Louis came together to discuss ways of helping in the civil rights thrust. Only by the grace of God were these diverse people able to communicate and plan together. The backgrounds were so different, the interests so varied, that at one point they were eternally at one another's throat. After 48 hours we came together again and hopefully worked out our differences ... What happened to the group as we went our separate ways that day? Mad, hostile towards one another, accusations made! Someone, or something touched each individual, especially those who were grinding personal axes— and somehow caused us to see the significance of our purpose, which far outweighed any other concerns.[99]

A seasoned observer who lived in St. Louis at the time was Rev. Dr. Luther Smith, Jr. [no relation]. A minister and scholar whose family later attended Smith's church in Atlanta, Luther Smith gives the Berea ministry of Dudley and Smith high marks.

> People were hopeful that this might represent something new for St. Louis. People weren't thinking about interracial communities. With Berea, it was such a hopeful possibility and sign of something else being possible. Berea was so active as a church in community formation and bringing people together. There was a

vitality and growth. They were black and white clergy with an interracial congregation—it was very inspiring. It is difficult for me to remember another ministry that produced such excitement about the ways they thought about worship and outreach to the wider community ... Together they modeled the kind of crossing of the boundaries that we look for in the church.[101]

Smith remembers one particularly successful community collaboration. In 1976, the Presbytery of St. Louis was asked to participate in the city's celebration of the Bicentennial. As Director of Race and Religion for the city, Rev. Smith was asked to coordinate some kind of programing. Drawing on his experience using music to work with children in Buffalo, Smith formed a choir with kids from the mostly white churches near Eden Seminary. He found a talented musician who composed and taught the choir jazz versions of classic Presbyterian hymns like "More About Jesus." The white children "had never had a jazz musician as a choir director before," Smith says, and there were some parents who were hesitant about allowing the music to evolve. However, when the choir performed at the magnificent Webster Groves Presbyterian Church, it was such a success that the local TV station, KMOX, asked them to perform it again as part of their Sunday series.

That same year, Smith was asked to write about the history of the black church for a Bicentennial issue of a local magazine, *Pride*. The issue was designed to address the lack of information and systematic research on the black church, and particularly the fact that "our early historians did not seem to recognize that the great humanitarian works of the church were worth recording."[102] Smith's article traces the development of the black church from the days of slavery through the Civil War to the Great Migration and beyond. He stresses the importance of black theology as a source of empowerment for a disenfranchised people and suggests that the church must be a font of political change: "The black church by word and deed is committed to the liberation struggle. It understands that it must move for fundamental change in the society in which it lives.*[103]*

Despite the significant successes of Berea and LaClede Town, the later 1960s were hard years. There is new weariness and recurrent anger in Smith's writing during this time. A journal entry dated 4/20/67 reveals Smith's thoughts about how much community work remained to be done.

> ... it seems programs are generally launched "after" the fact, rather than "before." The programs come after people have taken all they can stand and turn to the streets to release their pent up frustrations. Soon this country will discover that people are indeed the country and unless we begin to deal with them as peoples, we will continue to witness the bloodshed and wrath.[104]

Foreshadowing all too closely the strife over Michael Brown's killing by a policeman in Ferguson in 2014, Smith writes in 1967 about the shooting death of a fourteen-year old boy who was trying to rob a grocery store. He laments that the boy is not dead because he committed a crime, but rather

> ... because we (society) killed him. We caused his death because we are part of the system—we give consent and affirmation to it daily ... We should have provided a decent education. We should have given this boy an incentive ... What alternative does a Negro youngster have today? Death by the corner grocery or by a bullet in Vietnam?[105]

Smith's anger reached terrible new heights in April 1968 when Rev. Dr. Martin Luther King, Jr. was assassinated. With devastating suddenness, the man who had accomplished so much and who evoked both the ardent love and the virulent hatred of so many Americans was gone. In the final entry in the Service Supply journal, written several weeks after the fact, Smith's fury returns.

> How do you respond to death? Do you cry? Do you shout? Do you rebel? Do you condemn? ... When Martin Luther King Jr. was assassinated on a balcony, I was literally bitter and my first words were "damn the white people." I look back over those first moments and will never forget the panic, the feelings of hostility, the darkness of the day—the phone calls to various people whom I have known. And then the long night which never seemed to end. It just went on and on; the warm tears streaming down my face tasted like the water and bitter herbs that only a year ago I had tasted in that Maundy Thursday service. And when I took the herbs with the awareness that Martin had been taken from us—the taste will always remain as a reminder that man has not come to love his brother ...

Writing through his intense sorrow, Smith remembers their meeting at Talladega. With effort, he turns his thoughts to gratitude and the future.

> Some two weeks later, we are back to business as usual—we soon forget the venom that allows such an act to take place in the land we love so much. Where will it all end? I first met Martin [when] I was a bubbling senior at Talladega College and Martin came to our campus to speak. I will never forget that experience; his depth, his warmth, his piercing eyes; his folded hands. This surely was a man of God. Thank God he lived among us ... How long Lord, How long! Will we ever learn? Yet we are compelled now to turn the page and make Martin's dreams a reality.

To the great consternation of those who had shared their lives there, LaClede Town was torn down in 1995 after deteriorating through the 1980s and 1990s.[106] At present, Berea Presbyterian Church is once again the only thing left standing in what was once a thriving, creative, idealistic community. Rev. Dr. Luther Smith, Jr. has written that while there were

> ... larger forces at work beyond the church's influence ... it doesn't diminish the significance of Berea ... One can declare the significance and meaningfulness of what was occurring there as an example of prophetic ministry—the way a church may be involved in community transformations.[107]

There is a restlessness about Rev. Smith that has always led him into new challenges. During his fourteen years in St. Louis, he stepped fully into new roles outside of ministry. As a father, teacher, administrator, and researcher, he clarified his distinctive purpose at home, in the church, and in the world.

7

Dad, you have also given me as a legacy, your wit, your warmth, your ability to know, understand and be comfortable with all people. I have never once seen you angered because you were black. I had a hard time remembering when I first became aware of my blackness. You taught us how to live and love all people—strange, that for a greater part of my life at 137 North Carlisle, I never knew prejudice or hatred. That spark is still in each of us thanks to you.

Paul Smith, 1977[108]

The Spark in Each of Us

Rev. Smith's oldest daughter, Kathleen, was two when the family arrived in St. Louis. She remembers Odessa, the elderly lady at church who gave her and the Dudley children peppermints from her pockets.[109] She recalls hiding in the robes at her father's knees while he greeted parishioners on a Sunday at Berea. Only she could reveal that he was wearing his tennis whites under those robes so he could go directly to play after the service. For her, Berea was "a family," a place defined by "community."[110]

From Kathy's viewpoint as a teenager, there were few places that were not open to her and her friends. The city is dotted with dozens of distinct, residential neighborhoods of single-family homes. Away from the city center, many have gentle hills and winding roads. They tend to be bounded by low walls and entered through gates that announce their name. Within the city itself, there are orderly rows of sizeable houses in a rich variety of early- to mid-twentieth century architectural styles. Many are built to face each other in neighborhood clusters that are reached by driving or walking through arched gateways of varying design. No doubt, most had been all-white enclaves in the past. Yet the Smiths, their friends, and relatives bought houses and shared these neighborhoods for years with mostly white neighbors. Among the mansions on Lindell Boulevard overlooking mid-city Forest Park there is a compound where Kathy and the children of a black doctor played while their fathers competed on the family tennis court.

Between the city's commercial heart on the west banks of the Mississippi and these leafy neighborhoods lies the mostly concrete plain called Millcreek where low-income housing developments like LaClede Town have risen and fallen over the last century. The grounds of St. Louis University and Harris-Stowe State University converge where Berea now stands on the inner-city section of Lindell Boulevard called Olive Street. Today, this part of the city is characterized by blocks of unimaginative public housing alternating with old industrial buildings and empty lots.

The Smiths never did occupy any of the architect-designed housing that drew so many to LaClede Town. After about a year in their small apartment in the neighborhood, the Smiths moved into a house in Moline Acres, a quiet, mostly white, suburb north of the city. There, Smith made a lifelong friend—Lenny Wilkens, who later rose to Hall of Fame status as both a National Basketball Association player and a coach. Wilkens recalls that his family had already borne the brunt of the neighborhood's racial hostility when he heard that the Smiths had arrived. So when he saw Paul coming down the block to introduce himself, he didn't want to make it too easy for the newcomer. Though he was inwardly pleased at the overture, he pretended he didn't see Smith. Smith came after him, called his bluff, and the two have kept up a running banter ever since.

The families became close as Wilkens and his wife Marilyn had a daughter and the Smiths welcomed their second and third, Heather in 1965 and Krista in 1968. The two men are still joshing about the fact that it was Paul, not Lenny, who accompanied Marilyn to the hospital for the birth of their second child, Randy. By then a successful professional athlete, Lenny was out of town the day of the birth playing basketball for the St. Louis Hawks. Unable to let Paul's gallant assistance pass without comment, Lenny still asserts that what *really* happened that day was that he showed Paul how to have sons.

More seriously, Wilkens says that his friend has "that aura" that Wilkens found in Dr. King and in Nelson Mandela.

> [Smith] has great control of who he is. And a purpose. That's what he's there for. He never loses sight of those things. He has helped a lot of people …
> We played volleyball, tennis. We were very competitive at just about everything we did. But we respected each other. There are very few people that I think I'd put my life on the line for. And he would do the same for me.[111]

Frances remembers those years as a blur of teaching and caring for the children. The family of five later settled into the University City neighborhood from 1968–78. This community lies just north of Washington University itself. That institution, the city's pride and joy, is grandly sited at the top of a hill overlooking Forest Park. "U. City" was relatively integrated, being the home of many university people and Jewish families who were unwelcome in some other parts of St. Louis.

In stark contrast to the rise and fall of the urban developments in the heart of the city, Kathy says of well-groomed University City, "nothing here has changed." The Smiths' house on Princeton Avenue is the same dignified two-storey brick structure she grew up in. In her youth, there was a pool in the backyard and a pool table in the basement. The house was the frequent site of parties enhanced by her mother's memorable cooking. The children safely rode their bikes on the quiet, curving streets. Kathy remembers that kids in the area all played together, whatever their backgrounds.

Since segregation restricted many of the city's social clubs even in the 60s, African American people socialized mostly in their homes.

Former Smith home on Princeton Ave., St. Louis, Missouri. (Photo by author)

Those who could afford it built pools and tennis courts. As had been true for decades, people of color expected to share their homes with extended families, friends' families and visitors. Kathy says that there are people who never left their comfortable houses on Princeton Avenue; in several other cases, people of her generation have raised their own families in the houses their parents previously owned.

Through his friend the tennis-playing physician, Smith quickly met and began to work with highly accomplished older professionals. Accompanying her father on visits to homes and hospitals, Kathy saw how valuable his presence was to the sick and the dying. Unlike more conservative ministers of color, Smith has long been sympathetic to the role that can be played by hospice and end-of-life planning to give patients a greater voice in the circumstances of their death. Smith says he differs in this from pastors whose exclusive focus on Jesus' power to cure and comfort precludes thinking about more immediate ways to support a fatally ill person and their family.

Rev. Smith's reputation as a maverick blossomed internationally in 1971, when he and the family moved to Jamaica for the school year. The minister of a church in downtown Kingston was taking a sabbatical, so Smith was recruited to temporarily replace him. He was also asked to teach. "They wanted someone with a doctorate who could also teach liberation theology at the University of the West Indies Seminary across the street. Fran and I and our three girls lived on that campus."

The Smiths during their year in Jamaica, 1971.

The best-known articulator of black liberation theology is still Rev. Dr. James Cone, who has taught at Union Theological Seminary in New York for much of his career. Cone's classic treatise *Black Theology and Black Power* had just been published in 1969.[112] Dr. Cone was one of the sharpest critics of what he saw as a racist Christianity practiced by many whites in the United States since enslaved people were first brought here. His career has been dedicated to developing an alternative approach to Christian theology that speaks to and is inclusive of black Americans.

Cone drew on theologian Paul Tillich's work to assert that Christian love must be accompanied by justice and power.[113] Cone explored the idea that the sole purpose of the church "is to be a visible manifestation of God's work in the affairs of men ... The Church of Christ is not bounded by standards of race, class, or occupation ... Rather the Church is God's suffering people."[114] What followed was an idea that was as yet unheard of in white theology—if Christ brought God's love to the oppressed, and black people are oppressed due to their blackness, then "*Christ is black, baby,* with all of the features which are so detestable to white society."[115] Taking these ideas yet further, Cone wrote,

> It is the job of the church to become black with [Christ] and accept the shame which white society places on blacks. But the church knows that what is shame to the world is holiness to God. Black is holy, that is, it is a symbol of God's presence in history on behalf of the oppressed man. Where there is black, there is oppression; but blacks can be assured that where there is blackness, there is Christ who is taken on blackness so that what is evil in men's eyes might become good. Therefore Christ is black because he is oppressed, and oppressed because he is black. And if the church is to join Christ by following his opening, it too must go where suffering is and become black also.[116]

Cone suggested that to be free of hypocrisy, the church must be free of racism. Otherwise, the white church "makes racism a respectable attitude."[117] Further, he wrote that

> the biblical doctrine of reconciliation can be made a reality only when white people are prepared to address black men as *black* men and not as some grease-painted form of white humanity ... Reconciliation ... means that man can now be what he is—a creature made for fellowship with God. But that is only one side of reconciliation. To be reconciled with God involves reconciliation with the neighbor ... For black people it means that God has reconciled us to an acceptance of our blackness. If the death–resurrection of Christ means anything, it means that the blackness of black people is a creation of God himself. God came into the world in order that black people need not be ashamed of who they are. In Christ we not only know who we are, but who God is. This is the heart of the biblical message.[118]

It is not hard to imagine how radical these ideas sounded in the 1960s. When Rev. Smith arrived to teach the philosophy to Jamaican seminary students and parishioners, the Jamaican government was wary. He says, "The first month I taught in Jamaica, undercover people called the CID were in my classes every day. When my books came, they confiscated them. They had an undercover person in my class to be sure I wasn't coming there to destroy the country! They didn't know what liberation theology was."

As usual, Rev. Smith immediately attracted attention for his preaching. He recalls that "there were maybe thirty people in this huge church, downtown in Kingston. Within a month or maybe two, people were saying, 'You got to go hear da crazy minister at da church. He fascinating man!'"

Smith's intuition, magnanimity, and quick thinking aroused people's attention. On Easter morning, he remembers intervening on behalf of a congregant who was a little bit different from the others. "You know in Christendom you can do communion with a common cup or the little individual cups. Easter Sunday morning, the place was packed. I never knew her name, but there was a little lady with a nice little hat. For some reason, there was always saliva coming out of her mouth."

As Rev. Smith led the crowd through communion, they ran out of individual cups. "When I got to her row, I took the cup and gave it to her. Then because I could see what was going to happen, I took the cup right after her. After I had drunk from the cup, then everyone else took it after me. And then they said, 'Da crazy minister, he take da communion himself!' I just did it spontaneously. I knew instinctively the others wouldn't take communion after the lady with the saliva."

Smith seems to have both surprised and unsettled people with his equanimity and fearlessness. While the seminary had specifically asked him to teach liberation theology, Rev. John Hoad, who had been appointed President of the Seminary only a few years before,[119] at one point pulled Smith aside to ask, "Could you just tone it down a bit?" Smith is still laughing about this story today; as he says with gusto, "You can't tone down James Cone!"

When Smith was asked to give the commencement address at graduation, he said, "You need to hear from the man himself. James Cone is a friend … I called Cone and asked if he would come down to Jamaica to give the speech. He said, 'Are you kidding? I just got married. Of course I'll come to Jamaica!' Cone and his wife came, all expenses paid … [At Commencement, Cone] was up there being very smart, while the white faculty were huffing and puffing! They couldn't wait until he finished."

Upon returning from Jamaica, Smith began to preach more and more regularly at Second Presbyterian Church, just about a mile west of Berea. Hiring the gifted African American preacher was a step toward integrating the grand stone church built in 1896.[120] This National Historic Register edifice became the Smith's family church as the Berea era came to a close.

Smith also began to work for the government. In the 1960s and

'70s, he served as a Contract Relations specialist for the US Office of Contract Compliance, Defense Supply Agency. Companies getting government money were required to undergo a compliance review. Smith researched and wrote those reports. He describes it as a time of empowerment for African Americans. "Everything that was closed to me, the government was hiring me to [help change.]"

Smith relished the opportunity to have an impact. In contrast to many of his peers, he actually gave some companies bad reviews, reporting that they were not in compliance with government equal opportunity policy. Two of these he remembers were 3M in Minneapolis and McDonnell Douglas in St. Louis. He succeeded in getting their attention; in fact, he says, "They were pissed!" His bosses were flabbergasted. People were saying, "Rev. Smith is relentless! Get this guy off our backs!"

When asked whether he enjoyed upsetting people's expectations, Smith says mildly, "I didn't do it intentionally. I just did what I was trained to do. I didn't keep my light under a bushel."

St. Louis is a city with a strong Catholic presence. The magnificent Cathedral Basilica of St. Louis stands on Lindell Boulevard about halfway between Berea and Second Presbyterian. In the 1960s and '70s, this was the seat of Cardinal Joseph Ritter, the priest who had come to the aid of the local ministers in finding a flight to Selma. Smith eventually joined forces with the Catholic Church when he become the first St. Louis director of Project Equality, an empowerment program created to help black people gain equal access to employment. At that time, there were only two such offices, one in St. Louis and one in Kansas City.

With time, Smith was entrusted with the management of large-scale public funding. Smith helped run a $3 million Urban League anti-poverty program.[121] He worked with William E. Douthit who had been Executive Director of the St. Louis Urban League since 1954. In 1968, Douthit was reorganizing the Urban League in St. Louis to "meet challenges and opportunities coming from social and economic climate,"[122] and Smith had the requisite skills to help.

Smith had maintained his Urban League connections. When Whitney Young, the long-time president of the National Urban League, died in 1971, Smith attended the Lexington, Kentucky, funeral of his friend and Alpha Phi Alpha brother. Smith points to the fact that then-President Richard Nixon delivered the eulogy as evidence of the high regard with which both Young and the League were viewed on the national level.[123]

Meanwhile, word of Smith's work and influence had reached some powerful observers. Early in the '70s, he received word of his election to the most august black men's association of them all, Sigma Pi Phi. Founded in 1904, "the Boulé" as it is otherwise known, is "the quintessential organization for professional black men … it is considered by many *the* elite men's club and its membership has included the most accomplished, excellent, and influential black men in every city for the last [112] years.[124]

One cannot seek out membership in this national society; a nominee is vetted and voted in by his peers, generally at mid-career when he has proven himself to be the best at what he does. Across the nation, professionals are drawn into local chapters. Every two years, members meet for national conferences. Wherever they encounter each other in the working world, they are said to offer each other professional, political, and social support. These connections go beyond death; Sigma Pi Phi brothers perform special observances at each other's funerary rites. As impressive as the company may be, Dr. Smith does not hesitate to goad his fellow members into committing more of their resources to social service projects.

Smith's academic career took shape in St. Louis in the early 1970s at the grand institution on the hill, Washington University. His first appointment was as Assistant to the Vice Chancellor, where his role was to "implement and assess career development programs for all employees, with special emphasis on developing opportunities for blacks, and to encourage on-the-job training, career assessment, and educational development for the university's employees."[125]

He also began teaching, an activity that comes easily to this congenial and gregarious speaker. It is a part-time vocation that he has enjoyed in every city he has lived in since. His rapport is as powerful with students as it is with parishioners; people of all ages feel his concern, appreciate his experience, and respond to his message. At Washington University, his first teaching position was as a lecturer in Black Studies. Later courses focused on subjects including medical ethics and the works of Howard Thurman.

Smith moved easily up the ranks at the university. It was a time of war protest and political strife on college campuses, and he bonded easily with students, offering them a sympathetic ear. Building on the skills he had developed working with both youth and businesspeople, he was made Director of Housing. In 1973, his responsibilities expanded to include both Housing and Resident Life, and by 1974, he had risen to Assistant Vice Chancellor. Then-Vice Chancellor Robert L. Vigil, Jr. said of this appointment, "I feel Paul Smith is the ideal administrator for the created assistant vice chancellorship. He has an excellent method of working with students and of administrating the housing office on campus."[126]

—Ⅲ—

Having performed countless funerals for parishioners since his early start in Athens, Alabama, Smith has been called upon repeatedly over the decades to officiate at the funerals of family and close friends. One of the first of these intensely personal ceremonies occurred upon the passing of his grandmother, Odie Overby, in 1975. She was at that time living with her daughter Odie Mae in Niles, Michigan, just over the Indiana-Michigan border. Mrs. Overby's obituary[127] notes that both her grandson and the Rev. Charles Rowlett presided over the rites at St. John's Missionary Baptist Church, the family's house of worship in South Bend, Indiana. Though he was twenty years younger than the other ministers there, Smith says, he delivered the eulogy for his dear grandmother.

Granny was buried toward the northern edge of the verdant City Cemetery not far from her home on Birdsell Street. Her tombstone lies next to that of her parents, Ferd and Nancy Wingo. Now in his eighties, Smith has recently said he would prefer to not bury any more of his friends. However, he admits it is very hard to say no when he is called upon in this way.

Thinking ahead to his parents' final years, Rev. Smith wrote his father a letter in 1977. At 42 years old, Smith thanks his father for his wisdom.

> Dear Dad,
> I am writing this letter to you from Kansas City, Mo., where I am attending a meeting with the US Civil Rights Commission. My daughter Heather is with me. I have tried to take each of the girls on a trip with me so they can have time with me alone …
> You see Dad, I have been thinking about the greater things of life. My life is so blessed, and I have been fortunate in my job and community possibilities that I began to think about where it all comes from. As I sit here in the hotel, with my daughter, I realize that it began with you. How much I am like you is still a mystery, but I know that very early in my life I caught your spirit. Very early in my life, I knew the meaning of hard work and achievement. You taught it to me and even more you showed me by example. …
> I remember being at a ballgame at Kaley Park when the word came to you that Pappa had died. You greeted the person with a smile and the words "I knew that's what you were coming to tell me." You held me and Willie close as we went to the car. I can still feel the strength of your arms. Remember, we had just seen Pappa in Chicago the week before. That I shall always remember, because it showed me what a strong father had …
> One more thing—those Sunday morning prayers and the periodic quizzes are never to be forgotten. Do you realize that was my beginning as a servant of the Master? I didn't know it at the time, but I'm sure you

did … I remember our kneeling together and the first time I was asked to pray. It is very difficult to write the words as I recapture those moments …

Thank you Dad for giving me what you have. I will try to live up to all the fine and noble standards you have given, for they are reachable. I thank God for you for your strength and wisdom when days were dreary. I will strive to keep that spark always alive in me and I will pass it onto my children and they will pass it onto theirs.

Love your son, Paul

When Leonard Smith, Sr. died on April 9, 1983, son Paul helped lead that funeral as well. Having made a point of articulating his gratitude and love for his father, Smith was able to weather the storm.

"I know I am grieving but it is not as I expected. I got through the funeral just fine even though I could not say all of the things I had written. I will never forget the faces of my children, wife, mother, brothers, sisters, and friends. It was a sacramental moment indeed … I am not sure if I would or could cry in front of mother or Marlene—interesting. What I feel now is peace and wonderment … "[128]

8

Yours is a special calling and a very authentic mission.
Howard Thurman to Paul Smith, 1978[129]

Meditation and Mysticism

Rev. Smith first heard Dr. Thurman lecture at Hartford Seminary in 1958. He immediately became a devotee and took every opportunity after that to hear the brilliant scholar. Dr. Thurman was famous for his enigmatic talks and the sonorous intensity of his speaking voice. He delivered lectures at over five hundred educational institutions over the course of his long, groundbreaking career.[130] As the above line from a letter to Smith indicates, Thurman intuitively understood Smith's work and eloquently articulated his support for it. Their personal contact began in the 1970s and underwrote Smith's increasing midlife clarity about his mission in ministry. The only disappointment for Smith was that the relationship came to an end too quickly; Dr. Thurman died in 1981.

It was Berea parishioner Annalee Scott who enabled Smith to meet the man who had so inspired him. Scott was Director of what was then the black YWCA. The organization invited Thurman to speak in St. Louis each year. Dr. Thurman was a close friend of Scott and her husband, since they had provided a place for Thurman's daughter Anne to stay while the young woman pursued an internship at the

St. Louis Post Dispatch. As Smith remembers, "Annalee said, 'I would like you to meet Thurman since you talk so much about him in your sermons' … So she arranged for me and Carl and about five other black clergy in St. Louis to come have a private conversation with [him]."

On their way to the encounter Smith had dreamt of for years, reality intervened. One of the Smiths' daughters became ill, delaying her parents' departure from their home. This heightened the drama of Smith's first meeting with Thurman.

> … we were late coming to Annalee and Jim's apartment. We finally got over to that section of St. Louis and were climbing the stairs. As we get to the top, we hear Thurman speaking. We stop at the top of the stairs and look into the room, and he could see us.
>
> The best I can make out is that someone had asked him, "Who will carry on your work?" or something like that. Because Fran and I are standing in the vestibule, and there are about ten or twelve people listening, and without skipping a beat, he says, "Maybe that young man standing at the door with his wife." You can't make this stuff up! He said, "Young man, I'd like to get to know you better. Annalee thinks so much of you, so you *must* be something." So that's how our relationship began.

Once their personal relationship was established, Smith took every opportunity to visit, correspond, and collaborate with the man who understood him so well. Thurman was an exceptional minister, professor, and scholar. Born in 1899 and the grandson of a woman who had been enslaved, Thurman graduated from elite Morehouse College and earned a doctorate from Rochester Theological Seminary. He went on to teach and preach at Oberlin, Morehouse, Spelman College, and Howard University.

The full flowering of Thurman's mission occurred when he co-founded the first explicitly interracial church in America. The Church for the Fellowship of All Peoples was truly innovative for its time. Formed during the racial and cultural turmoil of 1944 San Francisco, the church drew the attention of powerful supporters like Eleanor Roosevelt. Thurman later left this pioneering ministry when he was asked to become Dean of the Chapel at Boston University, the first black theologian to do so at a major academic institution.[131] Reflecting on this history, Smith says, "consciously or unconsciously [Fellowship Church] was my model for my congregations."

Among Thurman's two dozen books, it is *Jesus and the Disinherited*[132] that is thought to have contributed the most to the civil rights struggle. It is apocryphal that Dr. King had a copy of this book in his briefcase when he died.[133] Thurman was attempting to address several crucial questions in this text.

> Why is it that Christianity seems impotent to deal radically, and therefore effectively, with the issues of discrimination and injustice on the basis of race, religion and national origin? [134]

> The masses of men live with their backs constantly against the wall. They are the poor, the disinherited, and the dispossessed. What does our religion say to them?[135]

For Thurman, questions about the practice of mainstream Christianity had troubled him since his childhood, when he had had painful encounters with rigid and uninspired clergy. He recounts that it was a man from a culture and religion completely outside his own who sharpened his thinking on these issues. When part of a delegation of black Americans invited to India in 1935, Thurman was asked penetrating questions by the Hindu administrator of a school where he spoke. The man asked how Thurman could be committed to a faith that had been so destructive to black people.

A five-hour conversation ensued that led to public talks and ultimately culminated in the publication of *Jesus and the Disinherited* in 1949. Written in an accessible style that belies its deep import, the study still yields fresh insights half a century later. Just as it guided Rev. Smith and countless others through the confusion of the sixties, it sheds considerable light on current turmoil in Ferguson, Baltimore, Chicago, and other cities.

Thurman's central point in the book is that when Jesus is understood as one of the disinherited himself, the true meaning of his message for all those who are subjugated becomes clear. Thurman emphasizes that Jesus was born into but ultimately severed from his ancient Jewish culture; he was poor; he and most of his fellows were subjects, not citizens, of the Roman Empire in Palestine. Thurman argues that Jesus spoke as one who understood people suffering under oppression that threatened their very lives. His message was directed to people feeling the terrible insecurity of being subjected to violence, repression, and humiliation in their own land.

Thurman illuminates parallels to the circumstances under which people of color have been living in America.

> The striking similarity between the social position of Jesus in Palestine and that of the best majority of American Negroes is obvious to anyone who tarries long over the facts ... For the most part, Negroes assume that there are no basic citizenship rights, no fundamental protection, guaranteed to them by the state, because their status as citizens has never been clearly defined. There has been for them little protection from the dominant controllers of society and even less protection from the unrestrained elements within their own group.[136]

In separate chapters, Thurman considers the corrosive effects of the Fear, Deception, and Hate that result from living in a state of such profound vulnerability. The terms of his argument are, tragically, still resonant today. In addressing Fear, he first dissects the methods whereby those without power can be controlled.

The threat of violence within the framework of well-nigh limitless power is a weapon by which the weak are held in check. Artificial limitations are placed upon them, restricting freedom of movement, of employment, and of participation in the common life. These limitations are given formal or informal expression in general or specific policies of separateness or segregation. These policies tend to freeze the social status of the insecure.[137]

The fear is compounded by the fact that the right to use violence is widely distributed. The many "deputies" of Jim Clark at Selma come to mind.

The threat of violence maybe implemented not only by constituted authority but also by anyone acting in behalf of the established order. Every member of the controllers' group is in a sense of special deputy authorized by the mores to enforce the pattern. This fact tends to create fear, which works on behalf of the proscriptions and guarantees them. The anticipation of possible violence makes it very difficult for any escape from the pattern to be effective.[138]

Dr. Thurman next points out the corrosive effects of responding to subjugation with Deception. "The penalty of deception is to *become* a deception, with all sense of moral discrimination vitiated. A man who lies habitually becomes a lie, and it is increasingly impossible for him to know when he is lying and when he is not. In other words, the moral mercury of life is reduced to zero."[139] At that point, reclaiming one's inner life becomes even more difficult. Thurman says that ultimately, Jesus's message is that sincerity to other humans and to God is one and the same; they are equally essential.[140] He concludes, "A man is a man, no more, no less. The awareness of this fact marks the supreme moment of human dignity."[141]

Turning to Hate, Thurman suggests that its roots often lie in "contact without fellowship, contact that is devoid of any of the primary overtures of warmth and fellow feeling and genuineness." His cardinal example is the "false fellowship" of the segregated South.

> ... there can be an abundance of sentimentality masquerading under the cloak of fellowship. It is this kind of fellowship that one finds often in the South between whites and Negroes. As long as the Negro is called John or Mary and accepts the profoundly humiliating position of an inferior status, the fellowship [between blacks and whites] is possible. [Thus] in the section of the country where there is the greatest contact between Negro and white there is the least real fellowship, and the first step along the road of bitterness and hatred is assured.[142]

With wisdom that is just as necessary today as in the post-World War II era, Thurman diagnoses "modern times" as being replete with circumstances which allow "the seeds of hatred to grow unmolested."[143] He underlines Jesus's recognition that hatred—on either side of a power struggle—poisons the haters themselves. From there, all manner of amoral behavior can seem justified.

> Often there are but thin lines between bitterness, hatred, self-realization, defiance and righteous indignation. The logic of the strong-weak relationship is to place all moral judgment of behavior out of bounds. A type of behavior that, under normal circumstances, would call for self-condemnation can very easily under these special circumstances, be regarded as necessary and therefore defensible ... Thus hatred becomes a device by which an individual seeks to protect himself against moral disintegration.[144]

Thurman outlines a process whereby people can instead follow Jesus's demanding counsel to love one's enemy. Thurman asserts that this work requires active effort on the part of those involved to recognize and build upon their common humanity. The powerful must relinquish the cloak of their status, and the subjugated must give up their hatred of the enemy.

> ... love is possible only between two freed spirits. What one discovers in even a single experience in which barriers have been removed may become useful in building an over-all technique for loving one's enemy. There cannot be too great insistence on the point that we are here dealing with a discipline a method, a technique, as over against some form of wishful thinking or simple desiring.[145]

Thurman condemns what he sees as the great tragedy of Christian life in America.[146]

> ... It is in this connection that American Christianity has betrayed the religion of Jesus almost beyond redemption. Churches have been established for the underprivileged, for the weak, for the poor, on the theory that they prefer to be among themselves ... The result is that in the one place in which normal, free contacts might be most naturally established in which the relations of the individual to his God should take priority over conditions of class, race, power, status, wealth, or the like—this place is one of the chief instruments for guaranteeing barriers.[147]

Ultimately, Thurman argues that every individual can and must seek opportunities to cross the boundaries and forgive if hatred is to be uprooted and equanimity is to prevail. This process happens, "in the white heat of personal encounter … rooted in concrete experience. No amount of good feeling for people in general, no amount of simple desiring, is an adequate substitute. It is an act of inner authority, well within the reach of everyone … At the center of the attitude is a core of painstaking discipline, made possible only by personal triumph. The ethical demand upon the more privileged and the underprivileged is the same.[148]

Dr. Luther Smith, Jr., published the first systematic consideration of Thurman's work in 1981, the year of Thurman's death. Strikingly, many of his observations about Thurman's worldview and theology[149] apply to Paul Smith as well. Like his mentor, Smith is ecumenical in practice and in thought, easily making members of other faiths an integral part of his community. He has committed himself to racial integration rather than separation and proven that interfaith and interracial communities are possible and rewarding.[150] Like Thurman, Smith sees combatting racism as one of the most urgent and creative aspects in the mission of Christianity.[151] In theological terms, both men emphasize the individual's experience of God more than the worship of Jesus as divine.[152] Their primary audience is the laity rather than other theologians and clerics.

Luther Smith's description of Thurman's effect on others articulates a central truth about Smith as well.

When others see how meaning flows through [his] life, something within their lives is aroused to discover their source for greater meaning and potential. [He] is not just an example but an inspirer; not just a leader but a maker of leaders; not the authority, but a revealer of authority.[153]

When Smith and Thurman began to actually work together in the mid-1970s, their mutual practice of contemplation and meditation formed the basis for their collaboration. Ahead of their time, Thurman and Smith began to develop retreat-like spiritual seminars where groups of like-minded people could read, discuss, and meditate.

In the course of this collaborative work, a series of letters passed between Thurman and Paul Smith that survive today. These missives help reveal the respectful yet playful texture of the men's relationship. The first letter typed and sent by Thurman asks for Smith's thoughts on the workshop they had just completed.

Howard Thurman Educational Trust
2018 Stockton Street
San Francisco 94133
January 29, 1975

The Rev. Paul Smith
7156 Princeton
University City, Missouri 63130

Dear Paul Smith:

My first concern, dear brother, is that the Holy Spirit did not take any radical chances with you on the highway, cause the traffic is not aware of the movement of the Spirit. When thoughts and feelings came upon you that could not be reduced to a manageable unit, I hope that Mrs. Smith was sufficiently rested to take the wheel.

You are a very exciting human being because of the way in which you honor thoughts and feelings that descend upon you with unerring vitality and specificity. I am sorry that we did not have a chance to visit but this will come later.

When you have a little margin of time will you sent

down in order, your reflections and suggestions for both our workshop experiences and future workshops?

Please give our love to Mrs. Smith and your young brood that keep their father on the straight and narrow.

Sincerely,
Howard Thurman.

In his response in February 1975, Rev. Smith answers Thurman's questions and reveals something of Thurman's effect on the participants (emphasis in the original).

> ... you are a very powerful presence and if one is not careful he may be overwhelmed. I got the sense that there were moments when we should have perhaps taken the time to hear everyone's response to that par-ticular moment when the quietness prevailed and all present were on the same agenda. Perhaps the silence (there were many) is enough but I guess I would have like to "check out" my thoughts against yours and the others present ...

The next section of the letter reveals some of Thurman's impact on Smith.

> ... Your meditations triggered a lot of thoughts. We have many pressures bearing upon us and I felt I had in a sense come to the Fountain. When my cup was full, I had no time to tarry. I needed time to rest -–my intake was too much. By Friday afternoon, it began to run over. I would hope there was more time for reflection.

Smith concludes in a light and joyous mood, describing moments of transcendence he experienced.

I would close by saying that my life was changed, refreshed and disturbed by this encounter. You have some idea because I am not frightened off by a group. When the spirit was in command you heard some of my cries. I have a better understanding of me; I feel closer to God and I am not ashamed of what I am in His presence. I have a better feeling for other human beings. I have not arrived, but I'm on my journey.

Two letters from Dr. Thurman then followed quickly one after the other. It is in the second that Thurman so beautifully expresses both his philosophy and Smith's (emphasis in the original).

Yours is a special calling and a very authentic mission. You <u>know</u> the meaningful contacts between people are more compelling than all the words, ideologies, prejudices and faiths that divide them; if such contacts are multiplied over a meaningful time interval they can undermine <u>everything</u> that separates.[154]

The years 1970–78 were a period of intellectual elaboration and consolidation for Rev. Smith. In addition to deepening his relationship with Dr. Thurman, Smith went back to school to earn his doctorate at Eden Theological Seminary. From 1970–1977, Smith attended classes at the seminary in a suburban neighborhood on the south side of St. Louis. Eden's campus is a quiet quadrangle of buildings graced by a majestic bell-tower. His dissertation, entitled *The Relation of Black and Jewish Students Living in the Residence Halls of a Multi-Racial Midwestern University*, was founded on original research into relations between students undertaken while he was working at Washington University.

The 1970s were times of protest and foment on college campuses riven by protest over the Vietnam War and the competition of competing identity groups beginning to voice their rights. Characteristically, Smith takes on a contentious subject in focusing on the relations between black and Jewish students. Smith states that his goal was to understand "their attitudes concerning each other and their relationships which are currently the source of tension and conflict in the general community of the university."[155]

The dissertation reveals much about Smith at around age 40. He begins by quoting Dr. Thurman along with Langston Hughes, writing: "Each of these men has had a significant influence upon my life and my ministry in a very special way."[156] Smith's analysis begins with an overview of the ways he believes relations between black and Jewish people deteriorated in the 1960s. He cites the conflict over schools in Ocean Hill-Brownsville, NY and the rioting in Watts as two examples of the growing volatility in relations between Jewish and black people. He asserts that despite their common history of oppression and discrimination, the experience of blacks and Jews in America has differed in significant ways. Drawing in part on his own experience handling housing complaints from black residents of west St. Louis, he asserts that the consolidation of Jews as property owners and blacks as workers and renters in the ghettos was bound to boil over at some point. He asserts that black people felt that their efforts had helped the Jewish cause but that Jewish people seemed to have forgotten that as they were more and more assimilated into the dominant white culture.

In his chapter on the social history and theological perspective of blacks and Jews, Smith eloquently articulates his view of African American experience. Echoing James Cone, he writes that the black experience has to do with moving from "Nobodiness" to "Somebodiness."[157] Since black people do not have a specific common history to work from, he writes, they use stories, tales, sayings, songs, prayers, and sermons to find their common ground.[158] He says, "the Black experience is the coming together of the Black community to affirm the meaning and positive worth of Blackness to an insensitive White world." He cites Cone's *Black Theology and Black Power* as asserting that the black experience "is self-determination and freedom whereby black people see themselves in a positive manner, with human dignity and worth."[159]

Smith is much less comfortable writing the section on Jewish identity. He asserts that Jews have had advantages in their positive self-image, their centuries-old culture, their color, and their greater psychological strength. He further states that the central concerns of Jewish people are their identity as Jews and their possession of Israel without interference from outside parties. He makes an effort to try and imagine a Jewish worldview. But he does not seem to have gained any real familiarity with a range of Jewish viewpoints on their history and theology.

At the core of the thesis are the data Smith collected in interviews with forty college students, twenty Jewish, twenty black. Though he uses fairly standard social science research methods, the design of the study would not pass muster today. His sampling methods were weak: Smith handpicked the black participants and a Jewish student recruited the others. The resulting sample size was too small to allow him to generalize from his findings. Smith did recognize his own "strong investment in the cause under investigation"[160] and knew he should try and avoid bias. Nevertheless, Smith's data essentially confirmed the views he brought to the project. These were that black and Jewish students had little knowledge of or contact with one another and yet had rather negative attitudes toward each other.

Typically for the time, Smith gives no clear definition of "race" in his analysis, except to say that there are two in the study —Blacks and Jews. He notes that he is using "Jews" and "Whites" interchangeably.[161] Using the language of scholars like Cone, he generalizes that "Whites" are the enemy and the oppressor, and "Blacks" are the oppressed and misunderstood. He is somewhat at a loss to know how to characterize Jews, since they have something in common with both groups.

Smith attempts to find a positive footing on which to end. He says that black and Jewish people can find common ground in their experiences of estrangement from their homelands and their diaspora experiences. He urges identifying "a universal oneness which accentuates the positive worth of both" and a need to "search for a common ground that claims them as children of God."[162]

It becomes clear in an informal addendum bound into the dissertation, however, that the most powerful part of this work occurred after the thesis itself was written. From Fall 1977 to Spring 1978, Smith and his advisors organized several learning experiences for him that greatly enhanced his understanding of his subject. Smith writes that the research had made him aware of prejudices toward Jews that he had had since he was a teenager and rediscovered in his administrative work at Wash U.[163] He describes how this became even clearer when the rabbi he had asked to read his thesis told him he thought it revealed anti-Jewish bias. In his characteristic way, Smith went to Rabbi Arnold Asher to find out more.

> Earlier I had learned that Arnie had read my thesis and in his opinion judged it to be anti-Semitic. This was a new label for me and at first I was offended by his judgment. I later invited Arnie to lunch and we seemed to hit it off so I decided to ask him if he would teach me something about Jews. He agreed, with the understanding that I teach him something about Blacks.[164]

What resulted was a series of encounters, readings, discussions, and workshops that were designed to bring the consideration of black/Jewish relations out into the light. Most powerful for Smith was the course of study he embarked upon with Rabbi Asher. He provided Smith with a reading list, and the men met once a week for discussions Smith admits were "challenging and often emotionally upsetting."[165] As uncomfortable as this work may have been, the thesis itself suggests this was the first real study of Jewish history, culture, and identity that Smith had ever undertaken. In the end, he says,

> … it helped me to identify some of my biases, engage in meaningful dialogue without fear of offending while at the same time learning new information, and having the opportunity to ferret out kernels that could be used creatively in my ministry.[166]

As his education progressed, Smith began asking Rabbi Asher if he could engage the rabbi's congregation in a similar discussion. Asher hesitated, informing Smith that some members of the synagogue had had negative experiences when blacks had moved into homes in University City. Smith persisted and eventually, an evening of discussion about his research findings was arranged. Both the reverend and the rabbi were unsure whether people would attend, how people would respond, or how Smith would be received. Nonetheless,

> Our fears were hardly justified as over 50 members showed up, greeted me with openness, and ask insightful questions and made salient comments. As we began the evening together, I knew almost immediately that my tradition and faith as a Christian pastor, as well as my ethnicity, had enough in common to enable dialogue and friendships to be established. Once again, my fears were allayed as well as theirs, because upon hearing my Black stories they found a kinship with some of their own ... [167]
> In May of this year, Rabbi Asher will stand before the congregation of Second Presbyterian Church and begin a similar dialogue, including preaching from our pulpit. This could not have happened were it not for our own encounter and sharing of experiences and information.[168]

Smith describes he and Rabbi Asher as being "from two entirely different cultures." Nonetheless, each moves forward in their understanding of the other. Smith, particularly, comes to a profound realization.

> ... that what I had been doing and saying in my thesis and discussions with Arnie, was trying to out horror him with my stories. I imagine he was attempting the same but he did it more gracefully with less rhetoric.[169]

Smith expanded upon these efforts by initiating contact with the new assistant rabbi on campus at Wash U. Their discussions again created a warm collegiality and led to plans for a course on Black-Jewish relations.[170] They then arranged a discussion session between Smith and three black students with Jewish students at Hillel House.

On his way to this event, Smith realized he had not set foot inside the building in eight years at the university. With typical candor, he writes,

> First, I realized how jealous I was of the symbols of Jewishness and Judaism, which were very obvious. The building itself is beautiful, comfortable, spacious and a center of gathering for the Jews at the university. When compared to the quarters for Blacks, there is none … What are our symbols I asked myself? All that really identifies us as Blacks is our color. Can it be that we need something more than color? Is there something other than color and if so, how is it perceived by others as well as ourselves? These questions were raised in my mind as I entered the room and remain largely unanswered even today.[171]

At the end of the addendum, Rev. Smith re-articulates his professional mission.

> … I am most comfortable in situations that afford me opportunities to be a bridge between racial, political and religious groups … Both as an administrator and pastor, my home is bridging the gap, initiating the points of contact, facilitating encounters and serving as an interpreter. Herein lies my ministry and the essence of my being.[172]

Thus, by the time he left St. Louis in 1978, Dr. Paul (as he was often known thereafter) had completed his education, diversified his professional expertise, and confronted some of his own prejudices. He saw where his strengths lay and was finding how they could be used for the greatest good. It was in Atlanta, Georgia, the family's next home, that he would be fully freed to allow these gifts to bear fruit in the world.

9

It was a "Paul Smith weekend" …

… The leave-takings began with what was billed as a "Welcome to Morehouse" reception at the [home of] Dr. and Mrs. Walter Washington and believe us, no [home] other than theirs would have accommodated the throng that responded to the call of the local alumni. Even the Morehouse president, Hugh Gloster, whose assistant Paul will become, was up from Atlanta for the occasion, and what a wonderful party it turned out to be!

St. Louis American, May 1978[173]

Headlines in Atlanta

Making the move to Morehouse College in Atlanta, Georgia, launched Paul Smith onto the national stage. The college had a unique mission, a star-studded history, and a special resonance for Smith. Howard Thurman had graduated from Morehouse at the top of his class in 1923 and later served as Director of Religious Life and Professor there and at Spelman College for women.[174] Morehouse was indelibly imprinted with the character of Dr. Benjamin Elijah Mays, the prodigious intellectual who led the institution from 1940–1967. Mays's most famous student, Martin Luther King, Jr., had graduated from Morehouse in 1948.[175]

When Smith was offered the chance to become Morehouse's first ever Vice President working directly with President Hugh Gloster, Smith felt destiny was at work. The family was excited by the idea of moving to Atlanta, Smith had his new doctorate in hand, and some years of academic administration behind him. He was ready to mount new heights in the intellectual world. The society pages in the St. Louis newspaper picked up the happy story.

Morehouse started out in 1867 as "The Augusta Theological Institute" and was transformed over the second half of the nineteenth century into a top-flight liberal arts institution. As an all-men's college serving African American students, the College still has a truly distinctive mission.

> At Morehouse, we are redefining the meaning of leadership. It's not about attaining the highest title or position, but about attaining skills such as compassion, civility, integrity and even listening. Morehouse is poised to become the epicenter of *ethical* leadership as we continue to develop leaders who are spiritually disciplined, intellectually astute and morally wise …

The chance to become part of the "Morehouse mystique" was a potent tonic for Smith. When he realized that the office he had been given contained Dr. Mays's desk, he took it as another positive sign. In fact, it seems likely that Mays's successor, Hugh Gloster, had had the furniture moved out of the President's office because he wanted to put his own mark on the place. Dr. Gloster had succeeded Mays in 1967 and had been leading Morehouse for about a decade when the Smiths arrived in Atlanta. As Vice President, Smith had been hired to oversee academic matters on campus, so Gloster would have more time to devote to his other duties. Gloster had just that year launched a medical school at Morehouse and was in the midst of a huge and successful fund-raising campaign that necessitated extensive travel.[176]

One of the first visitors to the VP's office in August 1978 was a freshman who had wandered through the administration building to find Smith. C. Howie Hodges II would later become one of the super-achieving surrogate sons that Smith has embraced over the years. Now a lawyer and Vice President of External Affairs at Time Warner Cable, Hodges recounts that Smith knew his family before Howie was even born. The lines of connection between the Hodges and Smith families are numerous. Howie's Aunt Marie had been a Talladega classmate of Smith's, and his parents got to know the Smiths when they all were living in Buffalo, NY. Howie's father, Clemmon Hodges, had been a Philosophy and Religion major at Morehouse. He and Smith were Alpha Phi Alpha and later Sigma Pi Phi fraternity brothers. When the younger Hodges arrived on campus, his family had advised him to get in touch with "Uncle Paul."

Hodges recalls going to find Smith's office in the administration building where the halls were bustling with new students and their parents. Smith gave him a warm welcome and soon suggested that the young man come by his office in the evening. Hopping into the same green VW Beetle Smith had been given in St. Louis, the two drove to the Smiths' house in suburban College Park for dinner. In a practice that continues to this day, Howie drove and listened, while Smith rode and talked.[177]

Hodges testifies to the impact Dr. Paul had on students at Morehouse. Smith had joined the College as Professor as well as Vice President, and he immediately began teaching. His Philosophy and Religion course was an elective open to upperclassmen only. The man whose classes had caused such anxiety at the University of the West Indies was now in an environment that suited him perfectly—teaching to gifted, dedicated students who were consciously striving to fulfill the dreams of those who had fought for black empowerment. Hodges says the classroom on the first floor of James P. Brawley Hall was invariably packed. Its location on the Morehouse students' direct route to Spelman was, not surprisingly, busy. That too ensured that Dr. Smith's crowded lecture hall gained a reputation.

Even though he was just a freshman, Hodges frequently got to attend because he was driving Dr. Paul home after class. He found the atmosphere electrifying; he took copious notes and was awed by the caliber of students in that room. Men like Jeh Johnson, Obama's

Secretary of Homeland Security, and Robert Mallett, an international health-care executive, have indeed earned stellar reputations in the succeeding years. Even Dr. John Wilson, a recent president of Morehouse, was a student of Dr. Smith's.[178]

The way that Smith wrapped Hodges into his family life was a huge comfort to the young man so far from his hometown in Buffalo. He says he escaped the dorms and spent most weekends at the Smiths' house that year. It was "a beautiful house, big, ranch-style—almost like a tri-level, in College Park, Ga. [It is] a beautiful, bucolic suburb, big tall trees, big yards. And that's where they lived—Paul, Fran, three girls and Sasha."[179] Sasha was a huge black Newfoundland dog, one of several that have been part of the Smith family over the years. Howie made himself useful by becoming the dog-walker and house sitter when the Smiths were away. Hodges says that caring for Sasha and an air-conditioned house with a car in the driveway was not exactly a hardship.[180]

The Smiths' home was a tightly run ship, though. The daughters were growing up, and they had all inherited their parents' intelligence and good looks. As a father of three girls who was working on an all-men's campus, Smith was quick to make clear that his daughters should stay clear of Morehouse. And as far as sharing the College Park home on the weekends, "Pappa Paul," as Hodges now calls him, made the rules crystal clear. Smith proclaimed that when Howie stayed over, he would sleep in Smith's study where there was a pullout bed. That room was upstairs right next to the Smiths' bedroom, a floor away from the girls' bedrooms downstairs. As Hodges remembers, Smith was serious but smiling when he delivered this news.

> I have got three daughters, and I don't want nothing to happen to them. And so I love you, but when you sleep, you're going to sleep in my office … I'm keeping you close. I love you, but I'm going to keep you right up here! [181]

Hodges says that Smith has always challenged him in subtle ways to be his best. He recalls that on one occasion, Smith told him to come over for dinner, just as usual. When they arrived at the house, he found Dr. Howard Thurman was the guest for the evening. That night, Dr. Thurman leaned across the dinner table and said in the measured, basso voice he was famous for, "We share the same first name. Young man, what is the purpose of your life?" Hodges says his first thought was, "I've never seen so many beautiful gorgeous black women in my entire life!" He then remembered the gut-wrenching D+ he had just received on his first college paper. Regaining his presence of mind, he mentioned neither. Instead he said, "I think I'd like to go into law. I want to serve. I want to give back. But I'm still trying to sort it out." Fortunately, that seemed to satisfy the famous scholar.[182]

A peak experience for Smith at Morehouse was even more illustrious dinner party. In November of 1978, Smith invited Dr. Thurman to campus to give a public lecture and meet students. At the speaker's dinner, Smith's dream guest list became a reality. Assembled around the table at President Gloster's house were some of the best-respected academics and ministers in the country, including Howard Thurman and his wife Sue, Hugh Gloster, Benjamin Mays, and Martin Luther King, Sr., a.k.a. "Daddy King." Smith says that he was the youngest person in the room, yet it was he who had brought the company together. The voluble Smith says that he mostly listened that night.

Even the more mundane aspects of his job were a pleasure for Smith. He relished the contact with students, and they responded quickly to his concern and attention. "I recognized them. I empowered them. Gave them a voice, a hearing. And I made sure that the ... Resident Advisors took their jobs seriously. They were there to help the students!"

Hodges describes how well things were going. "He was very popular. The guys liked him, other faculty members liked him ... Paul was interested in you, as an individual; [he was] approachable and didn't just look at the super gifted students."[183]

Now a lawyer and Vice President at Time Warner Cable in Washington, DC, Hodges identifies "the relationships" as among Smith's most powerful tools.[184] Upon arriving in Atlanta, Dr. Paul had quickly made friends and found tennis partners. His relationship with Ambassador Andrew Young was renewed now that the two were living in the same city. Atlanta's Chief of Police, George Napper, and Napper's chief of staff were soon playing tennis with Smith twice a week. Smith also got to know the Public Safety Commissioner, Dr. Lee P. Brown.

This kind of networking was utterly natural to Smith, and it soon paid off for Morehouse students. The College occupies a densely packed group of buildings on busy streets in western Atlanta. As Smith remembers,

> They had built a new administration building named after Gloster, on the other side of the campus across a street with no streetlights. It was dangerous for students to cross the street there. Gloster tried to get a streetlight for that spot, but he wasn't successful. The next time I played tennis with the Chief, I said, "Can we get a streetlight?" He said, " Of course I can do it." Within two weeks, we had a streetlight. Gloster had not been able to do it even with [Maynard Jackson] a graduate of his school as mayor.

One can imagine that being upstaged by his new VP did not please President Gloster. "He hated that," says Smith of the streetlight incident. Despite—or perhaps because of—the fact that Smith was proving so highly effective as Gloster's No. 2 man, relations between the two began to deteriorate. Smith did not share the details of what was unfolding with his young protégé. Hodges says, "He doesn't want to crush your spirit or have things that he's going through dampen your enthusiasm for the school. So he kept a lot ... to himself. But you could sense that there was less joy ... "[185]

Hodges says that even as an eighteen-year-old, he could see that Gloster and Smith were "like oil and water." From Smith's point of view, it was much worse than that. "I spent that year trying to stay alive because I thought I'd made a terrible mistake going to Morehouse. Gloster ... was very difficult to work with. I didn't know that going in of course. Mays loved me. The President didn't. Gloster tried to undo whatever Mays had done there."

The very day Smith went to tell Gloster he couldn't continue, he learned Gloster had just sent him a letter.

> I got fired and didn't even know it. I quit before I got the letter firing me. Instead of walking down the hall, Gloster sent a letter to the house. He thought I'd seen the letter when I went to talk to him but I hadn't yet. I wanted to say this wasn't working out, but Gloster got very defensive. He said, "You are the biggest disappointment of my entire career as an administrator!" I said to myself, "I'm just going to get up and knock the shit out of him!" I'm not proud of that. But I didn't. I said, "I'm sorry you have that opinion but the bad news for you is, the entire faculty and students disagree with you." And I walked out.

What Smith said was true. When the students learned he was leaving, they picketed Gloster's office and staged a sit-in protest. They had responded wholeheartedly to Smith's warm personality and his tough love. Hodges sums it up, "Paul was beloved by the students, had the relationships in the community to get things done, quietly. Gloster got jealous, because he could see more and more that students leaned on Paul, less on [him]. If you met Gloster you would see, this was a man who needed to have his ego fed."[186]

Smith wrote frequently in his journals about his struggles at Morehouse. On a day in late August 1979, he records that he went to Dr. Thurman for advice.

> Today I spoke with "my guru" in California. I had three major agenda items. 1) Coretta King's visit; 2) my career choices ... 3) consent to edit a book of meditations for me if his time permits ... he wished to give deep thought to the career choices from the context

of ME—where I was headed, the importance of this decision given the time in my life … I feel something stirring within me because my well has been low this past year. The long drought appears to be over and it has begun to rain again … [187]

With his administrative experience, education, and deft social touch, Smith might have pursued a college presidency himself. However, it was too soon to move the family again. So Smith decided to pursue a new pastorate he had heard about at an all-white church. He was soon one of forty-four candidates being considered by Hillside Presbyterian.

Hillside is an assemblage of low buildings built at the crown of a long, sloping piece of land in suburban Decatur, just outside Atlanta.[188] Church membership had fallen from over six hundred in 1970 to just above two hundred in 1979, and funds were running thin.[189] The neighborhood was "in transition;" historically, this has generally meant that whites were moving out because blacks were moving in. This time, though, rather than move or close down, the loyal white congregation wanted to stay and save their church by welcoming their new neighbors as fellow congregants.[190]

By October 1979, the search committee circulated a letter recommending that the church call Dr. Smith. The team described in already affectionate terms what had impressed them about him and quoted Smith's eloquent vision of their shared future.

We wish we could transfer to you the very strong positive feelings we have for Paul, but this is a pleasure you will have to experience for yourself … The following statement by Paul will give you some idea of the way he sees his role as a Minister and ours as a congregation:

I believe the church is the one place in the universe where God's people may gather together to work on problems without fear. There, they will find God who proceeds us in our concerns and who is able to address our fears. Here we are as one family; we are reduced to Oneness in God's house. No class, no race or clan shall be afraid here. Our task is to make the church that kind of place as we serve the Lord.

Smith wrote later about his unannounced initial meeting with the congregation.

The Communion along the river, downstate Georgia—October 1979 ... The setting was perfect, the occasion relaxed ... Topic of my meditation: The Sacramental Moment. The young people stayed near the water on the docks—they listened intently although giving the impression they were disinterested—after all, they knew where they stood on the issue. I knew if we could relate in this setting we would start on a new journey. Part of me knew also, that it was difficult to fail in this setting. Thus giving me a greater confidence and ability to be relaxed.[191]

The congregation voted forty-nine for hiring Smith and ten against with one abstention.[192] Smith worked thereafter to develop relationships with those who had had doubts about him. He later wrote how the communion service took on a special meaning for him at Hillside.

November 4, 1979 was my first Sunday in the pulpit ... 125 showed up; a large number of Blacks came that day. O. Jackson a colleague and friend from the Danforth Foundation in St. Louis was there. A memorable experience. B. Jones gave me a note I will always cherish, just minutes before the service began. He expressed his support and prayers for our work together—as well as that of his family. With that note, I gained the confidence and the spirit to serve effectively in this situation. The racial mixture on this first Sunday has remained for the last nine months. Communion took on a new meaning—even greater than breaking bread by the river—as brown hands broke bread, white hands received it. Now I understand how the table of our Lord is the dividing point; at the table, His table—we are all one.[193]

Members of the congregation said later that they felt that they had chosen the most qualified candidate, white or black.[194] Their offer to Smith was considered so unusual that it made the newspapers as far away as Miami[195] and Los Angeles.[196] The title of the *LA Times* article, "White Church in South Picks Black Pastor," shows that part of what made this newsworthy was the place where it occurred. However, a denominational journal also asserted that Smith was one of only a few black ministers in the Presbyterian denomination, and that being a black minister called to lead an all-white church made Smith "unique among the more than four thousand congregations of the Presbyterian Church in the US."[197] In interviews, Smith simply noted that he had done this several times before and that he had "not one reservation racially"[198] about accepting the job. He was poised to show people how it could be done.

The *DeKalb Sun* article provides telling details about the day-to-day ethos of Hillside Presbyterian under Smith's leadership. It quotes him as saying, "I know who I am [and] I am not afraid to discover who I am not." It praises the reverend for his "personableness, warmth and enthusiasm—plus his preaching abilities." A black parishioner is quoted as saying that Hillside's "outreach to bring a wholeness to the community" drew him to become a member and later a member of the Session.

Hillside member Lisa Demer, who wrote the *Sun* article, also mentions class as a factor shaping this new mix of people. As she puts it, Smith's "quiet, creative approach in the pulpit, often focusing on national issues … attracts middle- and upper middle-class people of both races." Demer quotes Smith and sketches his position on the class issues.

> "We are very upfront about integrating at class levels," says Smith. He points out that the caliber of blacks attending Hillside would be just as uncomfortable with a jive-talking street black as the whites would be with a potbellied redneck waving a Confederate flag. "Lower classes could feel comfortable here because of who we are," he says, "but they wouldn't like the music and order of the service. They look for a livelier, more emotional and spontaneous program."[199]

Smith's practice of ministry does not shy away from either poverty or wealth. He emphasizes commonalties between people that transcend differences in income level and status. In contrast to Atlanta, the congregations at both Berea and Second Presbyterian in St. Louis were mixed in their economic composition. In an article on interracial churches in south DeKalb County, he points out the actual demographic complexity of the area when Hillside was founded.

> "In 1954," Smith said, "this was virgin territory for the Presbytery. The present building was put together in sections, which indicates something of the new church's quick growth. It grew and grew and grew, and then the neighborhood changed."

After Smith's arrival and the newspaper coverage about it, black membership leapt to about 40 percent of the congregation.[200] Smith emphasizes that it was the church having black leadership, not just black membership that made the difference. By June of 1982, Hillside had over two hundred active members and a black/white composition of about fifty-fifty. Demer quotes Smith as saying, "I didn't come to this church with the intention of making it all black. I wouldn't be upset if that happened, but it need not. We are a culturally plural congregation and have a ministry here that meets the needs of a wide cross-section of people."[201]

Two parishioners became especially close colleagues of Smith's at Hillside: Dr. Joanne Nurss, a white woman with a PhD in Education and Dr. Prince Rivers, a black man with a doctorate in Chemistry who was very active in educational development in the Atlanta area. The pairing of black and white leadership has been one of the secrets of Smith's success. He has not only participated in such collaborations himself, he has used the principle to organize lay leadership in his churches. Nurss says that she and Rivers served as a sounding board for Rev. Smith.

> The three of us did a lot of things together, a lot of planning. Paul would bounce ideas off us, [asking] "What do you think?" … and we felt comfortable being honest with him. [We could say] "No, that's a crazy idea. It won't work!"[202]

Before she passed away in 2016, Dr. Nurss had much to say about being Clerk of Session and working with Dr. Smith at Hillside.

> What Paul was able to do at Hillside was attract a large number of both Caucasians and African Americans … They were all middle class and well educated, in the same professions, so they had all this in common, just we were different races. In the ideal situation, you're going to have a church with a mix not just of races but socioeconomic status. But it is very hard to do it in that situation. Among other things, style of worship and so on is so different.

The congregation quickly grew, but there was the perennial problem of how to help new and old parishioners get to know each other.[203] An old technique was used.

… We had a large group of people who got along very, very well. But we had people who had never socialized with people of the other race. So one of the first things that was [created] … was a program called Nurture Groups. We were divided up by area where we lived and the plan was that you would have a monthly meeting in your home. It could be a potluck, dessert, whatever. And in time, groups evolved differently. Some became singles, some became couples with young children. You had people of course, African Americans, who had never been in a white home and whites who had never been in an African American home. What you discovered was, "Oh your house is just like mine" or nicer than mine, sometimes we would find out.[204]

Nurss was in a position to observe Smith's abilities as a fundraiser and financial manager, and she asserts that Smith exceeded everyone's expectations. When he arrived, Hillside had debts that were difficult to pay off with only about 30 regularly contributing members. The church did not even have enough money to pay Smith's full salary. The Presbytery urged Smith to be realistic about what he could accomplish.

… [Paul] inherited a church that was falling apart … the Presbytery was paying a chunk of his salary—the church had gotten a second mortgage on the property from the Presbytery …
There was a plan that it would take five years before the Presbytery would stop paying part of his salary, and it [took] three years. The second mortgage was paid off, the first mortgage was paid off, bing, bing, bing. And so his goal was to build up a multiracial congregation that was thriving … and leave behind a vibrant church. Which he did.[205]

Despite the many steps toward racial incorporation that were taken at Hillside, Smith was not always successful in bringing in the new parishioners he sought. In March of 1983, he writes of his efforts to convince the new president of Agnes Scott College in Decatur, Georgia to become a member at Hillside. Agnes Scott is an elite women's college started by a Presbyterian minister in the nineteenth century.[206] In 1982, the college had just hired its first female president. Bringing her to Hillside would have been a real coup for Smith, yet his overtures failed.

> ... my reaction to seeing the new president of Agnes Scott, Ruth Schmidt at North Decatur Presbyterian Church ... was anger. After all, I had written her in Massachusetts long before she knew where Hillside ever was located. She only knew that it was in Decatur. I had invited her early on to visit; sent her an article from the *LA Times*. I followed up with a visit to the college. She came for a visit. I wrote another letter when I heard by the grapevine that she was thinking of joining N. Decatur. I wrote the letter in response to what I heard but not what I felt. Perhaps that was the mistake.[207]

Smith's frustration was that Schmidt seemed unwilling to take a risk for the cause of racial pluralism. He was also conscious of the loss to Hillside of the resources she would have brought with her.

> It is newsworthy for a black to come to an all-white church; it is different and challenging. We do these kinds of things all the time. Why not expect the same from whites? I tend to look at the rest of the world through the eyes of the Hillside experience that in itself is positive. Yes I have high expectations for myself and of course for others. It just seems natural, with all that was written about her, to at least visit Hillside enough to make an intelligent choice. But she will stay where it is safe; use the resources where they are needed, but

not needed as much as Hillside needs them. How will we ever become a self-sufficient church, truly racially plural, unless some whites like Ruth Schmidt and others take a stand, make us a statement (as George McMaster did) and join with us? It is clear to me how the white church continues to build itself. I am disappointed, but I am no longer as angry, now that I have written it down.[208]

A critical event for the Presbyterian Church as a whole occurred while Smith was working in Atlanta. That was the so-called "reunion" of northern and southern branches of the Church, which had divided in 1861 over slavery. In June 1983, one of the largest branches of the Presbyterian Church, the southern PC in the US and the northern PCUSA met in Atlanta and formally agreed to rejoin.[209] Smith wrote in his journal,

> Today it happened. After 123 years we PCUS/PCUSA became one. The music in the World Congress Center at the moment of the vote was a sacramental moment. Cheers, clapping, watching, rejoicing and the new church was off to a start. As I marched alongside of my wife I realized this was a very special moment in history in the life of our church. I thank God for the opportunity to be part of it.[210]

Smith was originally intended to have a special role that he clearly relished; he was scheduled to introduce Mayor Andrew Young to the crowd. He reveals a rare moment of bruised ego when he later writes about hindrances to the plan.

> It seems as though success is always just out of my reach. Of course that all depends on what I mean by success ... When the two General Assemblies of the UP [United Presbyterians] met in Atlanta, my job was to

introduce the mayor of Atlanta, Andy Young. He and I have been colleagues and friends through the years. As 8000 people marched from the Army in celebration of reunion I felt my heart beating with joy as we watched the steps of City Hall. Day was perfect and the people were happy ... I ran ahead to make sure everything was in place; particularly the mayor who is known to be elsewhere at times like this. And then it happened. The mayor was there and the staff was there. I was waiting for the opportunity to present the mayor. However the public address system was not there. It never arrived. There were too many people in the streets and surrounding City Hall that the truck could not get near enough to set up its equipment. I did introduce Andy with a bullhorn—significant of the occasion in yet another sense–for this is how we spoke to the marchers during the civil rights movement days.[211]

In another entry from 1983, he writes about a triumph that "confirms the validity in my mind of the racially incorporated church." Rev. Smith writes of attending the funeral for the father of a Hillside parishioner in Hoschton, Georgia, a small, all-white town about forty-five miles north of Atlanta. Smith's history in the Deep South made him hyperaware of how his arrival, unannounced, to join the family of the bereaved might be received. In the end, the experience affirmed for him the value of all he was striving for at Hillside.

The undertaker's helper, in a black suit, mud on his black shoes, and his belly hanging over his belt, was standing at the door of the church when we drove up. He looked as we parked the car and was there to open the door for us when we were about to enter. He was cordial, a bit startled but did not seem to mind, since we seemed to know where we were going. A black man, two white women and one black woman, made history as we entered the church. The door creaked as did the floors as we entered directing the eyes of all present toward us ... The family arrived shortly after and we were all asked to stand as they filed into the church. Those who had not seen us before could see us now but most eyes were fixed on the bronze casket ...

As the family was leaving the church, the man from Hillside saw Paul and the others and came to greet them.

I reached for his hand but he reached for me and put his arms around in a warm and moving embrace. With tears in his eyes he said, "Paul you will never know how much this means to us to have you here; just knowing that you cared enough means so much." It was a sacramental moment. The kind that can only come in a racially incorporated church. The symbolism of a white male, embracing his black pastor in rural Georgia in the midst of the very people [he and his wife had grown up with] could not have happened unless the first step had not been taken by Hillside three and a half years earlier. Now I am convinced that it is critical to have the church truly plural for that is the only way to authenticate the gospels.[212]

Smith carried this philosophy further by bringing white parishioners from Hillside to the historic downtown Atlanta church where both Martin Luther King, Sr. and Jr. had been pastors.

I have finished my second lecture on Jesus and the Disinherited at Ebenezer Baptist Church. It is absolutely fascinating to see the interest and enthusiasm of the Hillside members who have accompanied me to these lectures. It is clear that Blacks and Whites can indeed have an opportunity to dialogue and interact in

a setting which is totally black. That the whites from Hillside have participated at Ebenezer is significant. So many good things have already happened. Race, class, economics can be discussed without fear of intimidation
… The need for such opportunities as this is clear.[213]

Smith taught on Dr. Thurman's work elsewhere in Atlanta. Columbia Seminary was just a few miles down the road from Hillside Church. One of his students there was Mike Trautman, who has since had his own career in ministry. Trautman says the mostly white students there were unlikely to have read works like *Jesus and the Disinherited* in any other faculty member's class. It was a course Trautman would never forget.

It was a pivotal class for me. He was able to introduce Thurman's work, to share his personal experience of Thurman. [It gave us an] eye-opening sense of who Thurman was.[214]
[It was an] all-white seminary—we were not going to read non-Presbyterians. Thurman was a unique soul. I … would have [studied] James Cone, liberation theology, because I was very much interested in those alternative ways. But I never would have had Thurman without Paul.[215]

Trautman became involved with Hillside Church. He and his wife had visited Hillside the previous summer after relocating to Decatur. He recalls that they pulled up in the Hillside parking lot one Sunday morning, hoping to explore a church in their new neighborhood. He had no way of knowing what kind of difficulties the church was going through. He chuckles, remembering the welcome they received. "People rushed out to greet us so enthusiastically, that it actually spooked us!" Things changed after Smith arrived; Hillside later became the Trautmans' home church.

Trautman says, "I was intrigued by Paul and attracted by his charisma and depth yet wary, because was he for real? It didn't take me long to realize that his spirituality and insight was dynamic and life altering."[216]

Smith guided Trautman through his summer fieldwork training at Hillside in the summers of 1980 and 1981. Smith's easy, egalitarian style meant that the young seminarian had much broader fieldwork opportunities than many.

> He gave me the freedom to experiment. Took me on calls with him, and I got to preach. I went with him on visits to people, new members … He has an amazing gift of attracting people. People gravitate toward him because of his personality and depth.
>
> I had more opportunity to preach than many people would have. [He allowed me to be] part of the whole church experience, not just to work with youth or something like that …
>
> He helped me experience what it would be like to be a minister. I realized I had a lot to learn! The people skills, especially hanging in there with people who may not like a decision you've made. You have to learn how to handle folks who might be difficult for the life of the church.[217]

Of Hillside generally, Rev. Trautman says,

> Paul attracted such a wide variety of people. Hillside was a pretty progressive church for those days … Paul attracted a lot of socially mobile people, people with experience and power. He's never threatened by someone who in one walk of life may have wielded power. It took me a long time to appreciate what I learned from him.[218]

Trautman had grown up in a multiracial family and neighborhood in Bridgeport, Connecticut's biggest city. During his first year in the Deep South, Trautman remembers feeling uncomfortable that there was no discussion around the seminary of the Child Murders that had started in 1979. He soon found other students who saw the world more as he did.

> Columbia was pretty much all white at that time. There were two African American students, Elbert Darden, another guy that Paul adopted, and Will Coleman. [We] all became friends. We all felt—I didn't grow up with the southern Presbyterian Church and so it was [a] really strange place ... So we all kind of hung together. And Paul became the person who mentored us and cared for us and got us through that experience.[219]

Some of that "care" was rough-and-tumble and delivered on the tennis court. There, Smith contends, he ran circles around Elbert and Mike, two men much younger than he but not quite as good at tennis. As others, including Mayor David Dinkins, his future tennis partner in New York, will attest, the good minister has some competitive fires that can only be seen on the court. Mike Trautman admits that Smith's story is accurate.

> Elbert and I were Paul's guinea pigs ... Paul liked running Elbert and me all around the tennis court. It was the only place where you'd see Paul brag.
> Elbert was an all-American basketball player, part of the Southwest conference All-decade team. So he was a hell of an athlete. I was all right, nothing great. But he was a hell of an athlete, the best basketball player I've ever played with.
> But he caught on much faster than I did [to Smith's treatment]. He would say, "Mike, he's selling you wolf cookies!" It's an urban term—[it means] he's trying to

get into your head and intimidate you. [Elbert would say], "Don't let him do that to you![220]
[Smith] would talk stuff to us all the time. [The tennis court was] one of the places he had fun with it. I wonder how that worked its way out as a younger man. He had such an integration, a sense of who he was, where he came from, where he felt called to be and do in life.[221]

Rev. Trautman tells a revealing story about his former teacher. It occurred one day as Dr. Smith dropped him off at the seminary. Trautman had been mulling over a question from theology class, and he asked Smith what he thought about it. Smith's answer profoundly affected his interlocutor.

[The] question was—What would faith look like to you if they found Jesus's bones? Paul said, "That really doesn't matter to me." That was a huge shift of paradigm. I was a history major! But it changed my whole perspective. Paul said, "Wherever Jesus is, if I end up there, I'll be alright with that." To me, it captured Jesus's story and concerns … That was the base of being, the sound of the genuine.
That response has gotten more and more powerful for me as I've gotten older, as I see more and more people's own understanding of their faith. It has allowed me to be less judgmental of others … I'm now the age Paul was when I [first] knew him. That [perspective] has taken more and more root. It has made me a better human being, much more sensitive to other people's own journeys. He taught me—pay attention to other people's journeys.[222]

Rev. Smith's relationship with Dr. Thurman reached a glorious crescendo in 1980 when Thurman delivered the baccalaureate address to the fortunate women graduating from Spelman College in Atlanta.[223] Entitled "Listening for the Sound of the Genuine," the text of Thurman's speech has been widely reprinted and is the source of the title of this book. At least some of what Thurman meant by "the sound of the genuine" is captured in this excerpt (emphasis in the original).

> There is in every person something that waits and listens for the sound of the genuine in herself … Nobody like you has ever been born and no one like you will ever be born again—you are the only one. And if you miss the sound of the genuine in you, you will be a cripple all the rest of your life. Because you will never get a scent on who you are …
> So the burden of what I have to say to you is, "What is your name—who are you—and can you find a way to hear the sound of the genuine in yourself?"
> … I wonder if you can get still enough—not quiet enough—still enough, to hear rumblings up from your unique and essential idiom, the sound of the genuine in you. I don't know if you can. But this is your assignment …
> Now there is something in everybody that waits and listens for the sound of the genuine in other people. *I must wait and listen for the sound of the genuine in you.* I must wait. For if I cannot hear it, then in my scheme of things, you are not ever present …
> Now if I hear the sound of the genuine in me and if you hear the sound of the genuine in you it is possible for me to go down in me and come up in you. So that when I look at myself through your eyes having made that pilgrimage, I see in me what you see in me and the wall that separates and divides will disappear, and we will become one because the sound of the genuine makes the same music.[224]

Smith was in attendance when Thurman delivered this famous

lecture. He says it was a homecoming for Thurman, who had preached every week in the same church while teaching at Spelman early in his career. The audience was aware of the connection, and the talk was a huge success.

Starting in March 1980, Smith deepened his knowledge of Thurman's work by leading what became a monthly study group called the "Howard Thurman Ethical and Enrichment Circle." The purpose of this formally constituted body was to "perpetuate the memory and teachings of Dr. Howard Thurman."[225] It had several dozen members, including some from the Hillside congregation and honorary members such as Dr. Benjamin E. Mays and Rev. Martin Luther King, Sr. Co-leading with Smith was Dr. George Thomas of Shaw Temple AME Zion Church and the Interdenominational Theological Center in Atlanta.

In May 1980, the group hosted Dr. Thurman himself. After the sage died in April the following year, the Circle held a celebration of

Baccalaureate service, Spelman College, Atlanta, Georgia, 1980. From left: Paul Smith, Donald Stewart, Howard Thurman, Norman Rates. (Photo by Jo Moore Stewart)

the theologian's life annually in addition to their regular meetings. Their meetings made use of more than 100 recordings of Thurman's speeches and meditations. One of their main activities was fundraising to help build a Reading and Listening Room dedicated to Thurman in the new Woodruff Library at the Atlanta University Center.

Ardent members of the Circle made a scrapbook for Dr. Paul before he moved to New York in 1986. Included in the scrapbook are twelve hand-written letters of thanks from members of the group. They express deep affection and respect for Dr. Paul and wish him well in New York even though they are clearly sorry that he was to leave their company. They write, for instance,

- I have found you to be a person of love, gentleness, consideration, fairness, and humility. You possess the rare quality of being able to unite all who work with you into a coherent unit, because you take the time to know and understand those with whom you are closely associated.[226]

- This letter is written to express our deepest appreciation to you for bringing spiritual joy and comfort to our lives for the past six years. Your personal interactions with Dr. and Mrs. Thurman and leadership through Dr. Thurman's life's journey have enabled the members of the Circle to interpret his philosophy of living through you. Paul, we will truly miss you and your monthly Christian therapy; however, we realize that you must complete your tasks in life.[227]

- May God grant you continuing success as you carry on your ministry in New York. In the words of Sir Isaac Newton," I can see farther because I've stood on the shoulders of giants." Thanks for being a giant in our lives.[228]

Despite all his training and preparation, Rev. Smith was still stunned when he received word that Dr. Thurman had died in April 1981. His pages-long journal entry that day reveals his anger, soul-searching, anxiety, flashes of guilt, and search for meaning. He looks for logic in the way events have unfolded. After two pages of stream-of-consciousness writing though, Smith finds grounding in the solace offered by his wife and the inspiration of Dr. Thurman's own philosophy.

4/10/81 The news came today that Howard Thurman

had died. It is a fact that I cannot deny. Even though Luther [Smith, Jr.] and I spoke nearly 3 hours today about Thurman and the future (not knowing that he had died), the fact is—he is dead. Nothing can be done about it. It is so final and complete. Somehow, I knew I was being prepared for SOMETHING. First, the incredible news that the President [Reagan] and three others had been shot; then the news that Jim Whitaker had suddenly died of a heart attack—we had been with each other just a few hours before. Then the news that my father would need an operation on his heart for another time; and the frantic call from my sister in Detroit that my/our mother was depressed because of the phone call from our brother William; and the call to my father to explain that we all knew something which needed to be shared with him. Death appeared to be all around me, giving me clues that it was hovering around. Why! I ask, could I have not known that it had already called Jim as we talked on Sunday evening. If I had known perhaps I could have warned him. But what good would it do. Death cannot be put off from its course.

... the news came while Luther and I had been having conversations about Thurman—his thought, his life and where we might go from here. Little did we know, life had already escaped from its entombment in Howard Thurman. Can [it] be given onto someone else? Has it cared for Howard long enough and has decided now to move on to another? But to where I might ask ... he is gone; that laugh which utilized every ounce of himself has been silenced. Or has it? That ability to dramatize the words of the Bible—and the words of life itself, is no longer to be heard again ... It is further significant that Fran gently told me the news that Howard had died. The love of my life had meandered out to the driveway to first ask about Kathy's day at Agnes Scott—and then she told me–"Wait a minute they have been trying to reach you all day." In one breath she gave me the news and in the same moment I could feel her arms of comfort around me. A moment I will never forget and a reminder that those arms would enfold me again and again for moments such as this …

There is a sense in which we never come to the end of anything. I think this is one of Howard's many great statements. The truth of the matter is that he continues to live on the hearts and minds of many[;] that he left so many thoughtful words and challenges are not an accident. That he continuously challenges us each of us to find that spark in ourselves is truly beautiful. So his beginning is ours and as long as we see the genuineness in us, we will not only find it in others—but we will be challenged to live out our lives in creative ways.[229]

10

I was always very impressed with that church. Throughout Paul's ministry, I've never known him to have anything but a multiracial, multicultural congregation. I think he's probably one of the few preachers that can say that. Even his pastorates here in Atlanta were very well integrated before he went to Brooklyn.

Andrew Young, 2016 [230]

A Church for the Fellowship of All Peoples

The Call and Installation

If Rev. Dr. Paul Smith's achievements in Atlanta brought him attention in the national press, being called to lead First Presbyterian Church of Brooklyn (FPC) secured him a place in US history. Founded in 1822 and occupying its current home since 1847, First Church is a massive brownstone edifice on Henry Street in one of New York City's oldest neighborhoods. [231] Its imposing façade, a few steps up from the sidewalk, peaks at a bell-tower 120 feet high. Behind a high decorative fence, there are courtyards stretching to the back of the property. The first brownstone to the left of the church is the manse, a home built on a grand nineteenth-century scale.

The fine buildings and gardens of Brooklyn Heights rest on the prow of a bluff overlooking New York harbor and the skyline of lower Manhattan. The harbor is a salty mix of ocean and river waters with twice daily tidal changes of up to eight feet. At the north end of the neighborhood down a steep slope is the Fulton Ferry landing that Walt Whitman exalted in his poem "Crossing Brooklyn Ferry." There, one is at the edge of the surging East River across from the original port of New Amsterdam. Schooners, cargo ships, light ships, and water taxis can be seen at what has become the South Street Seaport tourist venue. Looking west across the river, the sun sets every night behind the massive skyscrapers of Manhattan. The landing itself is where General George Washington and his soldiers slipped away in boats from the pursuing British Army during the Revolutionary War.

Today, parks line the riverbanks, allowing people to stand at the railings to gaze upon the powerful river and the skyline. There is a floating theater where classical music is performed and an ice-cream shop serving the visitors touring Brooklyn on foot. Dominating the landing is one of the two huge, heavy footings that support the iconic and graceful Brooklyn Bridge, an early suspension bridge designed by the pioneering engineer John Roebling. The district is a nexus of visiting and commuting people, of commerce and quiet residential streets, of brand-new architectural projects and historic structures, of fresh water and salt. It is a neighborhood that offers the best of what urban living can be: people from all over the world, magnificent scenery, historic streets with gardens and trees, and transportation connections to all of New York City. It is hard to imagine a more inspiring place to live and work in any city in America.

About four short blocks east of the Promenade, First Church was given grand proportions and ornate woodwork by its mid–nineteenth-century architect, William B. Olmstead. It is graced by delicate, watercolor-like stained-glass windows by the renowned Tiffany and Cartier companies. The tall windows were sponsored by parishioners over the decades. The pulpit is high above the cushioned, carved wood pews, facing a generous balcony that can seat overflow Sunday worshippers. A large pipe organ rises behind the pulpit. Connected behind the church is a large wood-paneled two-story building that today houses a nursery school on the ground floor. Up a wide corner staircase is an enormous meeting room that stretches across the width of the church

First Presbyterian Church, 124 Henry Street, Brooklyn, New York. (Photo by author)

itself. An attached kitchen, a thick carpet, easy chairs, and portraits of early pastors create a gracious space called the Elliott Room where the congregation holds its social events. Just off the stairway landing is the pastor's study, a meditative cove with dark woodwork, tall windows, and a working fireplace. It was there that Dr. Paul spent twenty years, talking with all manner of people seeking pastoral counsel and spiritual solace.

Everything in the four-story manse next door has the same luxurious proportions. The main floor is reached via a set of stairs leading up to the front door, a full story above the sidewalk. Inside, the residence has large rooms with high ceilings, floor-to-ceiling windows, and a curving staircase in the main hall. It is so spacious that rooms on the upper floors have been rented out to tenants. Between the manse and the church, there is a driveway with parking space for several cars. All this is extraordinary in a community notorious for its small apartments, high rents, and nonexistent street parking.

When Rev. Smith received the call to lead the 163-year-old First

Minister's residence, First Presbyterian Church, Brooklyn, New York.
(Photo by author)

Presbyterian Church, he was poised to become its fourteenth senior minister and its first minister of color.[232] It was the strength of his preaching in St. Louis that led to his appointment. There had been an interim minister at the church for two years when, early in 1985, the only black member of the First Church Pastor Nominating Committee (PNC) submitted Smith 's name for candidacy. During his student days in St. Louis, William Edwards had heard Rev. Smith speak at Berea Presbyterian Church. As Edwards later told the *New York Times*, "[Smith] was one of the most dynamic ministers in all St. Louis."[233] After reading the articles about Smith's work in Atlanta, the nominating committee contacted him about the job in New York. Whereas Hillside had considered more than forty candidates, the search committee in New York was reviewing the resumes of more than one hundred.

Smith wrote of the process in one of his journals. In October of 1985, while accompanying youngest daughter Krista to look at colleges, Paul and Fran were hosted by parishioner Carroll Dickson, who lived a few blocks from the church in Brooklyn. Having been formally asked by the nominating committee to preach, Smith gave the sermon on October 27, 1985.

> I preached—Was received greatly; warmly. The setting was warm and open. The committee was favorably impressed. We returned to Carroll's living room … Gathered around his fireplace we met; the sacramental moment came. I knew and felt I would be asked to come as their pastor. I felt a bit strange in that moment because I realized I was going to leave Hillside. The thought had not crossed my mind until this afternoon. I would have to wait—they would have to wait; but the sacramental moment had come. When that moment comes each of us must ask—what will we do with it? All we could respond with—we will have to wait and see! Thank God for the waiting and for the sacramental moment.[234]

Afterwards, the committee unanimously decided to recommend him to the rest of the congregation. In mid-January, Smith preached again at First Presbyterian to a congregation that would vote afterward on hiring him. He wrote in his journal before and after the service.

Many thoughts running through my mind. Hard not to focus on myself, since this is my first sermon at the church. The vote of the congregation follows—A strange system—both congregation and preacher on the spot ... I wonder what the people are feeling? The names of previous ministers are etched on the walls! What must they be thinking now as they see this black man of God being nominated to the pulpit? I wonder what Mrs. Elliot really thinks as she remembers the 32 years her husband served here as the beloved pastor ...

1:26 pm. We sit together at the study desk; the fire is crackling in the fireplace. Fran and I are served a buffet lunch with a bottle of red wine ... The congregational meeting has been called to order by John McNabb. Fran and I are waiting to hear the results of the voting. I experience Fran in this moment, in a new and exciting way. Clearly, she is as happy as I am about our future here together. Clearly she has played a significant role in whatever decision is now being decided. She has affirmed me, the PNC, this congregation and this committee—this community. She will garner most of the yes votes for us—for this is a decision to welcome both of us to this ministry—me for church—Fran for the community and as my helpmate. Never has her presence been more important than now. So we wait together—in a joyful, celebrative mood (we feel the only vote can be yes) arranging in our minds the furniture in the study—what pictures will go where—what books there! Thinking ahead and feeling blessed. We kiss—a warm and tender kiss which says thank you for being who you are; thank you for 25 years of wonderful loving and caring. "We deserve this one," she kept saying. I agree.

Carroll Dickson comes into the room. How will we ever forget the excitement in his eyes; the glow on his face; the care and patience with which he says "Paul you are our pastor and they want you in the room." Slowly he climbs the stairs—his breathing is heavy/short. He has recently been to the hospital; his 80 years is beginning to catch up with him. And yet, there could be nothing to stop him from being the bearer of the good news of my call to the pastorate.

I remember Fran—excitement all over her face as we entered the Elliott room to the applause and singing of the doxology. People were smiling, I was crying and others began to cry … In that sacramental moment we became one voice; one congregation.[235]

According to the *New York Times,* the parishioners' vote by paper ballots that afternoon was sixty-seven for and twenty-three against.[236] After another vote was taken orally, the congregation was unanimous for calling Dr. Smith. Then,

The new pastor, who will move to Brooklyn in June, wiped away tears as he and his wife, Frances, were ushered into the room to a standing ovation. In a choked voice, he said, "I can assume you that this is one of the few times I will be without words."

He went on, his voice clearing: "This is the high point of my professional career. I pledge to you that together we will climb new mountains. I also pledge that we will have a lot of fun together."[237]

Regarding the possibility of leading a mostly white congregation, Smith told *Times* reporter David Bird, "I'm confident I can deal with it. It's a nontraditional thing and that's good for the church."[238] Smith said he hoped to be "catalyst, a visionary, a dreamer, to prod the interest of this church and community." He challenged the congregation to become "a voice in the wilderness." He said innovation had been the secret of his success at Hillside, where the membership had grown to three hundred.

In February 1986, Smith moved to Brooklyn ahead of Frances and the rest of the family. He soon discovered that there were still nine holdouts who had doubts about his skills. Knowing he needed to develop lines of communication with those people, he convinced the search committee to break the rules and tell him who they were. One was a pillar of the church who had voted no while his wife had voted yes. Smith soon found an opportunity to interact with the parishioner when he visited the man's wife in the hospital.

> Connie rises up in her bed to greet me. Jim says not one word, not hello, nothing. Connie and I were talking; she was saying she was looking forward to my being her pastor. Then she says she's getting a little tired. She says, "Jim, Dr. Smith doesn't know how to get around NY. Why don't you help him get to the subway?" Reluctantly, he goes.
> Jim has to walk out of the hospital with me and he obviously doesn't want to. We get down from the 8th floor in [the] elevator, and he still says nothing. We get four or five steps outside and there is a torrential downpour. We have to go back in. Then Jim says, "What the hell. We're going to take a cab." He says a few things in the cab. We get to the manse first; he lived one block over. I said—"My wife's not here, yours in hospital and it's dinnertime. Why don't we go get a drink and some dinner?" Jim said, "What the hell?" and he became my strongest advocate.

Smith visited each of the others who were resistant, saying he "wanted to know a little about them and they about me." Other opportunities arose that allowed them to see more of who he was.

> Jim … comes to see his daughter on Grandparents Day
> and finds Andy Young sitting there in the church. Andy
> told him, "I practically raised that boy!" about me. So
> it was validation. Andrew Young didn't just come to
> preach; he really knew me. From that point on, it was
> like, "Don't you ever say anything about Dr. Smith!" …
> It was a hell of a ride, a hell of a run.

In the end, all nine continued to attend First Church. With pride, a longtime parishioner at First Church was quoted in the *Times*[239] saying that hiring Smith was "the most historic event since the time of Cox," a mid–nineteenth-century abolitionist minister at First Church.

There were other hurdles to cross however. In New York, the Presbytery is comprised of some 115 congregations. The Presbytery has veto power; it can make or break a new minister's opportunity to answer the call of a particular church. First, the Presbytery has to meet with the candidate and approve the appointment.

> I had to go through a lengthy process … The Presbytery
> has the last word voting on you. They can keep you
> from [taking a] church. There were some arrogant guys
> on the Presbytery who had been turned down for First
> Church. They asked me ridiculous questions. I looked
> at them and said, "Does this have anything to do with
> being the pastor of this church?" They said, "We simply
> want to know what you think." I said, "What I think
> has nothing to do with what I can do if I become the
> minister here." They were interested in what I'd done
> at Hillside in Atlanta. Some of them wanted to know
> more about that than the theological questions. Then
> you leave, they vote, and you come back in to a round
> of applause.

Having quieted the naysayers in yet another group, Smith was ready to be officially installed as senior minister. The Presbytery organizes and pays for installation. Once again, Smith had surprises up his sleeve.

> You have to tell them who's going to speak. There was total disbelief when I told them Ambassador Andrew Young was going to speak for my installation.
> First Church was packed, even that big balcony. Must have been 50–60 years since anyone had used it. The church was packed, cameras, press—those old white guys were so impressed! They were saying, "Oh my gosh, who is this guy??" … They knew I was something different. To their credit, every one of those steeple pastors was very supportive. They were very generous to me. And I helped them.

An article in the local *Heights Press* reported that among the over 700 attendees were Hillside Church members from Atlanta, representatives from the mayor's and the borough president's offices, Councilman Abraham Gerges, newsman Gil Noble and various other well known executives and community leaders."[240] Former UN Ambassador and then-current mayor of Atlanta Andrew Young gave the sermon. There was organ and choral music, an Old Testament Lesson by the President of New York Theological Seminary, and an Epistle Lesson by Rev. Choong Sik Ahn from the Korean Church of Brooklyn, which was then sharing the church facility.

Elders from First Church, Presbyterian ministers, and other local clergy made up the group that led the actual installation itself. The leaders and the congregation recited some text emphasizing that there are different ways to serve God. At the end, the leaders placed their hands on Smith's shoulders as they asked him to pledge that he would serve faithfully according to the precepts of the church. After he had done so, the congregation responded with their own pledges to provide for his welfare, to stand by him in times of difficulty, and to honor his authority. Then all joined in prayer.

God of grace, who called us to a common ministry as

Atlanta Mayor Andrew Young speaking at Rev. Smith's installation at First Presbyterian Church, Brooklyn, New York, 1986. (Photographer unknown)

ambassadors of Christ, trusting us with the message of reconciliation: give us courage and discipline to fol-

low where your servants rightly lead us; that together
we may declare your wonderful deeds and show your
love to the world; through Jesus Christ the Lord of
all. Amen.[241]

The moderator of the event then said, "Paul, you are now minister
of the Word for this congregation. Whatever you do, in work or deed,
do everything in the name of the Lord Jesus, giving thanks to God
the Father through him. Amen. Welcome to this ministry."[242] The
Heights Press reported that Smith said, "he was called by God to serve
the church in Brooklyn Heights. His goal as the new reverend is to
develop a truly interracial and intercultural church in the Heights."[243]

Smith did manage to put a personal twist on the installation
proceedings by bringing his mother from South Bend for the service
and by organizing a series of seminars to be held the day before. The
seminar topics were all close to Smith's heart. For the mid-1980s, the
agenda was fairly progressive: Presbyterians and pluralism; Music as
a faith enhancing experience; the AIDS crisis; Medicine and ethics;
the Peace movement; the Church's position on Nicaragua; and issues
surrounding death and dying. These were subjects he later pursued
with his new congregation.

The Congregation

Smith stated after his installation that his intention "was to develop a truly interracial and intercultural church in the Heights."[244]
By all accounts, Smith was extraordinarily successful at First Church.
Over the course of two decades, the active membership went from
about 60 to 350–400.[245] The congregation represented in an increasingly conscious way, the perspectives of people in the black, white,
interracial, international, intercultural, interfaith, LBGT, believer, and
nonbeliever communities. Throughout his career, but most powerfully
at First Church, Smith created an amalgam of worship styles with elements of both traditional black and traditional white church practice.
Together with fellow seekers, he helped create a consciously integrated
community that celebrated its variety and its harmony. It appears to

have defined a set of values that have continued to be celebrated even after Smith's retirement in 2006.

Smith's instinctive ecumenicalism burgeoned in the cultural crucible of New York City. In 1987, when a parishioner whose foundation wanted to give an award to the Dalai Lama asked if the event could be held at First Church, Smith opened the doors of the church to him.[246] Smith remembers that Henry Street was blocked to traffic, the monks lined the sidewalks, and a neighborhood crowd gathered to watch. Over the years, other Buddhists, Sufis, rabbis, and leaders of other Christian denominations were invited to the church to speak, hold workshops, or join events with the First Church community. Andrew Young, Tom Foley, and other Congress-people, then-Mayor David Dinkins, Brooklyn politicians, Rev. Jesse Jackson, Marc Morial of the Urban League, and renowned law professor Derrick Bell are among those who eventually spoke to the congregation.

> Loretta Lynch [US Attorney General under the Obama administration] came to First Church. I worked pretty closely with her … At one time, there were 11 Harvard Law School graduates and their professor—Derrick Bell—at First Church. That was just magic, that time. At least four of that particular group are still there. One came here to work with Bill Clinton and then came back. Barry Ford, Lisa Mensa who is Obama's Under Secretary of Agriculture. We did well! And we had those not in lofty positions as well. A NYC bus driver. I still hear from her …

Parishioners who joined after Smith's arrival consistently point to the same factors that drew them to First Church. One was its mission statement, which defined the church as "openly inclusive—interracial and intercultural." Ellen

Oler, a therapist who was looking for a church in the late 1980s, said she had hoped to find a church dedicated to creating to a more racially and culturally integrated society. She also wanted a church she and her Jewish husband could feel comfortable attending together. It was a specific act of improvisation on Smith's part that gripped her.

> I went to First Church myself one Sunday. Paul, of course, greeted me warmly. I told him that I was five months pregnant, and he was very congratulatory, was very sweet. The following Sunday I went back. I sitting towards the back, and during the Prayers for the People, he said, looking straight at me, asked for prayers "for those among us who aren't born yet." He just looked right at me, and I just thought, wow—that's somebody who is paying attention. I felt like he just gathered me in, pulled me in … [247]

Mercia Weyand, another white professional woman who became a devoted First Church member, says she too had a powerful experience the first time she heard Smith preach.

> The Cathedral [of St. John the Divine] brought me back to church … I went to see First Church. I walked in and Paul was preaching. I sat in the back. He got all lathered up, saying, "When your back is against the wall, when nothing else works, when you feel alone, etc., etc., etc. [and then finally he said], God hears you." And I just burst into tears. So I started going to that church.[248]

Dr. Sam Murumba, a law professor from Uganda who joined First Church in 1991 with his family, was seeking a dynamic, politically active church after their move from Australia.[249] While coming from an Anglican/Episcopalian background, Sam and Keren Murumba's last church had been nondenominational, so the fact that First Church was Presbyterian did not concern them. They were attracted by Rev. Smith's history in the civil rights movement and the warmth of the welcome they received from Dorothy Gill, an elderly African American lady known for her embrace of one and all.

Marcia Smith and Ken Andrichik visited the church at Easter 1991 to hear Handel and were moved to find themselves sitting next to Arthur Ashe and his wife. That very first Sunday, Dr. Paul learned they were from the Midwest and told them, "You gotta come next week, okay? We're planning an all-church retreat and you have to come on that." They quickly found themselves in charge of planning the event. Both ended up serving for many years on session and in other key lay leadership positions.[250]

Parishioners quickly learned that Smith would draw them into all kinds of roles they had not envisioned for themselves. Smith's pastoral style was freewheeling, enveloping and enthusiastic. Dr. Murumba, for example, found himself asked to contribute to the service with little to no advance notice.

> Paul had a way of involving everybody. For example, he didn't feel that only the minister would do the pastoral prayer. He's very spontaneous. We'd start the service and then do the passing of the peace. Then he might walk by and say, "Sam, can you do the pastoral prayer today? … With Paul, there was no rigid form.[251]

Many members of the congregation mention the powerful way that Smith used his history and ongoing contact with key figures in the civil rights movement to bring political consciousness into discussion at First Church. Weyand's current church in Atlanta has an erudite minister, but the political awareness is missing.

> What's going on around you, and what your response should be as a Christian person, we don't talk about. Of course, some people think you shouldn't mix politics and religion. Especially in the South. But Paul would always talk about what was going on—and relate it to the Gospel.[252]

Responding to the burning political issues of the day was by now second nature to Smith. A few years into his tenure in Brooklyn, Smith wrote in his journal about some of the events he helped sponsor and the way they involved the wider community.

> ... FPC serves two very different groups of people. First, there is our actual membership who generally show up on Sunday or attend meetings which are important to the life and mission of FPC. I can always count upon this group, because for the most part, they have given much of themselves to the mission. They are present and accounted for. They are always there making their thoughts known.
>
> The second congregation represents the community with its varied interests. During the Persian Gulf 'crisis', which actually began in August of 1990, we focused the church's attention on a Christian/biblical moral and ethical response. On Christmas Eve, 1990 I made my first pulpit statement regarding the escalation of military machinery, manpower and personnel. That service gathered together some 300 people mostly from the community. On Jan. 17th, I put together an ecumenical prayer vigil which brought together over 700 (mostly from the community). This event was followed by a forum with Rep. Solarz, Major Owens, Rev. Goldie Sherrill and Rabbi Brickner, co-sponsored by Brooklyn SANE ... [253]

Among the many strong and distinctive personalities at First Church were the women Smith called "the two Dotties." Dorothy Gill, a lifelong Brooklynite, elder, African American, and key member of the congregation, helped express the ethos of the church.

> She was the mother of everybody. Everybody. It didn't matter [who you were]. Dorothy would go up and say,

"I love you." She felt it was important for everybody
to know that she loved them.[254]

The other Dottie was a white woman, Dorothy Turmail, who had
joined First Church long before Smith's arrival. She and her husband
were very active members who constituted part of the institutional
memory of the church. Dottie also developed an unusual talent for
sewing banners inspired by the ethos of the church; it was a banner
emblazoned with "The Coat of Many Colors" that brought Keren
Murumba and her son into First Church for their initial visit. Another banner hung outside over the front doors of the church simply
proclaimed "Struggle and Celebration."

Given the importance of tennis in his life, it is not surprising
that Smith knew before he even moved to Brooklyn that there was a
private racquet club a few blocks away from the First Church manse.
"The Casino," as it is known, is housed in a stout brick building with
a Dutch-style roof on Montague Street, the main shopping street in
the Heights. The club was built in 1904 and houses indoor tennis
and squash courts, a gym, and a restaurant. Inside, it offers the plush,
members-only quiet produced by heavy wood paneling and thick car-
pets. Whatever overt or de facto segregation it may have upheld in the
past, all one needs to become a member now is the ability to pay the
entrance fee and yearly dues. Smith contends that it was through fellow
tennis player and then–US Congressman Steve Solarz of Brooklyn that
he first gained entry into the club. Then as part of the negotiations
over his working relationship with First Church, Smith's membership
dues were paid in perpetuity. He was one of the few people of color
who belonged to the club at that time.

Another powerful friend made on the tennis court was Charles
Clayman, a lawyer with a long history in New York City who lived
down the block from the manse. Of their friendship, Clayman notes
dryly,

We were a perfect match. He was a young black guy

who grew up in the Midwest, went to a historic black
school and became a minister; I was [a] Jewish kid
from Quincy, MA who went to Harvard and became
a lawyer. We just had everything in common![255]

Nonetheless, meeting to play tennis and to eat breakfast once a
week at the Clark Street diner, Clayman says he and Smith "became
very close." Clayman says he found in Smith someone who was always
open to learning and interested in other points of view. "He was more
than willing—wanted to—talk to people and to admit what he knew
and didn't know. There is a confidence, but no arrogance."[256]

Over time, Clayman became Smith's "de facto general counsel."

I know a lot about politics. I'm a criminal defense
lawyer, been 47 years in NYC, general counsel to a guy
that was deputy mayor. [Paul] would listen. Sometimes
followed my advice, sometimes wouldn't. It was meant
for him to get a perspective from someone who only
had his interests at heart. No agenda.[257]

Clayman describes Smith's spheres of influence.

… he exists in a lot of different circles—be it Dinkins/
the government circle, friends of mine, lawyers, this
group of young black individuals, lawyers, accountants
and the brokers and the people he deals with. And
their friends. People in Washington in politics. He has
a wide, wide range [of contacts].

Over the years, Paul and Fran grew close to Clayman's family. This
culminated in Smith officiating at a wedding where his special brand
of sensitivity was appreciated.

… he was so much a part of our family that when my
older son got married in Kalamazoo, Michigan, they

asked Paul to come out and do the service ... I have a wonderful daughter in-law, a beautiful daughter-in-law. She was very nervous, before the wedding ... She walked up to the podium and Paul noticed how nervous she was and he leaned over and kissed her on the cheek. It was the most beautiful thing I've ever seen in my life. So that's who he is.[258]

Reviewing their many years together, Clayman emphasizes that his relationship with Smith is different than with anyone else.

... Paul is unlike most other people. There's something incredibly unique—it's not that it's holy. There's something unique about his presence. There are some people, when you're in their presence, it makes you feel better. With Paul, it is all the time. When he walks through the door, it's not that there is a light around him, but you just feel better. It is one of the most important things in my life, having a friend like that. It is something I never in the world would have imagined. And I have thousands of friends! That's what I do. But nobody like him.

Clayman recounts how events tended to unfold at First Church. In December of 1986, a few months after the Smiths arrived in Brooklyn, a now-infamous racially motivated killing took place in the Queens neighborhood of Howard Beach. Charles Joseph Hynes was the special prosecutor who successfully argued the case against white teens who attacked several black men, one of whom was killed trying to escape the mob. Hynes was a friend of Clayman's, and when he introduced him to Smith some months later, Smith invited the prosecutor to speak at First Church.

There was a nice crowd. Joe's one of these great Irish lawyers who can talk pretty well. And then Paul got up

and spoke. And it was just phenomenal. It was a little
of the southern black minister, a lot of passion, it was
poetry—it was beautiful. And Joe is a good lawyer and
I know Joe well, but they were on different planets ... I
would never have wanted to speak on the same program
as Paul. He's just miraculous.[259]

In the end, Clayman says, a number of people from the tennis
club liked Smith so much they joined his church.

Having moved to New York in 1988, Nathan Dudley, the son of
Smith's longtime collaborator Carl in St. Louis, joined First Presbyterian a few years after Smith assumed the pastorate. Dudley has a unique
perspective on Smith, the man who baptized him and watched him
grow up. He remembers being amazed as a child that Smith could walk
around the church and preach without notes.[260] After reconnecting
with Smith after many years in different cities, Dudley asked Smith
to co-officiate at his interfaith wedding in 2000 to Stephanie Jones,
a performance artist and Buddhist. Dudley, who has become a leader
at First Church, says of his old family friend,

> The church was incredibly open under Paul ... He ac-
> complished a great deal at First Church. The session
> took a huge leap of faith hiring him. And it was also
> a leap of faith for him to take that church ... [It] was
> a re-creation racially of the Thurman-esque church in
> San Francisco ... Spiritually, building-a-community-
> wise, it was obviously a success. It was like a dream of
> an integrated world.[261]

Now a father with interracial children, Dudley is incisive about
what the goal of a church should be.

> Integration as a word in the political sphere has
> disappeared, but it didn't die at First Church. Now
> "diversity" is the word. But it is not enough to just get

happy in our diversity. The question is [not just] are you diverse, [but] are you *anti-racist*?[262]

Another longtime parishioner, Jim Johnson, is an African American lawyer who went to Harvard College and Harvard Law School and has worked in the public and private sectors. He has known Smith since 1995. He first visited First Church after reading about Rev. Smith in Arthur Ashe's memoir. He explains further why just looking for "diversity" is not enough.

> Paul's church—I still attend—was home for me in a way that other places had not been. It was not diverse in the way that a lot of places are ... in the sense of the diversity of a crayon box—a lot of color but all wax inside? Instead [Smith] created space in which those who believed could commune with those who had questions. And those who had questions would not feel uncomfortable ... at a time when anti-Muslim sentiment was high, and it is even worse now, he had imams delivering messages and cantors giving Old Testament scripture. [263]

Johnson is still in close touch with Smith and has given a good deal of thought to what made Smith's ministry so successful. He highlights the physical warmth of the congregation.

> Paul blew up the hierarchy ... The power of Paul's ministry is that he doesn't worry about the law. He gets to the practices ... We touch each other [at First Church] ... we hug! There's five to ten minutes in which people will go around the congregation and everyone touches everyone else ... in a very robust way, in a safe way, [even] complete strangers ... There's one member of the congregation ... she may start a hug from eight feet away! The arms are up, the smile is big, and it is a

powerful thing. [264]

Fred Davie is a fellow Presbyterian minister and African American who has known Smith since the early 1990s. Currently Executive Vice President at Union Theological Seminary in Manhattan, Davie served as a parish associate at First Church for some years. A parish associate is an ordained minister serving in an unpaid support role to the senior minister. This can involve helping to celebrate worship services, baptisms and weddings, or representing the church at events that the senior minister is unable to attend. Davie is well-enough known and respected to have been asked to consider applying for the senior pastor position when Smith retired. Davie thought seriously about it but feels that administration, not parish ministry, is what he is called to do.[265]

Davie says that Smith is, at once, "a colleague, mentor, friend. He has a commitment to multicultural worship. He is intentional about it. It's about social justice and community change."[266] From his vantage point as fellow clergy, Davie says of Smith,

> Paul is deeply spiritual and reflective himself. He taps into God's presence, accessing the Divine out of a wellspring he's able to share with others. There is intentionality when he breaks down barriers. He has had an extraordinarily successful ministry in Brooklyn.[267]

In contrast to ministers who don't often let others speak from their pulpit, Davie says, "Paul never grasped for power. He loved to delegate, to bring in people."[268] And unlike his own calling, Davie says, "Paul in his heart, soul, and bones is a parish minister. He loves the liturgy and the ritual. He seeks a profound engagement in people's lives."[269]

Davie attests to the fact that at First Church, the choir, the session, and the congregation were all multicultural. He also reveals that he and another parish associate, Lee Hancock, were among those who pushed Smith to make his ministry explicitly welcoming to gay and lesbian people. One of the few criticisms voiced by former members of First Church was that Smith came late to recognizing that the LGBT community's quest for rights and justice was only the latest front in the struggle Smith had been a part of since the 1960s.

One lay leader believes that it was the heartbreaking loss of Smith's youngest brother to AIDS in the early 1990s that helped shift Smith's thinking on the issue. Smith later led a Sunday service at which he, Hancock, Davie, and another parish associate all gave sermons on gender and sexuality. Eventually, First Presbyterian became a publicly dissenting church within the denomination by supporting the rights of LGBT people. In the years since then, the wider Presbyterian Church (USA) has become more accepting. This culminated with a vote in March of 2015 to recognize gay and lesbian marriage.[270]

As young families joined the church and the membership grew, Smith's weekly routine grew busy with the rituals of a thriving congregation. He became especially well known for the way he walked new babies around the church to introduce them to the congregational family. In his sanctuary, there was an "unqualified celebration of children"[271] during services. A parishioner says, "He likes the sounds kids and babies make in church. He says it is part of the service. He'd say, 'The birth of a baby is life's answer to death.'"[272]

Smith's journals are filled with notes to and about babies he has baptized, couples he has married and funerals he has performed. Over roughly eighty months between January 2000 and October 2006,[273] Smith recorded details about sixty-nine baptisms, thirty-five weddings and twenty funerals. If each of these rituals is an occasion on which individuals and their families are literally touched by the church through the minister, it becomes clear how deeply and how often a clergyman like Smith gets to share his love and compassion with his parishioners.

Marcia Smith [no relation] served as Clerk of Session for most of Smith's tenure at First Church. She notes of his methods,

> People came because they were looking for faith, for a church home. It was still organized religion. It had some structure. But we had a lot of interfaith couples. A lot didn't even know what Presbyterianism was. Came because they liked the music and Paul and the

message—we're all in this together. He made it safe to
question the fact that black people don't like to talk
to white people and white people don't like to talk to
black people … now Latino and Asian people are part
of the conversation too. The conversation broadened.[274]

Working with Dr. Paul had its challenges, Marcia Smith says. "If
you wanted to work with Paul, you had to be flexible and go with him
in the service." She and the two Dotties are reportedly among the lay
leaders who also kept the paperwork between First Church and the
Presbytery flowing. Like Joanne Nurss and Prince Rivers at Hillside in
Atlanta, they provided the structure that supported Smith's spiritual
improvisations.

Asked about the well-heeled status of many First Church members,
Marcia Smith states she believes that Smith wanted to engage with the
elite because that was where the change needed to come from.

He wanted [to serve] upper- and middle-class white
people who weren't going to be taught about race,
rather than just talking with black people who were
marching. Because without that, it wasn't going to
cause change. He was about educating the people who
were in power.[275]

Congregants assert that Smith was unusually willing to share the
spotlight and the decision-making. In his characteristic way, he also
helped parishioners work through the inevitable conflicts that come
up in a congregation. "Paul used to say, 'If you disagree with someone,
that's when you need to take them out to breakfast,' and we still talk
about that."[276]

Around the time of Dr. Paul's retirement, Janet Dewart Bell, the
wife of revered law professor Derrick Bell, spoke formally at church
about her view of Smith's accomplishments.

I am and have been grateful to this church for being

the inclusive and caring community that it is, for being a model of diversity … I come to First Church to share God. This church and Paul have helped give me the courage to bear witness and tell my testimony … This is a wonderful and beloved community, where we have the freedom to be ourselves. We can be committed and joyful. We can even "disobey" Paul's and Beth's occasional dictates to "please remain in your pews during the passing of the peace."[277]

Mrs. Bell mentions the stories about Smith's Granny, Odie Wingo, that any repeat attendee at the church heard many times.

I debated with myself the title of today's talk: I almost called it "From His Grandmother's Porch." We all know how his grandmother brooded over him and helped him make his journey to responsible adulthood.[278]

Mrs. Bell says of Smith, "Dr. Paul has been our direct link with the legacy and inspiration of Rev. Dr. Martin Luther King, a participant in the Selma March and other 'sacramental moments.' Paul was there—side by side with Dr. King and Rev. Andy Young."[279] She quotes another parishioner on the mission of the church.

Sue [Carlson} has said that "real diversity is hard work." Let me repeat that: "Real diversity is hard work." It's not easy to get all our egos, set beliefs, and defenses in one place and surrender to a higher authority. Paul has been the inspiration, but we must remain true to the mission. It doesn't just happen.[280]

Many parishioners who were active members at First Church during Smith's tenure agree that his primary commitments were to diversity and inclusion, the theology and writings of Howard Thurman, and the struggle for justice. There was also a focus on introspection.

> Paul was multidimensional. We had a wonderful pastor in Australia … But he did not really have this inward thing that Paul has. I've never seen that much. Church leaders are more used to talking; there's very little reflection. [Smith's] Eastern methods, the quietness, the meditation—that was quite distinctive. The commitment to that is also quite strong with Paul … [281]

In his inimitable way, Dr. Paul insisted that the church elders on Session should be consciously multiracial. He changed the chemistry of the group with his methods. As Dr. Murumba remembers,

> … when I first got on Session, I thought we'd do admin business. But we met in Paul's office, and he said, "I want to go around and you tell me about your most moving experiences." He did the same on Session retreat. We'd do that all day. There'd be reflective meditative moments and then he paired us with somebody else. I was paired with Dottie T. It was a wonderful moment.[282]

> Ambassador Andrew Young spoke recently about First Church and his friend of many decades.

> Well, I think that everybody likes him, everybody respects him, and other than the problem at Morehouse, I have never known him to inspire resentment or envy. Everybody respects him and loves him. I don't know whether he was too young and aggressive or whether Gloster was too old and sensitive. But it's not unusual that good people clash over minor differences.
> But I tell you, the most impressive thing—I think two of the most effective people in government today were members of his church. And that is the Attorney General and the Under Secretary of Agriculture, Lisa

Mensa and Loretta Lynch. For a church to produce two members of a president's cabinet and subcabinet, is quite significant.[283]

Music as "an Antidote to Bitterness"[284]

Over Smith's years in Brooklyn, the choir became one of the most effective vehicles for building an integrated congregation. Particular music and hymns are a deeply felt part of the identity of both congregations and denominations. As Smith's daughter Krista put it while discussing her family's choice to attend a Presbyterian church in Summit, NJ, "I wanted the traditions I grew up with because that was such a part of my upbringing. Even to the hymns. I wanted my kids to learn the ones I learned growing up. The hymns are different in other churches."[285]

Aware of the way that familiar music grounds a congregation, Rev. Smith did not make changes in the music at First Presbyterian for a number of years. From the time of Smith's arrival into the 1990s, there were about eight people in the choir and there were four paid soloists, one each to lead the, soprano, alto, tenor, and bass sections. The hymns were chosen from the standard Presbyterian hymnal. There was a choir director and an organist. On several of the retreats at Ghost Ranch, gospel music was sung and discussed, and Smith hoped that the music director might be inspired to move in the direction of a more diverse style of musical worship. However, nothing changed until the impetus came from the congregation itself.

Around 1999–2000, Smith and the congregation together set a transformation in motion. First, a group of parishioners said they wanted to start a gospel choir. Eventually, two choirs formed, one traditional, one gospel. To Smith's chagrin, they settled out into two essentially racially divided groups (though there was one woman who proudly called herself the "token white" in the gospel choir). Dr. Murumba, whose wife and daughter sang in the choir, recounts,

When we first came, there was only one choir, all white, very traditional, classical stuff. Then suddenly a group of people decided they wanted to start a gospel choir … Paul said, "I can't have two choirs. They have to merge." Well, the gospel choir people didn't want to merge. In fact one or two left the church. Paul said, "We can't have it any other way. We can't have two separate choirs divided by race." That was around 1993–94. Then they merged choirs.[286]

Murumba points out that Smith has his limits. "Diversity was a very big thing for Paul. He was willing to go with the flow, but on that one, he was extremely rigid."[287]

At the time, Smith was on the Board of Trustees at the Brooklyn Academy of Music (BAM), the internationally known arts center just a few miles away in downtown Brooklyn. BAM had just initiated the "Sounds of Praise" gospel brunches intended to bring the powerful church music of Brooklyn to a wider arts audience.[288] It was in this context of renewed celebration of the art form that Smith began to push for more gospel music in the church.

Soon a new choir director was added to the mix. Amy Neuner joined First Church with her husband around 2000 after they moved to New York from Wisconsin. Both are classically trained musicians. The Neuners wandered into First Church to look at the Tiffany windows and were immediately drawn by the music and by Rev. Paul's sermon. Ron Metcalf, a prodigious musician with ties to Broadway, had just been hired informally to bring a gospel flavor to the music, and he was playing piano that day. Neuner says she knew nothing about gospel but found it completely captivating. After they joined the church, her husband Chris volunteered to play the bass for services, and Neuner began to assist Metcalf in organizing the music for the choir.

Embracing the move toward a more ecumenical sound, Metcalf hired a drummer and two gospel soloists. However, Metcalf soon moved on to other venues, leaving Amy Neuner attempting to fill his shoes.

The church really made an investment in the change.

They still had the other four singers who were classically trained. The [two new soloists] were a huge part of the ministry—Ben Smith and Bertilla Baker.
I never intended on having his job, but I kind of ended up subbing for him here and there. I said, "Okay I'll do it for a week," so I'd fill in. Then [Metcalf] just decided he was done—just wasn't there anymore. Paul said, "Ron told me that he trusts he can leave everything in your hands." Paul has such a genuine, loving, supportive nature. He was telling me, "You can do this." I didn't know gospel music. I was just learning from Ron … Paul said, "I trust you and you're going to learn." He was so genuine and loving. He said, "It is okay. We'll learn and keep on going."[289]

Neuner hit her stride after a colleague at the Long Island school where she was teaching music introduced her to the African American hymnal.

The African American hymnbook absolutely changed my life and the entire scope of my ministry at FPC. It was the key that unlocked the mystery of all the songs that were sung in black churches that I had been to. It was a transcription of the songs Paul hummed from the pulpit and Ben sang from the choir. It was the notes and the chords to so many songs that I had connected to emotionally and spiritually as I began to explore gospel music and spirituals.[290]

What Neuner learned from the notation in the hymnbook turned out to be essential to her success in developing new music and arrangements for the choir.

… for the first time, I could see the whole picture right in front of me. The notation made sense to me. It was the missing link. I had very, very little experience with improvisation, chord symbols, etc. The hymnal allowed me as a classically trained musician to sit down, play, and learn and experience hundreds of new pieces and in turn be able to teach them to our choir and congregation.

The body of work traditionally performed in black churches, as I understand it, was passed down through oral tradition. Not just the song, but the style and chords as well. And while you could find some of these songs in other hymnals, what was written down was not what you would hear in the church. Many "gospel" arrangements were not "true," in my opinion, to the spirit of the piece. The AA hymnal accurately reflects the structure of these songs and has been the bridge in my ministry between key phrases of songs and fully realized arrangements. In other words, we use the "bones" of the hymnal to create hundreds of pieces of our own.[291]

Neuner developed such a talent for leading a diverse choir in delivering a heterogeneous range of music that Rev. Smith gave her the title "Minister of Music" that is still recognized today. Neuner explains how Smith's philosophy helped shape the choir's goal of reaching everyone in the congregation.

We all have our own prejudices and things that really move us. Paul was always so intentional. The only reason this works is because we were not afraid to talk about this. He would say, "When we do communion today, it can't all be white guys. We have to do communion as we are actually represented." Paul was always very much—"and this is what we do and it is the diversity that makes us who we are" ... But everyone knows when they come, there's going to be something for them ... Paul was really into allowing people to be ministered to in many different ways.[292]

Over time, the choir has come to incorporate everything from spirituals to contemporary rock and even secular music. As Neuner relates,

> So we might start with a Presbyterian hymn "God of Glory, God of Grace" with the organ. Then we'd have something by the kids' choir. Then something a cappella. There will always be something for somebody to connect to.[293]

Eventually, a kind of shorthand developed between Smith and the musicians that made the music a spontaneous and integrated part of the mood of the service. As Neuner relates,

> Everything became much more improvisational. It was like, "If I ever start talking about Grandmother's porch ... " [there was music he wanted to start up]. He would be building to it. It was more a black style of worship. It is not really seen in Presbyterian churches ...
> Paul had a couple of songs I'd consider his signature songs. "I Don't Feel No Ways Tired"—when things were getting really deep and intense, we sang that song a lot. Sometimes he'd start singing something else like "The Lord is My Light and My Salvation." Paul would always sing, "Whom I shall I fear, the lord is the strength, who shall I fear?" They are both gospel but old traditional hymn-type gospel. They are out of the African American hymnbook.[294]

Professor Murumba says of Neuner,

… she became the interim and got so good. She has an amazing talent for bringing people together. In fact, Paul was right. Amy was really a pastoral figure. So the choir became like a mini-church. You'd go in Saturday morning and find them praying together. They help each other in all kinds of ways.[295]

It was in the process of choosing and rehearsing new music that the deepest community building took place. As Neuner relates,

We had amazing conversations at choir rehearsals—some of the deepest conversations about race and what some of the songs meant to different people.
The most recent [example was when] the pastor wanted us to do "Dem Bones" based on the scripture readings of the day. Jim Johnson raised his hand and said, "I can't participate in this arrangement. It is because of the choir who originally performed the song and what it meant in its time and place." And what that meant to him as a black man. We had a thirty-minute conversation about what these spirituals mean, how they can't all be lumped into one category. Those are some real conversations![296]

Both Johnson and Oler are long-term members of the choir that has become known in its own right. Johnson notes the part played by Bertilla Baker, a white woman who "sings gospel music with the gutbucket grandeur of Bessie Smith."

The music in most Presbyterian churches comes out of what is very much a Yankee kind of hymnal. Bringing together the gospel sound with that and having unpredictable voices yield that sound [was Smith's ministry].[297]

The choir developed a special relationship with Professor Derrick Bell who attended the church with his wife Janet. Bell, who was a few years older than Smith, had made a name for himself as a young lawyer working for Thurgood Marshall at the NAACP Legal Defense Fund in the 1960s.[298] Bell's uncompromising sense of justice led him to several highly principled decisions including leaving a tenured position at Harvard Law School in 1990 to protest the institution's unwillingness to tenure female professors of color. In 1992, Bell joined the law faculty at NYU and thereafter became a regular member of First Church. Sue Carlson remembers making a connection with him the very first time she went to FPC to hear gospel music—Dr. Bell too was a devotee and scholar of the music.[299] Eventually, Smith relates, a number of Bell's former students became regular attendees.

At some point in the early 2000s, Dr. Bell invited the choir to join him at the annual Race in American Society lecture he sponsored for freshman at NYU Law. Celebrated for its diversity and spirit, the choir appeared at the event annually, even after Bell's death in 2011. Their connection with Bell was so strong that when the congregation heard one Sunday that Professor Bell was in his final hours at nearby Long Island College Hospital, the choir spontaneously took action.

> … Amy Neuner rounded us up, and we left the service to go to the hospital. We went to visit Derrick's room and sang to him around in his bed. Paul was there and I was literally leaning on Paul. It was really one of the special moments of my life. It was really extraordinary. [Bell] ended up living another couple of days. We filled up that hospital room; there were about twelve to fifteen people.[300]

That kind of service to the community became a normal part of the choir's routine. They went where they were needed.

> There was a woman who had been a member forever. She lived alone with her dog. She started having mental

deterioration, no longer recognizing people. She was in an assisted living home. The choir would go there and sing for her![301]

Parishioners outside the choir testify to its power as well.

The music! That was the thing that brought people together unbelievably. I miss that so much. I would feel God through that music. A lot of African American spirituals and things like that—people moving and talking. It was electric. I left church high. I leave church now [in another city], and I ain't high. I do not feel like, "Wow, God is great!" I did at First Church.[302]

The powerful connections forged between members of the choir have continued even after Smith's retirement. Oler says she remains a member of First Church, because

It was a great congregation. They became my family. I stayed because they were my family. And the choir— that was a community within the community ... Members of the congregation also stepped up and took on important leadership roles. But Paul had set it up that way. He was never the kind of leader who wanted to have the power all for himself. He "nurtured a lay leadership." Not everyone would do that.[303]

Smith was comfortable allowing lay leaders to carry the energy of the church into many outreach programs. There is an active group organized by a lay leader that has been visiting and assisting a sister church in Cuba for many years. The current neighborhood Food Pantry where people can get a free bag of groceries developed out of an earlier ministry called the "Two Penny Lunch." Professor Murumba and his family were among those who cooked food and served it on Saturdays to homeless people housed at the time in the St. George

Hotel around the corner.

Neighborhood interfaith ties have always been a natural part of Smith's all-embracing pastorates.

> Under Paul, we've had lovely dialogues and conversations with a lot of religious institutions in this neighborhood. Congregation Mt Sinai. Now Brooklyn Heights Synagogue linked with us. Muslims on Atlantic Ave … [304]

In February 2000, FPC's adult education program launched a series of workshops entitled "Bridges: Embracing World Spiritual Traditions." A local newspaper noted that First Church's effort "was different from many presentations given locally in recent years in that the approach was meant to be personal rather than academic."[305] Parishioner Sue Carlson, who helped to create the series, told a reporter that the speakers had to be "devout in his or her own faith tradition." The first speaker, Tariq Quadir, spoke about basic practices and beliefs in Islam, emphasizing the Muslim view that Jews and Christians are "their cousins."[306]

Smith initiated contacts with several neighborhood synagogues including Congregation Mt. Sinai nearby on Cadman Plaza. Rabbi Joseph Potasnik of that synagogue collaborated with Smith over the years on radio and religious television programs.[307] Their congregations regularly exchanged choirs. Smith eventually instituted an annual Passover seder at FPC. Evidence of the warm relations in the neighborhood came, for example, in 1999 when First Church received a contribution check from a local Jewish couple. They wrote of FPC in an accompanying note: "This multicultural house of worship embodies the best traditions of our Borough."[308]

Interfaith ties became especially important after 9/11. Brooklyn Heights is so close to lower Manhattan that the cloud of dust and smoke from the falling World Trade Center towers blew across the East River and smothered the neighborhood. Amy Neuner had just taken the job as music director when the terrorist attack occurred, and she recalls Smith's response.

> He called and said, "Come to the church." I said, "What is our plan? What are we going to do?" He said, "We don't need a plan—just show up and [the] spirit will guide us."

After the collapse of the towers, neighborhood residents gathered on the Promenade, watching the fires burn at Ground Zero and sharing their stories and their shock. Within a day or two, Smith and Potasnik were both there when a group of Muslims assembled for a solidarity march with non-Muslims who wanted to support them. Smith says he noticed that the Muslims needed to communicate even more than the clergy, and he passed his megaphone over to them. Many such moments of generosity helped to soothe the sorrow of the succeeding days.

As the years passed, Rev. Smith and First Church began to use retreats of varying scale to further build and strengthen the congregation. In addition to daylong Session retreats, family weekends were organized around the national celebration of Martin Luther King Jr.'s birthday. Parishioners and their children lived together in a rented house outside the city, organizing their activities and meals communally. It was particularly effective for the children, who "bonded like you wouldn't believe. They had no preconceived notions."[309] Older children took responsibility for the younger ones, freeing parents to engage with each other. One participant said that the weekend was so powerful in uniting the community, she wondered what would have happened if there had been ten more years of such events.[310]

One of the most powerful retreat settings used by Smith and the congregation was Ghost Ranch in northern New Mexico, a property then owned by the Presbyterian Church. The luminous high desert terrain is so spectacular it inspired some of the artist Georgia O'Keefe's most celebrated work. Use of Ghost Ranch was by invitation only and rotated among the Presbyterian leadership. Starting in 1991, First Church visited the site for about 10 years running. Smith invited friends and parishioners from all his pastorates to commune with each other and the wild landscape of the southwest.[311]

Artist Sue Carlson, who was a long-time elder at First Church, participated in three of the Ghost Ranch retreats. She recalls,

> It is in Abiquiú, New Mexico … There was tremendous energy there. There was a strong Native American presence. The light there is so beautiful. There are some places on the planet like Greece where the light is so beautiful, people naturally start to believe in spiritual things … It had that kind of very unusual light.
> So people who were involved in Paul's ministry would meet there—people from St. Louis, Buffalo, Atlanta, Brooklyn. We all got to meet each other. I met Marvin Chandler and Nathan Dudley and his wife; at one point Andy Young came. Congregation members from all of those churches came too. It was beautiful. The energy was really great. If you loved Paul, it was all Paul Smith, all the time!

Incorporating many smaller workshops over a week or two, the retreat overall was called "Under the Tent." Smith relates that on one of his early trips, he began to think of how to bring groups there to do spiritual work together. He thought of a revival meeting as a model and imagined a tent under which the healing work could be done. The next year, a real circus tent was obtained and set up on site. The rule was that under the tent was a sacred space where anything could be said or asked. With important guests participating, the course started to attract people far beyond those with connections to First Church or to Paul Smith:

> We were trying to learn. You were free to say things then that couldn't get spoken. Under the tent was the sacred space … Other people wanted to be under the tent. Ambassador Young was sitting under the tent!

You had to sign up in advance … They had to cut off registration for my course.

Invitation to an "Under the Tent" workshop, Ghost Ranch, New Mexico, 1998

Carlson says that the central themes of the retreats were Howard Thurman's writing and inclusivity. However,

> It was mostly about the spectacular place and how we were all together. We'd go on walks at night in the desert. He would take people with a flashlight. He had this huge ten-foot rock he called his prayer rock. It had a flat top and he could bring people to sit together on the rock.[312]

Smith started a new journal on the occasion of his first journey to Ghost Ranch. He writes on his first morning there,

There is something quite extraordinary about waking up to the view of the mountains. I have had a similar feeling when I have awakened to [a] view of the ocean or any body of water. The Creator! Ah! that is who the Creator is. Creation is Creator and Creator is Creation. It can hardly be missed when in the presence of a body of water or majestic mountains … Just walking from my room to Cottonwood was so uplifting. It was as though the mountains and the quietness were waiting for me. I am energized in the moment I step on the path … I respond by saying, "Thank you Lord." And I do thank you Lord. [313]

On that trip, Smith writes of reading a biography of Langston Hughes, of workshops with Presbyterian colleagues, of hearing that Thurgood Marshall has stepped down from the bench, and remembering his road trip with Fran after their wedding in California. The scenery is continually moving to him, especially when he visits a place called Echo Canyon.

Hearing my voice/echo from this canyon beyond description. Only feelings can be expressed. I spoke out these words to this marvelous canyon. Peace, love, grace, celebrate, joy—wow. Hearing my voice from this point makes a microphone sounds shallow. It is awesome. The birds' melodies are clearly identifiable. When I hear my voice coming back to me I thought I was hearing God speaking to me. Perhaps that is what happens. Once the words leave my mouth it becomes instantaneously another voice. Awesome, powerful, moving and deeply spiritual. There is strength and energy all around. As I look up to the top of the rim my eyes fill with tears. The spirit of the Lord is in this place. That's it! You must be an apostle of sensitiveness to understand fully understand this power. Right now

I feel I am on holy ground ... Lord, let me bask in this beauty and power. Keep me looking upwards.[314]

As in other journals, Smith writes of his love for Frances and his gratitude for what was at that point thirty-one years of marriage. One day he takes Fran with him to Echo Canyon so she can experience it herself.

There was great anticipation in my heart as we slowly walked up the trail to the base of the great canyon. She had not seen Lion Rock on her previous visit so we had an opportunity to see this creation and artistry of the wind. Over two hundred million years have gone by and the wind has created this masterpiece ... We kissed and held each other for a few moments in thanksgiving of our time together. She spoke aloud the word 'peace' and heard her voice echoing back. Yes, there was something of great value being there with my Fran. As we came down from the canyon we both agreed there was energy spewing forth from this canyon. We are now recipients of that energy. Thank you Lord.[315]

These retreats gave rise to some of the most transcendent moments of Smith's ministry. One year early on, he and Fred Davie won a grant from the Ford Foundation to develop their retreat concept. The money allowed them to rent equipment like a good piano for the years when Rev. Chandler joined them in New Mexico. On one occasion, Revs. Chandler and Smith further developed their collaborative worship service style to great effect.

Paul and I felt each other's approach pretty well. We didn't try to analyze what was going on; we were just open to each other. His approach to religious experience is improvisational. And so is mine.
One time at Ghost Ranch, he started a meditation

and I started playing behind him. And it really was a very spiritual experience for everybody there. It was an intense moment in my life. An extraordinary moment of spirituality.[316]

Once Smith was installed in Brooklyn, Chandler visited First Church to perform his distinctive brand of musical sermons and give guidance to the music program. Revs. Chandler and Smith have an almost uncanny sense of connection that has not waned over the years. Chandler concludes,

> Paul is one of the most gifted people I've ever met in my long lifetime (and it has been long!) He's intellectually sharp, spiritually sensitive. He has a great gift of empathy for human beings. He has a wonderful sense of humor, laughs easily. And he cries easily. That is a great strength in a man.[317]

When asked what is special about Smith's day-to-day work as a minister, Chandler says, "Paul makes love real. At the same time he is not a sap. He's very worldly in his perception of what I think of as the dual character of life; the tragi-comedy of life.[318] Chandler elaborates.

> Paul doesn't make the profound simple, but approaches it in such a fashion that the encounter with the eternal—he does it with such simplicity—it makes it seem natural to do[319] ... Paul is a conduit person. He is always the receptacle for something that is moving.[320]

It is only this long-term, very intuitive friend who can suggest something of the toll the work takes on Smith.

> My own spirit reaches out to Paul because I feel a kindred acuity about the aspects of life we cannot really explain that are just as real as the material and

Revs. Marvin Chandler and Paul Smith playing jazz, Brooklyn, New York, late 1980s. (Photographer unknown)

physical ... I know him well enough to know that his heart aches a lot because of what he experiences. He looks for and longs for a sense of comradeship, for fellow seekers.[321]

11

*There's a difference between influence and power. Influence is
evocative; power is coercive.*

Paul Smith, 2016[322]

Working for Cultural Change

It seems inconceivable that in the final moments of the twentieth
century, a man like Rev. Smith—an erudite pioneer of racial inclusivity
and a man of God—should have to endure overt bigotry in his own
neighborhood. However, in March 1999, Smith was rudely reminded
that all of his accomplishments cannot confer immunity against the
racial prejudice that people of color can encounter at any moment,
anywhere in our country.

Dressed down in his sweatpants and baseball cap one Thursday
morning, Smith went into the Gristedes grocery store less than a half
block from his home. He had been diagnosed with Type II diabetes
in the 1990s, and he visited the drugstore there regularly to fill his
insulin prescription. At that point, he had lived in the neighborhood
for almost thirteen years.

Smith paid for the insulin and put it in his pocket. Then, on his
way out of the store, a white security guard stopped him and accused
him of stealing.[323] He asked what Smith had in his pocket; he replied,
"None of your business." The guard said, "I saw you take something

from the store." Smith says, "I thought he was kidding. I said, 'I'm Dr. Smith. I live right down there.' He said, 'That doesn't mean anything to me.' So I said, 'What's the issue here?'"

Smith tried to reason with the guard, but he was prevented from leaving the store until the manager of the pharmacy was called to determine if he had paid for the insulin. By that time, Smith was furious. He has been known to express his anger when reason is not working, especially when he knows he is in the right. He went on,

> I sure hope to hell you have a good attorney. You have just profiled the wrong person. I said, "I'm going to have to have something [some kind of apology] public. Otherwise, I will make sure nobody comes into this store" … The next morning the owner's on the phone with me [saying], "What can we do?" I didn't want them to just settle with me. I wanted them to know how egregious it was.

As news of the racially motivated episode circulated amongst First Church parishioners, community members, and other ministers in the neighborhood, outrage quickly gathered steam. In his sermon that Sunday, Smith says he mentioned what had happened, saying if it happened to him, it could probably happen to a lot of them too. After the service, he and about one hundred of the parishioners walked together to the store. They blocked the entrance in protest, demanding a public apology to Rev. Smith. Their plan was to organize a boycott of the store if they did not get a response. Eventually, the store manager did appear and made the apology, saying he had done so privately to Rev. Smith the night of the incident. The vice president in charge of security for the company that owned the store was quoted in the *Daily News* saying,

> It was a misunderstanding. It was embarrassing to the management of Gristedes and to the reverend. [The company] apologized and agreed to work together so

that nothing like this will happen again.[324]

The protest and the boycott were called off, and the security company said it would institute sensitivity training for its employees. However, the underlying systemic racism was not addressed and not corrected. When Dr. Paul asked the Session at his church how many people had had an experience like his at the Brooklyn grocery store, every black person in the racially balanced group raised their hands. Being black in America makes one suspect in a way that most white people are never aware of or subject to. Routinely, the benefit of the doubt is not extended to people of color. Routinely, they are treated with suspicion rather than respect. Routinely, they are guilty until proven innocent. The fact that this is not true for most white people, most of the time, has led to the development of the concept "white privilege"—that is, the acceptance, legitimacy, and inclusion that are so ordinary for most white people that they go unnoticed.

It is extremely ironic that the very man forced to endure the insult of being publicly taken for a thief had long been training neighborhood police officers to avoid these egregious mistakes themselves. In a way that seems especially farsighted now, Smith worked from early on to make connections with the local 84th Precinct of the New York City Police Department. He wanted to create a regular event honoring the work of police officers in the neighborhood. It turned out that he already knew the man he needed to talk with to make his idea a reality.

When I got to the Heights, I knew there were issues between the police and community. I thought maybe I should offer to do some diversity training for the precinct. Get to know them, have service where we honor them …

It just so happened that the new police commissioner had been the chief in Atlanta. Lee Brown. I had known him through Andy. We were good friends. He said, "What do you want to do?" I said, "Just get to know each other." He said, "When do you want to do it? I

am the commissioner!" Within twenty-four hours, a
police car pulls up with the precinct [captain] saying,
"My commissioner said I should meet you." He was a
nice guy. I told him what I wanted to do. Have a day
for your officers ...
Every February we had a service for the officers and
their families. They were all in their uniforms. We gave
thanks for the officers and families.
[The police] do a ritual before they go out on the street
for the day. I would go and have prayer with those guys.
We had established that rapport. I'd say, I don't have
to be right, but we have to talk.

Smith developed a workshop-style diversity-training program
that became standard for newly graduated recruits. Not all of them
were happy about it.

It was also mandated to have this time with me ... One
of the cops in the workshop said, "What the hell?? I'm
a good guy. Why should I have to do this training?" I
got into a real heated debate with him ... He was bel-
ligerent. They did not know he was the kind the guy
who could be like that. [His colleagues] had not seen
that side of him. So it was a perfect example of what
we were trying to deal with.

Smith had long before honed techniques for leading such groups.

I get them talking. I moderate, facilitate ... There
are some things that are basics. We need to recognize
differences. When you are policing a certain area of
Brooklyn, there are certain kinds of people there, and
you have to have respect for them. Don't just make as-
sumptions. You need to get to know them. And then I
say, "How do you feel about what I just said?"

Having good relations with the police department was mutually beneficial. Sometimes it meant that Smith had an opportunity to be a peacemaker in the community.

> One time there was a demonstration near the court-house in Brooklyn [a few blocks from the church]. There were a couple of thousand people. There was a massive police presence. It was getting a bit tense. The precinct captain called me and asked me to come take a look at this. I knew immediately there were too many police officers. I said, "Do you need that many people? You'll get applause if you take a hundred of these officers and leave." He said, "I can't do that!" I said, "Why?" He said, "Well I guess I can." And he did it. And the tension went down just like that.
> A couple of months later ... a [police officer] commit-ted suicide. His wife had been at one of our services. She was a staunch Catholic, but she said Rev. Smith is doing the ceremony [for her husband].

Sometimes it meant that he could get special access to help a parishioner, even when they were involved with another precinct.

> In another case, one of our Hispanic kids was falsely accused of a crime and put in jail ... His mother called me and said, "He's in a holding cell." I said, "It is not this precinct," but she said, "Please come." Because I had a relationship with the 84th, the people at the other precinct let me go back to the cell with Dorothy Gill. The precinct captain knew I was working with the 84th. They wouldn't even let his mother in there to see him, but they let Dorothy Gill and me. If you have that kind of relationship with people, you can do almost anything.

That access proved vital after the terrorist attack on the World Trade Center on Sept. 11, 2001. Thich Nhat Hanh, the Vietnamese Buddhist and peace activist, came to New York City and wanted to go to Ground Zero. The Buddhist knew Andrew Young because Hanh had been in communication with Rev. Dr. Martin Luther King, Jr. about the Vietnam War. Hanh contacted Young who suggested that perhaps Smith could help them get access to the site, which was off-limits to the public. Smith contacted the precinct and was provided with a police escort to Ground Zero. A policeman there recognized that them and allowed them to enter.

> Thich Nhat Hanh wanted to climb "the pile" and Andy [Young] went with him. Fred [Davie] and I and the other monks stayed behind … The onlookers who were being kept away from the site went quiet when they saw the whole group arrive. Everyone recognized Andy. Andy later said it was one of the most profound things he had ever done.

During his years in New York, Smith's influence has taken on new dimensions through his activities as a consultant, mediator, trustee, and teacher. His advice has come to be sought by business leaders who value his wisdom on issues of civil rights, community relations, multiculturalism, and diversity. In particular, he is known for his integrity. As another Presbyterian minister puts it,

> It's not just that Paul can turn a phrase, but the phrases are so clearly woven into his manner and being. It's … genuine. That's the power of Paul's preaching—it's the life he lives that matches the words he preaches.[325]

Macy's Inc.

Two internationally known companies have developed long-term relationships with Smith as a consultant, relying on his experience, his network, and his straight talk in developing their hiring, employee relations, customer service, and other policies. Both Macy's Inc. and Honda Motors see Rev. Smith as an enormously valuable corporate asset. In these contexts, Smith's impact is felt far beyond the streets of Brooklyn.

Macy's is known across America but is especially high profile in New York City. The company operates more than seven hundred stores in almost all fifty states and employs around 150,000 workers.[326] Standing twenty stories high, the flagship store has anchored 34th Street in Manhattan since 1902. The massive building was recognized as a National Historic Landmark in 1978, and the company has recently invested $400 million to renovate the store to better attract international shoppers and millennials.[327] Macy's sponsors both the famous Thanksgiving Day parade with its gigantic balloons and marching bands and the gargantuan, annual New York City fireworks display on the Fourth of July. This is a company that takes its public image and its relationship with the community seriously.

One of those who have worked to create those community connections is Edward Goldberg, who retired in 2015 as Senior Vice President for External Affairs. Goldberg joined the company in the mid-1970s and spent the last twelve of his years there in both public affairs and as an advisor to the Chairman. As part of his responsibility for Macy's diversity issues in the early 1990s, Goldberg was asked by management to meet with Rev. Smith. Goldberg traveled to Brooklyn to meet him at First Church and says they "instantly" had a rapport. Goldberg quickly became convinced that hiring Smith as his advisor made excellent business sense.

> He comes to the table with a great deal of experience and credentials from the religious aspect, diversity strategies, and the development of community relations. From the very outset, I thought it would be very valuable for Paul to be an advisor to me and the Macy's team. Over the years I utilized his services on many occasions which included review of policies and procedures, development of community relations, and in

sensitive situations so that we would be sure to remain ahead of the curve in the retail industry.[328]

Goldberg remembers that when he began working for Macy's in New York in 1987–88,

> … race relations were at an all-time low … As time went on, it became apparent to me that either you get involved and develop your relationships with communities or at some point in time, you will lose the respect and loyalty of the consumer.[329]

Rev. Smith was put to use in creative ways, depending on the problem being addressed.

> I recall that we had a serious issue in our Delaware store where there had been some customer complaints about store associates in which insensitive remarks or lack of service was mentioned.

> I asked Paul to become involved and in a short time he visited the store posing as a customer and after several days of careful study he developed a plan to meet with all of our employees in groups over a period of days in order to discuss and teach. Needless to say Paul won over the store associates and the complaints in that arena went way down. For several years after, the employees would always ask for Paul.[330]

With stores all over the country, Goldberg knew that they needed to look at how the company's policies affected communities of all kinds, urban and suburban. Smith, he felt, had the right connections and experience to help with this.

> … he was very actively engaged in the Brooklyn com-

munity, but Paul also has a national and international posture. He knows people all over the world. Paul is a member of the Boulé, which is a very highly prized membership of [a] very influential organization of African American gentlemen. So Paul, I knew from the very beginning, had his finger on the pulse of things that were happening community-wise, particularly African American community-wise, throughout the country ... [331]

Goldberg says the company already had a proud history of progressive hiring practices.

Macy's cares very much about the communities that we serve. Macy's has been a leader in diversity before the word diversity came into everyday usage. The company has been a champion for women's issues again long before the topic gained the national attention that it deserves. Back in 1888 Macy's promoted the first female to the position of vice president well ahead of any other store in the retail industry. Over the years we have continuously promoted African Americans, Asians, Hispanics into middle and upper management positions because the company philosophy was always find the best people for the many executive positions that we have ... getting the best people was important to the community so that it was clearly understood that Macy's delivered on its promise to be a good corporate citizen day in and day out. Paul was an important part of this philosophy during the years that we worked together.[332]

Over many years, Goldberg developed working friendships with many African American religious and political leaders as well as the publishers of journals like the *Amsterdam News*, the *Carib News*, *Impacto Latin News*, the *Christian Times*, and *El Diario/La Prensa*. He helped Macy's develop relationships with communities by "sincerely doing what we're supposed to be doing as good corporate citizens."[333] Among other things, that meant opening stores that created good jobs in the local neighborhoods.[334]

From left: Edward Goldberg, David Dinkins and Paul Smith at a Macy's celebration for the publication of Mayor Dinkins's memoir, March 2016. (Photo by Margot Jordan, *Afro Times*)

Goldberg says he and Smith settled into a pattern of speaking every other week or so to discuss policy developments and/or current events. They often met at one of the restaurants in the 34th Street store. Smith helped introduce Goldberg to key people in the reverend's huge network of contacts and colleagues.

> Paul introduced me to Marc Morial when he came up from New Orleans. In 2000–2001 Marc took over leadership of the National Urban League ... From time to time, the leadership especially of HBCUs, Paul would set up dinners and I would come and meet with all the folks, the administration and the leadership of the college conferences or the colleges themselves.[335]

Smith's congregants learned to expect surprise guests who come to speak at his services. After he discovered that Goldberg had been trained as a cantor in the Jewish faith, for example, Smith began inviting him to participate at First Church.

> I would go to Paul's church a couple of times a year on a Sunday, and I would give the readings from the Old Testament. Since I was trained in liturgy and music, I would sing some of the Old Testament for the congregation. So it was not only our relationship but also the relationship with Paul's congregation. Paul would tease me every once in a while and say, "You know I'm not going to let you come anymore. They are asking for you more than they are me!"

Frequently over the years, Goldberg and Smith have attended the same annual conferences of organizations like the Urban League. Goldberg also regularly attended the annual conferences of Rev. Al Sharpton's National Action Network and Rev. Jesse Jackson's Rainbow Push Coalition. In the context of such events, Goldberg and his wife socialized frequently with the Smiths. Eventually, they came to know each other's children and grandchildren.

The benefits of the relationship flowed both ways. In 1998, Goldberg presented the Brooklyn congregation with a check for $15,000 from Macy's to use as the church board and lay leadership saw fit.[336] After Goldberg became a Trustee at Smith's alma mater, Talladega College, Smith says that Macy's funded the refurbishment of the famous Amistad Murals and supported their exhibition in eight art galleries around the country between 2012 and 2016.[337]

Rev. Smith's contributions have proved especially important in the last decade, when Macy's and other large retailers have been accused of racially profiling shoppers. In 2004–5 and then again in 2013–14, Macy's was sued by individuals who felt their rights were violated after they were unjustly detained and accused of shoplifting.[338] On both occasions, the NY state attorney general's office investigated the complaints and secured agreements with Macy's to forestall future episodes. Goldberg asserts that the mistakes were not due to company policies, but rather were the product of overreach by security and police personnel. Nonetheless, the *New York Times* has reported that Macy's has twice paid around $600,000 to settle lawsuits brought by shoppers who were detained after being wrongfully accused of stealing. In both cases, Macy's private security personnel were accused of violating the rights of shoppers, disproportionately those who were minorities.

In fact, all employees, including those in security, agree in writing to abide by all of Macy's policies regarding proper procedures for interacting with the public. Goldberg says the company has a zero-tolerance policy when it comes to breaching these good governance standards. But with more than 100,000 employees across the country, Goldberg says, a few are bound to make mistakes. One way to make sure that employees are complying with the company's policies is to have someone like Smith go into a store as a shopper and then report on how they are treated. Smith says it is a common loss prevention practice used by retailers.

In the case of the flagship store in particular, the sheer volume of people moving through the building on a daily basis is enormous. Twenty million people visit the store each year, and hundreds of millions of dollars worth of business is transacted there; 4400 people work in the building every day, and the number rises to 6500 during holiday periods.[339]

> You have to put it into perspective. The 34th Street store is in fact a little city. It occupies more than 2 million square feet of space. Each year, we deal with an incredible amount of people. Some are truly nefarious people. Some come there looking to steal.[340]

According to a New York State statute known as the "shopkeeper's privilege," people caught shoplifting can be made to pay the cost of the item if it is not in condition to be resold, as well as a penalty of up to five times the cost of the item.[341] These arrangements can be settled at the store without a trial, and afterward the person may be free to go. But the New York City police can also be summoned, especially in the case of a repeat offender or when a person appears dangerous. Under those circumstances, some arrangements must be made for holding the individual until law enforcement arrives.

The *New York Times* reported on some of the methods used by the in-house security system at Macy's stores in 2005.[342] Goldberg states that in his day, company policy simply called for a store to have a holding room with a table, chair, and a lockable door. But in some cases, the security personnel appear to have created more intimidating places to hold people suspected of crimes.

> Dozens of security officers patrol the Herald Square store, Macy's flagship, where people suspected of shoplifting are fingerprinted and detained, often behind metal bars in a holding cell.[343]

Given his own experience with profiling and that of many people he knows, Smith found even the rare use of such methods chilling. He was asked to investigate at the 34th Street store and to write a report on his findings. He did so but was not in a position to insist that his recommendations be implemented. However, given the numbers of people involved, Macy's appears to have handled the large proportion of these cases in a way that has produced few complaints.

> In 2002, more than twelve thousand people passed through detention rooms in 105 Macy's stores, including more than 1900 at the flagship store. Fifty-six percent of those people were handed over to the police, though most of those detained confess and quite a few pay the in-store penalty before leaving, company officials say.[344]

Together, Goldberg and Smith worked hard to ensure that Macy's record of creating job opportunities and making investments in communities does not get drowned out by the media attention surrounding cases like these. Smith's contacts and credentials as a minister and diversity professional were especially important in such efforts.

> When the situation arose both in early 2004–5 and again in 2013–14, I asked Paul to become intimately involved in developing a plan to resolve the issues. After extensive discussion we decided to create a list of community contacts in order to set up meetings in which we could further discuss the issue and develop strong community partnerships and support. Of course there were other retailers involved, and executives from all disciplines formed committees to work out resolutions.
>
> Our meetings included leaders like former NYC mayor David Dinkins, Marc Morial, the leader of the National Urban League, Rev. Calvin Butts, Ossie Davis, former State Representative Frank Diaz and many, many others. In each case Paul was a driving force for constructive change.[345]

An important part of Smith's contributions was helping to write the "Customers' Bill of Rights" that is posted in all of Macy's stores today. Smith says he fought hard to have details included that he felt were important. While this is not meant to resolve all the legal challenges that have been raised about such tactics, it is an important articulation of how the public, even people suspected of a crime, should be treated by the company.[346] Goldberg says it has become a mainstay in the industry.

Dr. Smith's mediation skills have also been used in more direct ways. In one case, he trained managers and other staff in a midwestern store to deal appropriately with Muslim customers. Not everyone was open to the idea, but they spent four full days in Rev. Smith's workshops. He also helped the company navigate the local waters when Macy's acquired the iconic Marshall Field's store in Chicago. Marshall Field's had been a fixture in downtown Chicago for over a century and was part of the city's lore. Smith and another Macy's representative were asked to run focus groups to learn how customers were reacting to the rebranding. What they uncovered posed a formidable challenge. Thankfully for everyone concerned, Goldberg and Smith rose to meet it.

> There were sixty thousand signatures objecting to Marshall Field's becoming Macy's! They were saying, "We are going to be turning in our credit cards." … four days later, Ed [Goldberg] comes. I said, "You have some pissed off people!" We had to find a way to bring them back. We had easily fifty top community leaders at the dinner table at Macy's flagship store in Chicago. They were all together in one room. [Ed got up to speak] saying, "We made a huge mistake. We didn't take into account the history the community has with Marshall Field's." Ed said, "Now that I know what I know, we made a mistake." And that completely defused the anger … Then we had a good meal and started talking to each other. With sixty thousand signatures! It changed on a dime. He defused it, because he was honest …

Honda Motors

Rev. Smith is also the only consultant working for the Honda Motor Company who holds the title, "Senior Diversity Counselor." In the middle of the 1990s, African American leaders had made it clear to the growing Japanese company that they didn't have sufficient numbers of African American auto dealers in their network. Rev. Jesse Jackson threatened the company with a boycott if they did not make some changes. Executives at Honda, who had been focusing on growing their business in the United States, realized they needed to pay attention to critical diversity issues.

Jeffrey Smith [no relation] was one of the Honda American managers given responsibility for this change. In 1998, he became project manager for a new venture in the South. The firm had identified an

Alabama location where they wanted to build a new automobile manufacturing plant. The site was in Lincoln, Alabama, seven miles from
Talladega College. As they began to develop their plans, someone suggested Paul Smith could help facilitate the process. Jeffrey Smith recalls,

> We formed an Executive Task Force on Diversity, and
> I felt that it would be helpful to have some knowledge-
> able guidance and counsel as we moved forward. I
> interviewed many "diversity consultants," but without
> much success. Everyone I spoke with told me that
> money was the answer.[347]

Within ten minutes of meeting with Dr. Paul in New York, Jeffrey Smith says he knew that the reverend was the man they needed to
build community with the people of Alabama. As he puts it in terms
that Smith taught him,

> When I met Rev. Smith through a mutual business
> acquaintance, Rev. Smith did not talk about money
> being the key to success. He talked about Honda's need
> to be genuine, intentional, strategic and authentic.
> Honda is a very philosophical, values driven company,
> so this sounded right to us. This was the beginning of
> a wonderful and invaluable relationship between Rev.
> Smith and Honda that has lasted until today. He is an
> instrumental guide, a sage counselor, a tough critic, an
> inspiring catalyst, and a moral conscience.[348]

Jeffrey Smith knew that paying attention to culture was going to
be essential to the success of the Alabama facility.

> We were pioneers ... It was [a] $140 million invest-
> ment, 1500 associates [employees], 120,000 vehicles.
> The company was thinking about the business reality
> of that; some of us were thinking about the cultural

aspect of that. Going from mostly white Ohio—moving to well below the Mason-Dixon line, to an area that had been the epicenter of the civil rights movement—I felt before we turned a single piece of ground over to build that plant, we had to understand where we were going.[349]

The two Smiths soon traveled to Alabama together. The population in Lincoln in 1990 was approximately three thousand. Jeffrey Smith says the town was so small, it did not even have a stoplight. He remembers noticing that there were no nets on the basketball hoops and that grass was coming up through the blacktop. When the group stopped their car at a small roadside shop to get a cold drink, the Honda exec asked Rev. Smith if he wanted a cold drink. As they all went inside, the Reverend mentioned that when he was in college, he would never have gone inside a store like that, because he couldn't be sure that he would come out again. Jeffrey Smith found this personal history deeply moving.

Drawing on his extensive knowledge of local business people, religious leaders, and politicians, Rev. Smith set up meetings between Honda executives and the mayor of Birmingham, the head of the local NAACP chapter, the Southern Christian Leadership Council (SCLC) in Anniston, the President and Board of Talladega, the head of the Birmingham Civil Rights Museum, and the publisher of the African American paper, *Birmingham Times*. The idea was for Honda's Japanese employees to learn about the history, politics, and way of life in that part of the country.[350]

Smith knew the whole project could be seriously undermined if Honda did not gain the support of elected state leadership. He had the Honda representatives meet with members of the caucus of black Alabama legislators. He ensured that Honda representatives contacted the two black churches in Lincoln. The company needed one thousand workers to start with, far more than Lincoln alone could provide. Rev. Smith wanted to be sure that local people had the training they needed to compete for these new jobs. As the Honda executive recalls, "We put up a training facility real fast with a miniature assembly line and all these different tasks you can do. The training [was going on] before the plant was up and running."[351]

Later, when Japanese employees moved to Alabama to build and work in the new plant, Dr. Paul was asked to help them make the transition. His first step was to show them parts of the Public Broadcasting Company documentary series, "Eyes on the Prize." Then he called on Marguerite Archie-Hudson, a former classmate, who had become President of Talladega. She met with executives from the company to explain the history of Talladega and its success in producing high-achieving graduates. The college was subsequently commissioned to develop a sensitivity training program that became mandatory for every Honda executive who was going to work in Alabama.

Honda's position, according to Jeffrey Smith, is that "the population inside the plant should look like the population outside the plant." They knew their operations would be under scrutiny to confirm that they achieved what they promised.

> We see what the population looks like and want to be sure we reflect it. And we have always met it or exceeded it. While getting ready to operate, we had leaders in the African American communities like the National Association of Minority Auto Dealers who said, "We're going to watch you." And I said, "We are going to report to you how we're doing." And that's what we did.[352]

Rev. Smith was also responsible for designing and carrying out sensitivity training sessions for Honda employees in other parts of the country. On his first visit to the company's US headquarters in Marysville, Ohio, it appeared to Smith that not one woman or person of color was working in the local manufacturing plant. It was not long before the president of the company made it clear that everyone would be taking the sensitivity training workshops that Smith was developing. The workers complied, though some were resistant to the idea.

You get them to talk first. You acknowledge them, honor them. You say, "I know you don't want to be here, but we're here, so let's talk. Why don't you want someone like me to come talk with you?" And they heard themselves. They realized, to stay in this job I will have to embrace some of it. They had to sit in an all-day session with me.

Jeffrey Smith, now a vice president at Honda, says of the reverend,

He is deeply loved in this company for helping us advance our commitment to inclusion and diversity. Since we began up to today, he is considered an invaluable human being and resource to us ... When I say he is deeply loved in this company, I mean it. He's been at many, many meetings, and when he gets up [to speak], he is listened to. He's been with us from the beginning.[353]

Starting in 1999, Rev. Smith also began to work closely with Marc Burt, an African American executive hired to help develop Honda's diversity policies. Within seven years, Burt says, "in many ways we became thought leaders in the industry."[354] In 2007, they formed the Office of Inclusion and Diversity and made Burt senior manager of the department. A few years later he was promoted to System Vice President, and in 2013, his office moved to Marysville. As happened with Jeffrey Smith and Ed Goldberg, Smith and Burt have developed a close personal relationship over the years.

Rev. Smith has worked with Burt in several capacities. Most often, Smith is a listener and advisor. Burt says,

... [Smith] plays a multifaceted role. He's a confidant that I can bounce things off of, that's pretty obvious and pretty frequent. But he also sits in on all of our strategic meetings relative to diversity. His purpose there is to act as an outside voice, an outside counsel. Other companies frequently will have outside diversity counsel, and they will be people who just come in for meetings, once a quarter, a couple times a year ... But we would rather have those who give counsel be part of what we do. So rather than us having to explain to Paul the context, when we've established a strategic direction, he knows it because he's been part of those meetings. We feel that's better.[355]

Burt has given a good deal of thought to where the roots of bias lie.

There's no outward, expressed opposition, but there is this unconscious bias, I think, that slows down our progress. It's not that people are intentionally trying to get in our way or make us less effective, but it's not an easy thing to do. I tell people all the time that what we are involved in is culture change. And culture change is never fast and it's never easy.[356]

Smith recalls an occasion when twelve Honda executives had dinner with him and Andrew Young in an effort to educate them about the African American experience in this country. Young invited the guests to visit his midtown office where much of the memorabilia from his years with Martin Luther King is on view. Smith says it is always a powerful experience for people to see those materials and hear about them from Young himself.

Burt has learned a great deal about the unconscious level at which bigotry operates.

We have to allow each other to be curious. And one of the reasons why we have this really, really bad epidemic of unconscious bias in this country is because if we don't know each other, we fill in the blank. We fill in the void ... we unconsciously fill in the gaps because we've not really engaged. So we just fill in the gaps with what we do know.

Using the example of a woman he met in a doctor's office who was covered in piercings, Burt explains how things could be done differently.

> ... I'd never seen so many piercings in anybody's face. She literally had bolts in her face. So like everybody else, I just kind of wanted to look away, not really want to get into any kind of conversation that would make anybody uncomfortable.
> But I looked her in the eye, and I said, "Did that hurt?" And I don't know, I smiled. She sensed that I wasn't judging her. She looked at me, she got this bright smile on her face, and she said, "You know, only this one." And I can't remember which one but there was a story behind it. But she said, "With the rest of them, you'd be surprised! You know you kind of get used to it." And we just chatted it up a little bit and I learned something that day.

Burt believes that if we allow ourselves to be curious and non-judgmental, we may find that we can relate to people unlike ourselves. Using Dr. Paul's language, he says, "If we don't know, we ask. That's all. People can tell if you are faking. You really have to be genuine"... He makes you feel important, that you matter, that the work that you do matters. He just has a very encouraging spirit.[357]

Over the years, Burt and Smith have helped Honda develop distinctive programs to engage people and contribute to the public good. One of these, the Honda Campus All-star Challenge, celebrates the historically black college and universities (HBCUs].[358] It is an academic competition in a quiz show format that pits the HBCUs against each other in friendly competition for the prize of top school in a given year. Jeffrey Smith says,

It has been in existence for more than twenty years. Graduates include nuclear physicists, astronauts, brain surgeons … They are young people who are academically plugged in, ambitious, want to strut their stuff for their school.

Another annual event sponsored by Honda for the HBCUs is now being called "HBOB" or the "Honda Battle of the Bands." The event has been held every year since 2003 at the Georgia Dome in Atlanta.[359] It combines pride in the HBCUs with the enormous popularity of marching band and drum line performances. Bands from the schools compete during football season and then some are invited to meet in Atlanta in January to perform in the Invitational Showcase. There are grants awarded, and an HBCU recruitment fair is held before the main event.

Throughout his years with Honda, Rev. Smith has attended many of these performances. But in 2012, he will be remembered for bringing his powerful brand of compassion to a family that desperately needed it. That year, he was asked to visit with the family of a young drum major named Robert Champion who had been fatally beaten by his Florida A&M band mates in a hazing ritual on a bus in November 2011. The young man's parents had attended the event many times to watch their talented son perform. His mother recalls sitting on a couch with her husband in a suite at the Georgia Dome.

> … we were introduced to many people, even [Georgia Congressman] John Lewis. They all expressed their deepest sympathy and offered to help us if needed. Then we were introduced to Rev. Dr. Paul Smith. We had no knowledge of who he was, but little did we know that was not important to him.
>
> He pulled up a chair and placed it closely in front of us and sat down facing us both. He took my hand and looked deep into my eyes and the tears began to fall. It

was as if he could sense my pain and agony through my tears. He did not say a word at first; he just sat there to absorb what we were feeling; what I was feeling. And he began to speak. He told me it was okay to cry and hurt, don't try to hold it back. I wondered how he knew this was what I had been doing since my son's death. He talked in a low soft voice and seemed to have said all the right words we needed to hear.

He provided so much comfort to us and encouragement. No one has ever taken the time to do what he did for us. He took the time to [acknowledge] our pain and agony, while conveying God's inviting words of comfort … [what] I will never forget was his unspoken words of compassion while he held my hand and looked deep into my eyes.[360]

The Arthur Ashe Institute for Urban Health

In St. Louis, Smith played tennis with the doctors. In Atlanta, it was Andrew Young and the Chief of Police. In New York City, it was inevitable that he would meet the Honorable David Dinkins, the first, and as yet only, African American to be elected mayor. Dinkins will forever be remembered as the New York City public official with the greatest interest in the game. It was through his efforts that the US Tennis Center in Queens became the international-level venue that it is today. Smith met Dinkins around 1990, early in Dinkins's term as mayor. As Smith tells it, he found himself playing doubles against investment banker Ronald Gault and the new mayor, complete with security detail.

We kicked their butts! They couldn't believe it. Some preacher comes in here and beats us! [Dinkins] said, "We should get to know each other." I said my son-in-law is from Trenton. David knew the son-in-law's parents. He said, "Stop by the office and see me." I said, "City Hall?!" He said to one of his people, "This is Paul. Make it happen." So I went to his office.

After that, Dinkins spoke many times at First Church, and Smith had occasion to return the favor. Smith played master of ceremonies at a book party at Macy's celebrating the publication of Dinkins's autobiography in February 2014. The public was invited to a floor in the Herald Square store to meet the mayor and buy an autographed book. VIP guests included Dr. Roscoe Brown, one of the Tuskegee Airmen, the African American pilots who performed valiant duty during World War II. Goldberg introduced the whole event by welcoming everyone as part of "our family at Macy's." As is typical of the banter between Smith and the former mayor, Dinkins took the microphone to tease Smith for his advantage on the tennis court: "It is unfair playing with Paul, because he gets God on his side!" Privately, Smith admits that Dinkins "is a helluva tennis player" who often beat him, even when Smith slyly brought the tennis pro from the Heights Casino as his partner.

Cementing their relationship was another mutual friend—Arthur Ashe, the African American tennis champion and activist. Ashe, of course, had had a celebrated athletic career, which included three Grand Slam championships and holding the No. 1 ranking in men's professional tennis.[361] After giving up tennis in 1980 due to heart disease and later contracting AIDS, apparently from a blood transfusion after surgery in 1983, Ashe used his fame to help fight apartheid and to raise awareness about AIDS/HIV. Also part of his legacy was several health-care foundations he created. Among them was the Arthur Ashe Institute for Urban Health (AAIUH), founded in 1992 and based at the State University of New York (SUNY) Health Science Center in Brooklyn. Ashe knew Mayor Dinkins well, and close friend Andrew Young had performed Arthur and Jeanne's wedding ceremony. Given all the connections, it is no surprise to find that Dr. Smith was involved in Ashe's Institute from the beginning.

It was a further shared passion that brought Rev. Smith and Ashe together—the work of Rev. Dr. Howard Thurman. Ashe had found

Thurman to be "the supreme example of the black American's capacity for achieving spiritual growth and maturity despite the incessant blows of racism."[362] Further, he found solace in Thurman's ideas about "centering down" within oneself and pain being sacramental. Along with Rev. Jefferson P. Rogers, Ashe helped get Thurman's birthplace in Florida recognized as a National Historic Register site.[363]

Smith and Ashe began to study Howard Thurman's work together around 1991, after Young asked Smith if he would consider being Ashe's pastor. When Smith asked why Ashe needed a pastor, Young revealed the AIDS diagnosis to him; at that point, few others knew the news. Ashe was later forced to go public with his health crisis after journalists caught wind of the story.

Through Young, Ashe expressed a desire to obtain a copy of Thurman's *Jesus and the Disinherited,* which had gone out of print. Smith sent his own copy via Young. Though Smith has many famous friends, the chance to meet the tennis great had special resonance for Smith. The prayer in his journal reveals his thoughts before the meeting.

Tomorrow I will visit with Arthur Ashe. Lord help me to be used by you and to keep my channels open to your spirit. I must remember it is his need that is important; mine can surely wait. Help me to focus upon ways I may be used by you O Lord to break through any barriers that might be there. Let me know that the first get together may not produce your desired results. Help me to wait upon your spirit and upon your presence. More than anything Lord, please work your miracle in his life and in the life of members of his family. Help us find a cure for the disease of AIDS. Hold Arthur in your hands and bless him and heal him Lord, by the power of your holy spirit. Be with him in his questioning moments—those moments when questions outdistance answers. Not my will O Lord but yours as we come together tomorrow.[364]

After his encounter with Ashe in a restaurant the next day, Smith wrote again.

> Met with Arthur Ashe today. It was a sacramental mo-
> ment. He is a follower of and a believer in Andy Young.
> They met across a tennis fence in Washington, DC
> when Andy was a Congressman. Arthur never forgot
> that first encounter.
> We began with our introductions of each other ... I
> also gave him my copy of The Negro Spirituals Speak
> of Life and Death by Howard Thurman. We had a
> wonderful time sharing stories and exchanging ideas.
> He mentioned that he had considered going to Calvin
> Butts but felt now that God had brought us together
> through Andy—and that as a result we would be seeing
> more of each other. He is clearly an outstanding and
> caring person. I especially liked his simplicity and his
> care for his 2½ yr. old daughter ... Before the time was
> up he had mentioned something about his adjustment
> to the "fact" of his illness ... He said it was "just one
> of those unfortunate circumstances and therefore, I
> don't think about it."
> He spoke of moving back to Manhattan so he could be
> nearer his doctors at New York Hospital and that he
> would be taking things one day at a time. ... we each
> began to see something deeper and more significant
> in our conversation. Roger Staubach came over and
> we were introduced—but clearly Arthur wanted to
> get back to our conversation. From that point on we
> looked one another in the eyes. Thank you Lord for
> allowing me this opportunity and for writing ahead of
> time in my journal.[365]

Paul Smith and Arthur Ashe at First Presbyterian Church, Brooklyn, New York, circa 1991. (Photographer unknown)

From then on, about once a month, the two men talked on the phone or met in person. Their mutual regard for Thurman, the gravity of Ashe's circumstances, and Smith's pastoral experience made it easy for them to become close. Ashe visited Smith's study at First Church and occasionally attended Sunday services. As Ashe grew gravely ill, Smith provided his characteristic pastoral support. Ashe wrote with gratitude of a hospital visit by Dr. Paul and Andrew Young: "Before they left, in a moving moment, Paul, Andy, Jeanne and I held hands in a circle and prayed."[366] The last time Smith saw Ashe, the athlete was giving him and Andrew Young a thumbs up as he was wheeled into a hospital after collapsing near the end of his life. Smith later participated in the Richmond, Virginia, funeral and the memorial service for Ashe held at Cathedral of St. John the Divine in New York City.

Just a few months before his death, Ashe established the Institute with the goal of finding ways to provide underserved people with community-based health care. It was Smith who helped him make the connection with SUNY Health Science Center.[367] Smith was a founding member of the AAIUH Board of Directors, which came to include Ed Goldberg among other associates of Smith's. For many years, Dr. Paul helped raise funds for the Institute, which addressed issues he had long held dear himself. AAIUH celebrated a twenty-year anniversary in 2012 and remains active in community health care in Brooklyn.[368]

Long Island College Hospital

Another long-term Brooklyn-based project in which Rev. Smith became engaged was the fight to save Long Island College Hospital in Brooklyn Heights. Until 2015, LICH was a five-hundred-bed teaching hospital just up the hill from where Atlantic Avenue dead-ends at the East River. Though formerly a nondescript stretch of waterfront occupied by commercial warehouses, a series of public parks have been built along the river below Brooklyn Heights.[369] The real estate on which the hospital sits has became extremely attractive to buyers who want to build high-end housing overlooking the new parks and the river. A years-long battle has been waged for control of the hospital and the rights to build on the site. The fight involved private developers, doctors' groups, neighborhood activists, the State University of New York, the Governor's office, and Rev. Dr. Paul Smith.

With his interest and experience teaching medical ethics in Atlanta and later in New York, Smith had been tapped to become a board member at the hospital after he moved to Brooklyn. As has been true many times over, he was the first black member of the board. Though he has had to step down from boards that never made him feel welcome, at LICH he was chosen to chair the Ethics Committee. It was there that he met John Wren, the CEO of Omnicom Group, one of the largest public relations firms in the world. Smith says Wren initiated conversation with him at board meetings. It seemed Wren wanted to know how it felt being the only black person in the room. Smith told him, "The races didn't start together. One had a head start."

The two became friends and saw each other frequently at the hospital where the meetings were held. One day Smith took Wren on one of his regular visits to the hospital wards.

One time at the LICH board meeting, I asked him,

"Would you go up to say hello to a young man who has AIDS and is dying?" About 8:00 pm, we went up on a ward to see the kid. Wren was deeply touched that I asked him. I wanted him to see how the hospital was caring for this AIDS patient. I don't think he ever forgot that.

Smith recalls that as they sat by the man's bed, the dying man reached out and hugged Wren. Wren was surprised, but Smith had already demonstrated that there was nothing to fear in touching the very sick man. Wren later asked Smith to visit his own mother when she was at LICH during her final days. Smith did so and says he served as her pastor until she died.

Smith's relationship with Wren flourished in the context of their mutual work at LICH. Over many years, dozens of physicians, bene-factors, and community leaders like Smith worked to ensure that the 150-year-old institution remained open to serve community needs. Smith's principal part in the affair was speaking for the community in that part of Brooklyn who would be losing a much-needed emergency room and other medical services. He rallied local black churches to help save the facility.

Despite the community activism, the hospital was not profitable and had begun to accrue debt. Its demise began in 2008, when the health-care company that owned and ran the facility proposed selling some of its buildings to pay its debts.[370] In order to save it, the hospital was purchased by SUNY Downstate Medical Center; Smith was one of the people behind the scenes who helped garner a $50 million com-mitment from then-Governor David Patterson's office to facilitate the merger. Then two years later, just when it seemed that the battle had been won, the Board of SUNY voted to close the hospital altogether. Labor and neighborhood groups challenged the decision with strident protests and action in court. [371]

Veteran New Yorker Chuck Clayman describes Smith contribu-tions to the effort.

I'd say there wasn't much the board could do; there

was a lot that Paul could do and did do through his relationship with the people at Downstate hospital and other places. It is all personal …

I think he was very much the spiritual leader with a small "s" to get people to do, to move, to talk. He has a will of steel when he wants to have a will of steel. So I think he was able to talk to a lot of different sides. I think he was very important.[372]

Clayman did not really expect a more positive outcome. "If you view the history of the city, there's the real estate interests and then there's everything else. That's the business of New York."[373] Nonetheless, Clayman describes what he thinks made Smith successful overall during his years in Brooklyn Heights.

… I think it was more the nature of his personality, his intelligence, his ability to compromise, to understand how things go … I think when people were approached by him and got to know him, they saw him as a man of God and that was important. But that was the beginning, not the end.[374]

The closing of the hospital was a huge disappointment to Smith and many others who had given years of their time and huge infusions of cash to buttress the institution. Smith had made innumerable visits to patients there during his twenty years in Brooklyn, often accompanied by First Church congregants. Sue Carlson remembers donating some of her artwork to hang on the walls of the chemotherapy waiting rooms. However, all the services provided to people there could not forestall the inevitable; the property had become hugely valuable. In 2014, the SUNY Board approved the property's sale to Fortis Property Group for $240 million.

12

Dear Brother Paul,

I want to offer you robust and sincere congratulations on the epic occasion of your "official" retirement ... It seems to me the end of an era here in Brooklyn. On behalf of this church, I want to thank you for standing by her in times of true trouble and craziness. This church could easily have gone down but your "tough love" helped her to stay afloat.

David Dyson, 2006

Legacy

Before he retired, Rev. Smith had several more occasions to bring his powerhouse colleagues into communion with his congregation and the neighborhood. On April 3, 2005, the thirty-seventh anniversary of Dr. Martin Luther King's death, Ambassador Andrew Young Day was celebrated at First Presbyterian with speakers including David Dinkins and Marc Morial of the National Urban League.[375] Young himself delivered the sermon. In typical fashion, Smith combined the event with a Question and Answer session after the service. In addition to Young, Dinkins, and Morial, the panel included Loretta Lynch, who served as US Attorney General under President Obama and who was a frequent worshipper at First Church.

The following year, a grand send-off was organized for Smith

Rev. Smith's First Church retirement service, 2006. From left: Paul Smith, Andrew Young, Marc Morial and son Mason, David Dinkins. (Photo by Don Evans, *Brooklyn Daily Eagle*)

himself who retired in June 2006 after twenty years as senior pastor. Speakers at that occasion included local public officials, David Dinkins, and Ed Goldberg. Angela Breland, an officer from the 84th Precinct, read the scripture. The program was laced with music including Professor Murumba playing guitar and singing "I'll Never Let Go of Your Hand," as promised. Smith's sermon "Following Your Yes," sounded a final optimistic note. His parishioners wrote in the program,

> During his time here Dr. Smith, using the guidance of his mentor Dr. Howard Thurman and his experience in the American civil rights movement, has created one [of] this country's most diverse churches. We who are members are enormously proud of this accomplish-

ment and most determined to continue on the road Dr.
Smith has shown us … To say that Rev. Dr. Paul Smith
will be missed would be to grossly understate. His love
and leadership have caused the institution to flower.
We hope to live up to the ideals he has shown us.[376]

Smith's friend and fellow activist Rev. David Dyson of Lafay-
ette Avenue Presbyterian Church in Brooklyn (now retired) added a
personal note to his letter of congratulations on Smith's retirement,
quoted above.

> … I am profoundly grateful to you. You have been a
> role model for me in so many ways. Your picture, on the
> day of my installation, sits right over my right shoulder
> as I sit at my cluttered desk. I have always thought that
> is a good place to have you—looking over my shoulder,
> but having my back as well. That picture will stay there
> as long as I have anything to say about it … So God
> speed on this next chapter in your amazing life … [377]

Congregations, like all communities, take energy and time to
build, and by nature, they are ephemeral. Families move in and move
away, children are born, and people age and pass away. Even the best-
loved ministers move on or retire. Many congregants from the years
of Rev. Smith's pastorate are still active members at First Church, and
they say they are as committed as ever to the Church's mission. Yet
finding the right person to carry on when such a charismatic leader
leaves is a complex and emotional task.

One measure of Smith's impact is the size of the void created by
his departure. While the Presbyterian polity does not appoint new
leadership, it does prescribe the nature of the search process. In the
Presbyterian Church (USA), interim pastors cannot be called by the
congregation, no matter how well liked they may be, nor can a minister choose his or her successor. To find a new pastor, a formal Pastor
Nominating Committee (PNC) made up of elected lay leaders must

be formed. The PNC considers all the resumes submitted, vets and interviews candidates, and finally makes a recommendation to the rest of the congregation. The whole process may take a year or more.

It has taken 10 years for the First Church congregation to find a replacement they could wholeheartedly agree on. There have been three PNCs active over the past decade. Each of the searches took enormous amounts of energy and commitment. The community experienced significant conflict over the first two individuals who were formally called, and that took time to resolve. After 20 years of Smith's improvisations, some want to reassert the principles and procedures set down in the Presbyterian Book of Order. Others are resistant to re-applying the guidelines too zealously. The fact that the first interim minister insisted that Rev. Smith not set foot in First Church for a year after he left angered some of Smith's loyal supporters and Smith himself when he heard about it. The stricture turned out to be impossible to implement; parishioner Dottie Gill's grandchild was born during that first year, and most agreed that she could ask Dr. Paul to officiate at the baptism. He did so, but not everyone felt that contravening the interim's authority was the right thing to do.

In June 2016, First Presbyterian announced it had called a new pastor – Rev. Adriene Thorne. Having been a dancer in an earlier career, Rev. Thorne delighted the congregation by tap-dancing part of her installation sermon. Tall and elegant, warm and articulate, Rev. Thorne brings effortless style and an unforced reverence to her work. There is no doubt that First Church has found a new and inspiring leader.

After retiring in 2006, Rev. Smith appreciated not having the continual responsibilities and deadlines that had ordered his schedule for so many years. He and Fran moved out of the Henry Street manse and settled permanently in Maryland. They travelled, visited their daughters, and thoroughly enjoyed spending more time with their four grandchildren: Kathy's daughter Paula (b. 1994), Heather's son Lloyd (b. 1998), and Krista's two children, Stephen (b. 1998) and Krista Ann (b. 2002).

Rev. Smith is frequently asked to preach, and he continues to advocate for health and end-of-life care. In July 2007, he was the opening speaker at Marian Wright Edelman's 13th annual Samuel DeWitt Proctor Institute for Child Advocacy Ministry held at the former farm of Alex Haley in Tennessee. His contributions in Brooklyn were recognized the following year when Medgar Evers College made him a Legacy Award Honoree. In 2011, he returned to Talladega College as the invited speaker at the 14th Annual Founder's Celebration.

Most significantly, as he was preparing to end his twenty years at FPC, Smith's relationship with John Wren of Omnicom took a dramatic new direction. Smith had long wanted to better meet the needs of people of color in urban areas, who often lack access to health-care resources. Wren, who wanted to give back to his home borough, had been making contributions to First Church for some years.

> John would ask how the church was doing … If we were not okay, he gave me three blank checks with his signature. He said, "You write in any amount to take care of any deficit and whatever else you want to do. I want to make a contribution." He never, ever questioned what the checks came out like. Wren did this at least three times. So there's a history of him trusting me with his money.

On another occasion, Smith was in South Africa visiting a former student who is a Presbyterian minister there. He relates the following story.

> Maake asked me to come see his mother in Pretoria who was very sick. I've been around a lot. I've seen blight, poverty … But I have never been anywhere like this hospital. I think it was the smell. I went to the bedside, prayed with Maake and his mom. I later told Maake I wouldn't send my cat to this hospital.
> So I called John in the US … I said, "I don't know what you can do, but if you can send something … " Wren

said, "We have an office in Jo'burg." Two days later we go by their office, and there was a $25,000 check.

As Smith approached his retirement, Wren made a remarkable offer that speaks of the bedrock solidarity in the relationship between the two men.

> [Wren] said, "I want to make a proposition since you are retiring—I want to give you some money to do something in Brooklyn." I said, "I will need to talk to my wife—this is not what she has in mind." John said, "We'll do it formally."
> So the three of us met in Wren's office. He said, "You will have $5,000,000 at your disposal. I don't want you to have to ask me for money every month." I was to use the money as I saw fit to help people.

At first, they considered handling through First Church the funds for the nonprofit they would call Healthy Families Brooklyn. But since Smith knew he would be stepping down and probably moving out of the area, they decided to channel the money through the Arthur Ashe Institute where Smith and Wren were serving as board members. Smith was awed by the trust placed in him.

> Here is a corporate CEO, a white male, from Brooklyn, independently wealthy, and this African American minister who have come to know each other so well. He also wrote [a] check to LICH. So he wasn't just doing this for me. I was one of his many charities.
> [Wren] never in five years asked me for a financial report. I sent it to him anyway, of course. It is extraordinary when you think about it. I took Andy Young to John's office some years ago. People there were flabbergasted when Andy walked in. I said to John, "Andy is working in Rwanda. He'll be afraid to ask for money

so I'll ask on his behalf." John said, "I want to give the Ambassador $35,000." He didn't have to do any of this.

Healthy Families Brooklyn has developed in a robust way since its launch in 2007.[378] Rev. Smith became Executive Director of the new nongovernmental organization, and he hired Necole Brown, a community health specialist then working at the Arthur Ashe Institute, to be the program director and deputy executive director. Brown is one of the people Paul Smith considers his "daughters" along with the three he raised with Frances. When asked about Smith's influence on her, Brown quotes Howard Thurman's line, "Find what makes you come alive and go do that. The world needs people who are alive ... When people are in his presence, they feel uplifted. Being in a world that is always trying to press people down ... around Paul, you feel uplifted. You genuinely feel his love for you because it is real."[379]

Brooklyn Healthy Families programs were planned for two public housing complexes, the Gowanus Houses and Wyckoff Gardens, both not far from LICH and FPC. The plan involved training and later employing local people to serve their fellow residents as community health workers called "Healthy Families Advocates." Brown, who has been mentored by Smith for many years now, says, "Our main focus is to get people connected to a primary care physician to prevent disease."[380] The success of the program was detailed in a scholarly paper published in 2010.[381]

Eventually, Healthy Families got its own 501(c) tax-exempt status and began to assert its independence from the Institute. Despite many years of collaboration with the Institute to address public health issues, Smith was gravely disappointed when a serious conflict arose with someone he had mentored there. While spending months trying to resolve an impasse over money, Smith wrote long passages in his journals trying to understand what had occurred and to find a resolution. Eventually, the issues had to be settled in court. Despite his strong feelings about the Institute and its mission, Smith stepped down and has not been involved with the organization since 2014. His readiness to place trust in people much more cynical than he is one of the few character flaws his many admirers will give voice to. This has been one of the few cases in his life where he feels that trust was betrayed.

Nonetheless, Brown relates that in the last ten years, the Healthy Families program has evolved and continued to empower and teach people. Brown met Smith when she began working for the Arthur Ashe Institute in the mid-1990s. Her first project seemed like a "no-brainer" to her—meeting with Brooklyn churches to share information about HIV/AIDS.[382] With Smith as her guide, her hope was that she could help black churches develop ministries around a public health crisis in the black community that was beginning to receive attention.[383]

Despite her strong communication skills and ardent concern for the communities involved, Brown made little progress. She did convince clergy to allow her to meet congregations, but when she arrived on workshop day, no one came. Persevering, she eventually discovered that she had to address head on the fact that HIV/AIDS is not just a disease of young homosexuals. Brown also discovered that there were people within these communities who were willing to share their experience with HIV/AIDS. One in particular became a powerful witness: a married mother and nurse, daughter of a preacher and a minister herself, who had discovered that her husband was HIV positive. Here was the case of a woman "doing all the rights things and still now HIV is in her home—not just knocking at the back door."[384] Brown finally made inroads after finding collaborators like the nurse.

Healthy Families put Wren's money to powerful use training community health-care aides, and Brown shared the success of the model with health workers in Philadelphia among other places. Since then, the nonprofit has moved on to a partnership with the Jobs Plus initiative of the Bedford-Stuyvesant Restoration Corporation.

The lasting power of Healthy Families' work was demonstrated during a recent public health crisis. In 2012, the storm surge from Hurricane Sandy swept up New York harbor, inundating everything at the city's shorelines from Staten Island to the easternmost reaches of Brooklyn. Brown remembers that two days after the storm hit, she received a phone call from former health-advocate trainees. Cut off from immediate aid for two days, the trainees organized assistance for residents in their housing complex. They found food for those who had none, visited the elderly, and assisted those stranded on upper floors. They reached out to Brown when they had learned what kind of help they needed and knew that it would have to come from entities far larger than themselves. She was amazed at all they were able to accomplish with no assistance from city agencies.

The powerful mentor/mentee relationship that has flowered for nearly twenty years between Necole Brown and Rev. Smith exists with a number of other accomplished women as well. Smith has been a long-time mentor to Lisa Mensah, who was the Under Secretary of Agriculture for the Obama administration. Ms. Mensah grew up in Oregon with an African immigrant father and a mother who was a "former Iowa farm girl."[385] Earning her degrees at Harvard and Johns Hopkins, she and her family live in Maryland. Mensah recently participated in Smith's latest effort to engender a spiritual context for the discussion of racial realities at a white church in Connecticut.

Rev. Smith continues to mentor Rev. Beth Waltemath who served First Church in a variety of capacities from 2003–2010 and who now leads North Decatur Presbyterian outside Atlanta, a church Smith knew well when he led Hillside Church. Rev. Waltemath co-pastors at North Decatur with her husband, Rev. David Lewicki. Smith also supported Rev. Julia Kristella as she became an ordained Interfaith Minister. Kristella has served at churches in New York City and is associated with the Psychotherapy and Spirituality Institute where she specializes in using art, spirituality, and journaling as therapeutic tools. One might guess that Dr. Paul's closeness with these impressive women could cause conflict to arise with Smith's real daughters. However, daughter Krista says that her father brings these surrogate children into the lives of everyone in the family, so they all learn to care for them too.

—◆—

Much like his grandmother a century ago, Smith stays in touch with an enormous network of people. Despite his age, he uses all the latest tools—cellphone, email, blogging, texting, Facebook. He has been taught how to navigate these waters by asking for help from younger people, like his surrogate sons. At present, there are at least three with whom he is in close communication. Two of them, Jim Johnson and John Utendahl, have been long-time members of First Church in Brooklyn. Johnson is a Harvard-educated lawyer who was Assistant Secretary and then Under Secretary of the Treasury during Bill Clinton's administration. Of that work, he says,

> ... I oversaw the AFT, the Secret Service, the Customs Service. ATF is the Bureau of Alcohol, tobacco and firearms—the people that the NRA hates. All in all, I had twenty-nine thousand people reporting to me directly or indirectly and an operating budget of about 4.6 billion dollars. I finished that job on my fortieth birthday.[386]

At times, Johnson says the responsibilities of that job were overwhelming. For instance, "having the Secret Service report to you means you are responsible for the security of the President." Johnson's purview was extremely wide-ranging, and he could never predict what task would fall to him.

> You may remember that in 1995–96, churches were burning in the south. People thought there was a national conspiracy targeting African American churches. The Bureau of Alcohol, Tobacco and Firearms (ATF) was responsible for investigating those fires, and I was responsible for the AFT. So President Clinton appointed me to be the co-chair of the National Church Arson Task Force with Deval Patrick who became Governor of Massachusetts ... we did such a good job of being ambassadors to the ministers, that by the time we finished our first four months, the congressional black caucus moved from a place of complaining about the ATF to trying to get more ATF agents in their districts.

At the same time that was going on, there were "pastors for peace" … four of the pastors decided they were going to go on a hunger strike. One of those pastors was a friend of Paul's, Lucius Walker. As things evolved, on the one hand I was developing this sense of trust with the ministers, with African American ministers nationwide; on the other hand there was another group of ministers opposed to me because of another one of my bureaus. The ATF was great; Customs was a problem. And in the middle of this mix, people were starving themselves to death.

Under such pressures, Smith became an essential advisor to Johnson.

When you are in a senior position, there are few people you can really talk to on a confidential basis. And one person I could talk to was my minister. It wasn't me talking to a lawyer to get legal advice, which is one form of privilege, but it was more in the nature of advice that was protected by the privilege between a pastor and a penitent. So that was a safe space for me. I talked through a bunch of different issues. We worked together actually.

… I opened up two tracks of negotiation; one with the legal side with the general secretary of the Methodist church where the pastors were being housed, and the other was the spiritual side in which I was talking to Paul late at night and very early morning. And he was talking to the ministers … I was talking to Paul and he was talking to the leader of the group, Lucius Walker, about the duty of people of faith in positions of power.[387]

When things got really bad, Smith dispensed tough love.

And he would just listen and then he would pull me back into perspective, sometimes in ways that were just sort of blunt. He'd say, "You have an extraordinary privilege. This is hard, but we are not enslaved. There are people who have gone through things, a generation before, that were much harder. And part of this hardness is your own internal conflict; it is not what is happening to you on the outside." This was not one of those, oh Jim, let's sing Kumbaya. He was very, very straight with me. Because I had this position, there were not a lot of people that were willing to be straight with me. Unless they were above me, and then, this being Washington, they would say whatever the hell they want. And they did.[388]

More recently, Johnson has been applying his law degree and political skills to help build deeper relations between law enforcement and the communities. He helped found the New Jersey Institute for Social Justice, a group he says strongly coalesced after Eric Garner was killed by a police officer in Staten Island.

The Institute has been kicking for more than ten years. It is focused largely on urban issues of social justice, economic development, restoration of lives kind of decimated by the time in the criminal justice system. And after the Garner decision in Staten Island, a group of people came to me and said we want to do something other than have another protest or another vigil. We want to do something meaningful. And I had already been working with a handful of people on urban violence and opportunity issues ... the people who came to me were the head of the NAACP state conference and the black issues convention. I was able to broker an agreement between the NAACP and the NJ State Associations of Chiefs of Police to work together to build bridges.

They came to me because I had chaired the Advisory
Committee on Police Standards in New Jersey in 2007.
Governor Corzine pulled us together to decide whether
or not the state troopers had made enough progress
with issues related to racial profiling so that they could
get out from under a Federal consent decree.[389]

Much like his mentor, Johnson has been honing an approach
to diversity issues that can be learned and applied anywhere to help
create change.

... We've now held community forums with a view
towards actual action items, in Newark, Trenton ...
We are going to be working in Camden, Atlantic City,
and Jersey City. All with a view towards coming into
relationship with each other—not just talking at each
other, but relationship. And then developing a practice of engagement, which means more conversations,
which means joint service projects between police and
members of the community, all sorts of the small things
that actually knit people together ... Basically the work
of diversity is close-in work. [390]

In 2015, to honor the fiftieth anniversary of the events in Selma,
Johnson invited Smith to speak at Debevoise and Plimpton, his law
firm. As he has done in many settings over the decades, Smith shared
his experiences with a room full of professionals. With him was Dick
Leonard, the white Unitarian minister who had replaced James Reeb
in the marches after Reeb died. Leonard and Smith had never met,
but together, the two civil rights veterans brought the struggle of the
'60s to life for people too young to have experienced it for themselves.
Johnson says of his mentor's honesty about his experiences at Selma, "It
just points up that nonviolence is very, very hard ... It creates a space.
It says we're not perfect. And [Paul's] power is in his imperfection and

willingness to own it and challenge himself and everybody else."[391]

Asked about Dr. Paul's legacy, Johnson speaks of how the reverend changed church practice.

> Sometimes the law ushers in cultural changes and sometimes the cultural changes are what make possible [changes in] the law ... The practice of the church ... the routine ritual—you cannot go to First Church without touching somebody. You cannot go to First Church without hearing music that speaks not just of the theology of Christianity but the deep yearning of the soul for something different, higher.
> The choir that he envisioned—we are a motley looking bunch in some respects because we are very diverse, we are ethnically—even from the religious spaces from which we move, but we come together in a spirit of love. That is transmitted even if we don't get all the notes right all the time. And so, that culture is something that people then carry with them. That's what's transmitted. And by changing our practices, you change what you do every day, for thirty days ... you've actually changed your mind.
> If [Paul's influence] only resided in him, and he didn't teach other people to do it [it would not continue]. There's always [that] danger.
> I'm deeply interested in, why do we do what we do? When it's conscious, when it's unconscious. You know trying to understand racial profiling is about understanding not just bigotry and the conscious decisions that are wrong but also the unconscious biases that we have and why we make split-second decisions that can be horrific. And then how do we train against that?[392]

Johnson believes that Smith's characteristic honesty, spontaneity, and warmth have had a lasting effect on First Church.

… There are folkways that have to change and there are practices. And the power of Paul's ministry is that he doesn't worry about the law. He gets to the practices … [At First Church] we hug! There's five to ten minutes in which people will go around the congregation and everyone touches everyone else … There are some people in the congregation and one of them is the one of the church leaders, when she starts to hug someone, she may start a hug from like eight feet away! The arms are up and the smile is big and it is like a powerful thing. When you are brought in close, everyone is made physically secure. And that's a cultural transmission too.

The church envisions a hierarchy. The Presbytery, the church … You've got this whole bureaucratic structure. Paul blew up the hierarchy. The reporting lines were largely moved from a [bureaucratic] structure to say a hub and spokes in a wheel … Paul became central to it, which put in some jeopardy the move to the next phase, at least from an administrative perspective. Administratively things needed to be tied together.

But what I didn't see from an organizational perspective, that I understand much better now, is that the rim of the wheel was the culture and that enabled this sort of messy structure to go forward, because the culture was so deeply embedded in the church.[393]

In the spring of 2017, Johnson ran in the Democratic primary for Governor of New Jersey. While Johnson lost the primary to the long-established candidate, he made a strong showing with his inclusive message of prosperity and quality of life for *everybody* in the state.

—◦—

Another "son of Paul" who is a member of FPC in Brooklyn is investment banker John Utendahl. Now Executive Vice Chairman at Bank of America, Utendahl is best known for having founded the Utendahl Group, one of the largest African American investment banking companies in the United States. Utendahl first met Smith when he and his wife attended First Church in the early '90s on the spur of the moment one Easter Sunday. His story of their first encounter is vintage Smith.

> We walk in and see a black preacher, a predominantly white congregation, a diverse population of black and white. Paul was preaching. He didn't sound like Calvin Butts, but he had a delivery that was very effective and sincere.
>
> [After the service] he walked by and we shake hands. He says, "How ya doing? You play tennis?" I'm six foot seven so I usually get asked about basketball. I was playing tennis a lot, so I said, "Yeah I do." And he said, "You want to play?" I was really into it. I said, "Yeah, sure. But I don't play outside in cold weather." He said, "Let's play in the Heights Casino." I'd been trying to get in there! I couldn't figure out how ... Here I am supposed to be this big Wall Street banker, and I couldn't get in the door. He said, "I'm a member. Do you want to play?" I said, "Yeah" and he said, "Meet me over there at 3:00." That's how it all started.
>
> To my surprise that man beat me that first day! I was expecting an old man game. Every serve was a first serve. He actually hit me with the ball. That set me back. My wife at the time said, "Did you take it easy on him"? And I said, "He beat me! And he hit me with the ball!" Then I went in my room and got quiet for about an hour. [394]

Smith and Utendahl have been speaking on the phone regularly ever since. When asked what the reverend has done for him, Utendahl says unequivocally,

Paul represents somebody who saved my life. I owe him a large part of my success. My perception and the way I look at things have a lot to do with Paul. There isn't a thing I wouldn't do for Paul. He's a hybrid. He can see me as a dear friend, and he can also see me as a surrogate son that he never had ... It is a very close relationship, very special ... Paul is a rare individual who perhaps has no equal. He's a force of nature.

Smith and Utendahl have served on boards together, and the banker says he too was invited to visit some of the terminally ill patients at Long Island College Hospital.

There was one morning he asked if I would go with him on a normal morning run to LICH. It was six in the morning. He was spending time talking with AIDS patients, early on before we knew very much about AIDS.

I've got to admit I was nervous. I was like, "Let's do this." But I was thinking, am I supposed to fear death? And that answer is no, given my religion. I was thinking, am I going to catch this? I remember going into the room, greeting everybody. Most of them were in bed. Paul went over and hugged a particular guy. I looked at him and that individual. I thought this is truly a special, special man, if he is a man at all. I don't know anyone, even in the movies, a man like this. He gave me so much strength to accept, recognize the flaws in my thinking. And put me on a path to strengthen that position to be on a path where he is ...

Like Smith, Utendahl has daughters, so childrearing is another subject of their conversations. Utendahl says that his mentor has helped him develop a daily practice that sustains him.

He has insisted, the way out of good and bad times is to keep my routines, keep my faith strong. I get up at five, five-fifteen, having a sip of espresso, take a nutrient drink, reading the Bible for about an hour, exercising for about an hour. If I do that routine every day, it allows me to deal with any problem, any situation.[395]

More than anything, Smith supports Utendahl's understanding of his Christian faith.

I don't know how I could get through any day, any moment without God and Christ. Paul has literally been the rudder of that ship for me. He has helped me keep a consistent thought, routine, strength through moments when it's been very challenging. I had to endure divorce, which was very traumatizing for me. I've had moments where I wouldn't say it challenged my religious beliefs, but it did challenge my views on individuals. It brought moments to me of utilizing those negative tools, like anger and anxiousness, things that will lead to some form of physical and mental destruction. I didn't lose heart in God and Christ, but I wasn't applying what the armor of Christ has given me in dealing with people. Paul has said, "You're human. You will have moments when your judgments have been challenged."

... Everybody has some talent, skills, and then you have gifts. If we can find out what our gifts are in our lifetime and go to that, that is a beautiful thing ... The gifts are the things that separate you from anybody else. Paul is always telling me to focus on the clues ... those gifts are God. It is there. You have to access it. You have to start to believe. It is interesting when you find that thing and you can believe, how many doors open up and how hope becomes even visible, very visible. And you can't quantify it. I've been amazed at how the boundaries have just blown wide open and the probabilities and possibilities of things happening.[396]

Smith's legacy is also carried forward by Howie Hodges II, his surrogate son from the Atlanta days. Hodges is still chauffeuring Smith to conferences and family events. He says that he finds himself using Paul Smith-isms regularly at work: phrases like "Don't take the via negativa; choose the via positiva," and "factual minimums and meaningful maximums." Asked to describe the most important things he has learned from Smith, Hodges says,

> The thing that I learned most from Paul, particularly in the Morehouse days ... I guess the word to use is grace. Just being able to talk to and appreciate that everybody's got value. Everybody's got something to offer.
> I'd say before then, I was slightly less than listening. I thought that I was like BMOC, Big Man on Campus. But then when I got to Morehouse, not only just the school, but the academic regimen, molded you into something bigger. To think of more than just yourself. To be more compassionate ...

Hodges, who lives in Washington, DC, drives to Charlottesville, Virginia every weekend to care for his mother, who has Alzheimer's, and his elderly aunt, Smith's former classmate from Talladega. Smith often rides along.

> I get a lot of quiet time with him in the cars driving. So he's been with me these last three years back and forth to Charlottesville to visit my aunt/his classmate and good friend probably six or seven times. I drive and he's in the passenger seat and we talk about life, relationships, how he and Fran met, the things that he hoped to instill in his kids and his grandkids. He

talks about things that he fears or I'd say, is concerned
about, at this age of his life ...

Asked what kinds of things Smith worries about, Hodges mentions,

> ... just being prepared. Not being a burden on his
> children. Not being a burden on his wife. Wanting to
> have the best health as long as possible.
> So I'm there listening. I think the thing that probably
> struck me the most was, on one of these trips when
> we're going to visit my mom and my aunt, he says,
> "Howie, I've really admired how you watch and take
> care of your mom and your aunt. I'm taking notes!"
> He always says that," I'm taking notes." I said, "I'm
> here for you," and he said, "I know."

Hodges recalls with frustration that he was out of town and unable
to come when Smith called him for help after having a heart attack in
the fall of 2014. Since then, Smith has had several more heart attacks,
surgery, and eventually a quadruple bypass in November of 2015 just
after his eightieth birthday. All three of his "sons," whose own fathers
have already passed on, visited him immediately after the surgery.
Smith has been diligent about doing the requisite rehabilitation, and
he has been clear about having to make changes in his life. During
one of his periods of rehabilitation, he was able to play tennis again.
But he has decided to give up the game that has been at the center
of his social life, saying, "Why do I need to play tennis? If I fall and
break my hip, I'd really be sorry." Happy to be healthy again, Dr. Paul
is not complaining.

The caliber of the next generation of Smith's colleagues speaks
for itself. This is a man whose spiritual philosophy is being usefully
carried into all levels of public life in this country. He has been forced
to slow his pace down, but this gives him more time to counsel those
who need him. It has also allowed him to see that those he guides are

also ready to return strength to him. This is fortunate, as in the last few years he has faced some of the darkest days of his long life.

13

I was never afraid. Open-heart surgery—never afraid. I'm afraid now. And when you're afraid, you're dangerous.
                                                    Paul Smith, 2016

Black Lives Matter

Despite all his accomplishments, Dr. Smith's powerful faith has been shaken by public events in the last few years. Smith has been haunted by the flood of news stories about black people killed for little or no cause. In 2012, there was Trayvon Martin, a teenager killed by a neighborhood vigilante sheltered by the stand-your-ground laws in Florida. An ever-lengthening litany of names has followed: Eric Garner in Staten Island, Michael Brown in Fergusson, Missouri, Ezell Ford in LA, and Tamir Rice in Cleveland in 2014; Freddie Gray in Baltimore, Walter Scott in South Carolina, and Sandra Bland in Texas in 2015; Alton Sterling in Baton Rouge, Philando Castile in St. Paul, as well as five police officers in Dallas, all of whom died within three days of each other in mid-July, 2016. The tragic litany shows no signs of abating.

Rev. Smith suffers acutely over the news of these fatal encounters. As a dear friend and fellow empath says of him,

> He gets too overwhelmed, too in touch, too empath-
> ic … in a wonderful, beautiful way. But the question is,

is it harmful to him? He's so deeply involved in what's happening in the news. He's highly sensitive ... I wrote him before the most recent surgery that he can't fix the world ... He somatizes all that feeling. It manifests in his body. The feelings go right back into his shoulder and his heart ... He internalizes everything he can't fix. I tell him, you can't fix it. You have to learn to take care of you.[397]

Smith's reserve of optimism has been drained low by the relentless regularity and senselessness of these deaths. He has also struggled mightily with the election of President Trump and the Republican Congress's obsession with undoing everything President Obama accomplished in his eight years in office. As always, Smith has used writing to work through the anger, fear, and sadness. Prescient about the times to come, he wrote in his journal in 1989, "These are difficult days for white men. The world is changing their power base. Once that happens they may be willing to fight to hold onto what they have."[398]

In May of that year, he appeared on a national television program to speak about the Central Park jogger attack in which five young men were accused of savagely beating and raping a white woman. Smith assailed the comments made by fellow New Yorker Trump.

Billionaire Donald Trump paid for an ad in the New York Times that argued and more directly lobbied for the death penalty [for the "Central Park Five."]. Cost: $89,000. I responded on the t.v. show that his act was one of the most irresponsible and racist actions of any which have come forth ... Clearly, Trump's anger and avowed hatred for the kids who attacked the woman in the park is but a response (knee jerk) to a very tragic event ... I can think of better ways to use $89,000. Nevertheless, I am saddened to think that Trump is so taken by this attack in central Park that his inner hatred comes ringing through. To be proud that you hate no matter the justification is a terrible thing to comprehend ... [399]

During Obama's time in office, Smith saw what he believed was an up-tick of what have been called "micro-aggressions," hurtful actions and speech made unconsciously on the basis of racial stereotypes.

> I often wonder how my parents and their generation withstood the steady berating of them simply because of their color ... President Obama's two time election as POTUS has opened up a huge backlash of resentment and anger by mostly white men. I am a target for this anger and resentment. As I was walking to my car which I had parked [at a commuter train] lot in Summit, NJ, a white man walking a few steps in front of me was also looking for his car ... I was dressed with a suit and tie and was carrying my briefcase. It did not matter! The white man turned and asked me if I would move the cars blocking his? I was stunned momentarily until he said "Aren't you the parking attendant?" 2013 a black man dressed professionally could only be an attendant ... I would not describe him as a white racist. He is used to black people in menial jobs and an assistant in the Transit ticket office. What else could a black man be in Summit, N.J.?[400]

The fact is that Smith is frequently in Summit because his daughter and her family—including his white son-in-law—live there. Thankfully, he was brought back down to earth when his granddaughter happily greeted him a few minutes later.

Without a regular schedule of sermons to deliver, Smith has begun thinking out loud via blog posts to an email list created for him by former First Church elder Sue Carlson. Between March 2014 and the present day, Dr. Paul has posted more than a dozen essays, trying to find a spiritual way through events in the national news and in his own life. In some ways, these essays have replaced the sermons that Smith no longer preaches on a weekly basis. In "Something to Think About," written in mid-February, 2014, he reveals some of the hard truths his health crisis has taught him.

> First, I cannot continue to be the "joy maker" for everyone. This is difficult for me personally because of my role and profession as a pastor. I have strong bonds and relationships with people from all around the country. I must learn to say no which for me is very difficult. I have continued strong ties with many of the members of the congregations I have served …
>
> Secondly, I must recognize that I cannot always solve the problems of communities where I no longer reside. Recently, I resigned from two boards in NYC where the expectations were unmanageable and time consuming … It took two mild heart attacks for me to get this message …
>
> Last year, I conducted three funerals of very dear and close friends whose families would not have anyone other than me to speak on behalf of their family member … What I realize now and did not realize earlier is the toll these memorial services were silently taking on me. The deceased were like my own family members and their children were like my very own … [401]

On August 1, 2014, Smith wrote through his anger about the Trayvon Martin and Eric Garner cases. Martin's death especially hit close to home.

> I am mortified by the events taking place around the world and within our own country … Trayvon Martin who was murdered was the age of my grandsons. His death could easily have been my own grandsons and your own sons. So imagine my horror when I saw the

video coverage of an NYPD cop viciously grabbing Eric Garner by his neck along with other cops dragging him to the ground in chokehold! Eric called out 11 times that he could not breathe but that was not enough to stop the cruel and brutal murder by a white cop. Most disturbing for me was the comments from Mayor de Blasio and Police Commissioner Bratton who said "race was not a factor" in the death of Mr. Garner. Who do they think they are kidding?[402]

After the death of the young man in the hoodie, Smith wrote to his grandsons with instructions about how to behave when they interact with police. Lloyd and Stephen, the sons of daughters Heather and Krista respectively, were both born in 1998. In the fall of 2016, they both left home for college. As devastating as the loss of a child would be to any family in America, parents and grandparents of young people of color have long had to consider the possibility that a family member could die at the hands of the very people the rest of the country expects to protect them. It is shocking that the fear of racial violence that Smith feels for his grandsons as they go off to Amherst and Villanova is little different from that felt by his parents and Granny when they put him on the train to Talladega in 1952. Granddad Smith says,

I wanted them to know that regardless that they are middle class kids, they need to be aware of what to do, how to act, when and if they are stopped by cops:

- First thing, be respectful. "Yes, sir. No sir."

- You need to be sure to say to them, "I'm going in my pocket now to get what you asked me for." Follow their instructions and give them specific info about what you are getting from your pocket.

- Never be argumentative. You are not going to win … Do not be argumentative even though you know you are right.

- Get the day, time, officer's name …

- Listen carefully to what the police officer is saying, so you can write it down afterwards …

- Let your parents know so they can record it as well. Let [the police] know that your parents are concerned.

Speaking about his grandsons reminds Smith that he continues to be subject to extra police surveillance, even today.

> I got stopped twice on the way to Columbus last year … A policeman was following me. The first question he asked me was, "Is this your car?" They are not supposed to ask that, but he has the gun! … I was looking at the GPS trying to find the hotel. It was 1:30 in the morning and I didn't put my directional on. The cop says, "You can't do that in this town."
> [The other police officer] said, "The reason I stopped you is because you were driving too close to the person in front of you." On Interstate 70. In my Mercedes. You can't get close in that car! He's already pissed because I'm driving a Mercedes. This car almost drives itself … It won't let you get too close to the car in front of you!

In the future, August 9, 2014, will be known as a watershed moment in the awakening of the rest of America to these realities. On that day, the news broke that eighteen-year-old, unarmed, Michael Brown had been killed by police officer Darren Wilson in Ferguson, Missouri. The encounter was set off after Brown and a friend were seen on video camera stealing a package of cigarillos.[403] The young men left the store and were walking back to the Northwinds apartments in an eastern corner of town, when Officer Wilson, who had heard a dispatch describing the robbery suspects, spotted them.[404]

Wilson radioed that he thought he'd seen the men, followed them, and blocked their path with his car. There was an exchange of words and a physical struggle ensued with Brown outside the car and Wilson still in it. Wilson discharged his gun twice, one bullet grazing Brown's thumb. Brown began to run away, and Wilson got out of the car and followed. After going some distance, Brown turned to face him and, Wilson says, charged toward him. Wilson shot ten more times, hitting Brown in at least six places. Brown died facedown in the street, more than 150 feet from Wilson's car. It was only after an autopsy was performed that Brown's body was removed from the street.[405] His crime had been only petty theft.

When news of the shooting spread, public meetings and protests were organized in Ferguson and greater St. Louis by local, young peoples' advocacy groups including Millennial Activists United (MAU) and Tribe X. It was during this period that the #Black Lives Matter activists began shaping their message. They began organizing regular protests that went on for months.[406] With shared and predominantly female leadership communicating via social media, these groups represent a new generation's social awareness and political views.[407] They were effective in keeping up the pressure for a thorough investigation of Michael Brown's death and do not appear to have been responsible for the subsequent violence that so preoccupied the media.[408]

Absorbing the terrible loss of yet another young black man, Smith wrote a blog post two weeks later that expressed his anguish over the incident and its aftermath. In "In Search of Common Ground," he retells the story of his work at Berea and the ministers' trip to Selma and laments what he sees as a very different kind of protesting.

> Like many of you I have been watching the events taking place in Ferguson, Missouri and wondering whether common ground can ever be found. I confess that early on the images of armored vehicles, rubber bullets along with tear gas being thrown at the police could easily have been anywhere in the Middle East. It was not the Middle East rather it was an American city where 52 years ago I spent time as a very young pastor ... [409]

Of central concern to Rev. Smith is the fact that the multiracial nature of protests in the '60s seemed to be missing.

> The Ferguson of 55 years ago is not the Ferguson we have seen on the screens of televisions the past two weeks … What is troubling me is the seeming lack of white ministers and whites in general at the protest marches. I raise the question, where are they? Did the civil rights organizations try to reach out to them? If not why not? Whatever is or is not negotiated going forward will necessarily have to include white people. They must be at the table to make sure they hear the plaints of blacks and vice versa. Dr. King was always open to sitting at the table with the oppressor. Why can't we? …

Smith gives voice to his frustration and writes of realizing he must temper his anger (emphasis in original).

> As I prepared to preach at a predominantly white congregation last week in Bethesda, Maryland, I realized I had not gotten over some of my own personal anger and outrage over the shooting deaths of Michael and Eric by the guns of white policemen. I was a real mess until I received two e-mails from close friends and colleagues who ended their message to me with these words: *"There is still reason to celebrate."* It was not until I saw these words in front of me that I realized I could not preach a sermon reflecting my anger and grief and disappointment over the shooting deaths. I turned immediately [to] 1 Corinthians 13 Paul's letter to the church in that city. The words of Scripture spoke volumes about how I was approaching my situation in the wrong way. It has been said this particular epistle is the best definition of love ever printed. I allowed Paul's

words to touch my head and my heart and it made a difference in my feelings. I knew there was no way for me not to be open and prayerful in my tone. I had to provide an opening for myself before I could find an opening for others ... [410]

A few weeks later, Smith was lifted up by a surprise—he received an email from one of those white ministers. Rev. Mike Trautman, his former student at Columbia Seminary in Atlanta, is now senior pastor of Ferguson Presbyterian Church, the very church mentioned in the blog. He had found Smith's post online and wrote back asking for advice. He had not been in close touch with his professor since Rev. Smith preached his ordination sermon in 1982. After twelve years pastoring at other St. Louis churches, Trautman had been called to First Presbyterian Church in Ferguson in 2001.

Trautman wrote to say he was going to demonstrations but was looking for insight and support, having found himself in a town that had gone from ordinary to infamous overnight. As the demonstrations and violence in Ferguson continued through August into September, 2014, Trautman was sustained by what Smith taught him.

Especially, when Ferguson began to be torn apart—at that point I felt I had to reach out to Paul. I reread Thurman's *Jesus and the Disinherited*. It was a really important book to reread, to see what kind of opportunities for ministries were happening. I reached out [to Smith] in a deeper way, saying here's what I'm thinking and feeling. And he started connecting me with people from all over. They were people who have been through things like Ferguson ... He offered to get me connected with [then Attorney General] Loretta Lynch, another "daughter" of his.[411]

As Trautman tried to navigate the troubled political waters in Ferguson, Smith activated his network in support of his student. Jim

Johnson, with his experience dealing with racial issues in policing, was one of those Smith connected to Trautman. Johnson in turn circulated Mike's name as a possible contact for others trying to find solutions to the conflict.

Rev. Smith wrote again about Ferguson late in September 2014. In "The Need for Constancy, Not Consistency," he airs his frustration over the state of America's race relations and suggests a spiritual and emotional response to the continuing protests.

> … In listening to the residents and others expressing their thoughts on this tragic death which has torn apart its citizens one thing is quite clear: the great racial divide with blacks and whites in America continues. One need only listen to comments from both sides to realize America has a long ways to go … Without constancy in addressing our issues I am afraid it will be difficult to reach any sort of agreement …
> Constancy is preferred because the God of my life is constant in loving me, in correcting me, in nudging me, in encouraging me to launch out into the deep … And if you do not believe in God that is your right and privilege and you would be welcomed at my table. I will not cut you off from dialogue and conversation as so often is the case. I believe now is the time for us to recapture the dreams of those on whose shoulders we stand.[412]

Rev. Trautman's response reflects Smith's effects on him.

> Thanks Paul. You have given me much to think about in the coming days. I hear you about that need to be constantly moving on the path to forgiveness, risking listening to the sound of the genuine that alone can break down the barriers that divide us. I realize that I haven't created the space within me to allow that God

sound that comes through the voice of the "other" to find a resting place with me. I'm too busy trying to do away with what disturbs me to make space for the genuine, which alone can set us free … [413]

Smith wrote back a few days later with questions intended to guide his former student through the crisis.

Who is working with the Ferguson Police Department on strategies of working with the protesters? Who has done sensitivity training for the 53 police officers? … Is there an identifiable leader or organizer of the protesters? Is there a central place where protesters can gather to rest, discuss, refresh and otherwise get information as to next moves? Would your church be such a place? … What clergy are involved and do they have sway over the protesters or are any members of their congregations a part of the city administration/police officers? As one on the outside looking in the police are making some huge mistakes and that only irritates the protesters. Protesters are also on edge and must have someone they may work with that can intervene on their behalf. Are there off-camera meetings, conversations taking place with officials, protesters and clergy? These are just a few thoughts coming up for me that I pass on to you … Hope you are holding up and doing well in this entire situation. You and your colleagues remain in my prayers. Paul.[414]

Much of what Smith was asking about was in fact occurring. In a recent book based on interviews with protesters and clergy in Ferguson and in St. Louis, Leah Gunning Francis, a professor at Smith's own Eden Theological Seminary, chronicles the ways that clergy tried to support the protests. They spoke to officials and prayed for police, visited activists arrested in jail and helped win their release, and opened their churches to protesters organizing as the weeks went on. Many felt empowered by participating in the protests. Francis reports that the people involved seemed to have gained awareness of and respect for each other.[415]

Ferguson is not the urban tinderbox portrayed in media reports. Trautman says that the town has actually moved a fair distance in the direction of racial integration.

> The sad tragedy of Ferguson is that you never hear about that. In the '70s and '80s lots of people were active to get laws against redlining and to get the integration of the schools. Many whites left, going to places like Chesterfield and St. Charles. But there were people who stayed even as the African American community grew in numbers. They wanted to live in communities that were diverse. In Ferguson, the housing stock is solid and the school system is really solid and they wanted that diversity too.[416]

Once a community where black people were not shown houses, Ferguson is mostly made up of neat, small, private houses owned by people of color as well as by whites. The population is about 60 percent African American. The heart of the city is considered to be the stretch of South Florissant Road, which runs parallel to West Florissant Avenue at the eastern edge of town. South Florissant Road is where the city hall and police station are now located. There are strip malls, churches, and a historic railroad station. It is an entirely ordinary, modest small town.

Rev. Trautman's church, Ferguson Presbyterian, is just two blocks off South Florissant Road, the epicenter of the nightly protests. His parishioners are mostly white homeowners who had planned to ride out the demographic shift. As the protests over Brown's death settled into a pattern with local residents and people from other parts of the country joining in nightly demonstrations, his congregants were upset and surprised by the way things were unfolding.

Most of them are lifetime residents who have been here through thick and thin, and there is great dismay at how quickly things unraveled ... People who once talked easily across the fence are now more guarded. They're fearful of saying the wrong thing, of not being sensitive. But they're trying to come together.[417]

The administrative structure of St. Louis County is part of what creates the complexity of politics there.

St. Louis has all these little tiny municipalities. One hundred and sixteen different taxing districts in the county of St. Louis. Just in the county. Some of them are like fire departments and other kinds of taxing entities. But most of the little communities at one time had their own police force and then they would share whatever larger communities—fire departments, things like that. That was part of the problem—you've got all these little municipalities with their own self-interests and their own little fiefdoms and many of them were reliant on the revenues [generated by those bureaucracies].[418]

In an interview in October, two months after Brown's death, Trautman emphasized that such factors were not being mentioned by the media. "There's been some successful living together of African Americans and Anglos. That gets lost." Nonetheless, efforts were being made to discuss "police brutality against people of color. The sense that the police have this sense of arrogance about them and the vulnerable are victimized by the police force ... Ferguson is known as a place where the police don't mess around.[419]

In words that echo those of Professor Smith, Trautman said,

First we have to acknowledge the gap is there between

people of different backgrounds. We have to listen to these kinds of different perspectives. People need to hear "of the pain and the hurt and the history of black oppression. And we don't want to hear white folks say, 'well it is not my fault' … That's where churches can be helpful. It's a place where, at our best, we are able to bear this kind of hard conversation.[420]

Asked what others could do, Trautman said,

… The best thing you can do for us is to have these conversations now in your own time and place, without the added pain of what happened in Ferguson. Leave your anger at home, and just open your hearts and hear what is going on. Feel the hurt and the pain that is very real here in Ferguson. It was bad enough that Michael Brown was shot and killed, but to have his body lay on the ground four and a half hour[s] was inexcusable. That reminded so many folks of the power of lynch[ing], when the bodies of victims were intentionally left on display.[421]

Trautman participated in the so-called "clergy march" on Moral Monday, October 13. On that day, several hundred people assembled in the rain to march from Wellspring Church on Florissant Road to the police station a few blocks away. They took up positions opposite the line of police officers stationed there in full riot gear.[422] The clergy had explicitly decided to support the younger activists, not to lead them. Many there said afterwards that this was a moment when they felt the presence of God and the rightness of their cause and participation.

Nonetheless, after word came in November that Officer Wilson would not be indicted, violence fell for the first time upon businesses on South Florissant Road. Trautman says that white residents who had been sympathetic to the protesters became angry that this part of town was being damaged as well. The "I Love Ferguson" campaign smoldered again. White and black were becoming more and more polarized.

In March of 2015, a brutally frank Department of Justice (DOJ) report[423] was released, excoriating both the police department and the court system in Ferguson. It took a full year for the DOJ and the Town Council to agree on how to comply with the recommendations in the report. One step toward the "entire reorientation of law enforcement in Ferguson"[424] that the DOJ report called for came with the hiring of a new police chief. In May of 2016, Major Delrish Moss, from a small city in Florida, took up his new post.[425]

Trautman emphasizes that, "What happened in Ferguson could happen anywhere within St. Louis County."[426] Shortly after Brown's death, the deeper causes of this urban unrest were beginning to be explored. An article in the *St. Louis Post Dispatch* on August 11 asked, "Why did the Michael Brown shooting happen here?"[427] The journalists found that the uprising "seems to have had as much to do with socioeconomic factors as [with] opinions about race relations and police brutality."[428]

As downtown developments like LaClede Town were torn down in the 1980s and 90s, urban residents of St. Louis have looked outside the city for a better quality of life. The cluster of low-income, privately developed apartment buildings in the far southeast corner of Ferguson where Brown was living was an attractive place to start. However, in the last twenty years, the Canfield, Northridge and other apartment complexes have become overcrowded.[429] The interests of private developers, surrounding residents and state representatives together have combined to ensure that the low-income housing is clustered in neighborhoods like Brown's. The result has been in the clustering of the town's poorer residents in "one of the highest concentrated areas of low-incoming housing the state of Missouri."[430]

A new generation of African American scholars is writing about the effects of these conditions on urban youth. Journalist and professor Marc Lamont Hill[431] argues that to fully understand the plight of Michael Brown, Trayvon Martin and others like them, one has to recognize that there are class as well racial issues involved. He characterizes the young men who have been abandoned by the state and subjected to its violence, as a "disposable class." He writes of Michael Brown,

> His physical presence on Canfield Drive was due not only to his personal experiences and choices but also a deeply rooted set of policy decisions, institutional arrangements, and power dynamics that made Ferguson, and Canfield, spaces of civic vulnerability.[432]

Rev. Smith was also called to help when violence erupted in Baltimore, Maryland, later in the spring of 2015. After Freddie Gray was pulled out of a police van in a coma with a spine so badly mangled that it later killed him, Baltimore too exploded into a series of violent protests. There were injuries, arrests, and buildings set aflame before a state of emergency was declared, and the city quieted temporarily a few weeks later. When Rev. Christa Burns of Faith Presbyterian Church in the northern part of the city went on sabbatical in the late spring of 2015, Dr. Smith was asked to fill in for her three-month leave. Fortuitously , Smith was able to bring his mediation skills and experience working with police officers and the public to bear on another city in crisis.

> … Baltimore was a powder keg at that time. I met with probably fifteen ministers at Christa Burns's request. And we just talked. Kind of like what we did with the 84th Precinct in Brooklyn. Why couldn't they do something like that? It broadened what we did—it was not—do what we did, but something to that effect. It can happen. It is not about what kind of sermon you preach but were you there. It's a model.

As usual, Smith drew on his network and made himself available to whoever sought his advice.

> Again, I'm 90 percent of the time behind the scenes. Through Jim Johnson, and the work he's doing, he told the chaplain, community relations officer, and a third

person that they needed to talk to me when they came to Baltimore. They came and they were really learning and listening. They were people, police officers [from] communities outside of Baltimore. So they came to see what they needed to learn. They came to listen.

By the time the trials were over in late July of the next summer, all charges against the law enforcement personnel involved in the death of Freddie Gray had been dropped.[433]

In June 2015, Smith's blog post contained both joy and sorrow. He wrote about a moment that involved one of his surrogate daughters.

> A couple of weeks ago I was invited to the swearing in ceremony of Loretta Lynch our new Attorney General and a dear friend. There was hardly a seat in the Warner Theatre in Washington, DC where the ceremony took place. President Obama was at his very best in praising Loretta whom he has known for a long time. I had not seen the president so happy and it showed on his face and in his interaction with the crowd who had come to witness the ceremony.[434]

The tone of the post then shifted to address a particularly horrifying episode of violence against upstanding black citizens, this time the killing of nine Christian worshippers by white supremacist Dylann Roof.

> Little did any of us know how soon the President's smiling face would quickly turn to one of grief and frustration upon hearing of the massacre in Mother Emanuel AME Church in Charleston, South Carolina. The President's cup like my own had "runneth over." What does one do when ones cup overflows with unbearable agony and grief upon hearing the news of the

tragedy? That the tragedy occurred inside of a house of worship during bible study is unimaginable and too hard to understand. So, what do you and I do?[435]

Rev. Smith wrote that first one must acknowledge that the event had taken place so as to be able to deal with one's pain. Second, he wrote,

> I had to acknowledge my anger was real, so real that I was ashamed of myself longer than I am willing to admit. My anger is the same kind of anger all of us have and when it gets out of control we become as dangerous as Dylann Roof.[436]

Third, he revealed that he had

> … learned about the real essence of forgiveness and faith coming from those who had lost the most … They were and have always been people of faith and forgiveness … My flow began to stop when I heard the testimonies and I saw how the God of my life and theirs is the only answer to the experience of the tragic fact. Scripture tells us: weeping may endure for the night but in the morning cometh joy. And morning did come.[437]

Just a few days after the cluster of deaths in July 2016, Smith spoke of finding his public voice in these difficult times.

> I think my role is emerging. Calvin Butts[438] spoke at our convention of the Boulé
> … They asked me if I would do the scripture and the prayer at the end. For a lot of these guys, if they are not the main speaker, they don't want to do scripture and do the prayer … The mega-preachers! So they came to me. The good news was that they could come to me.

Calvin spoke and [people] were literally up cheering at points. He was fantastic and erudite … It was like when you make a basket in the last two seconds of the game? "The crowd goes wild!" I had to follow that!

But rather than try and compete with the nationally revered speaker, Smith followed his own instincts.

Here's 2000 people been brought to the mountaintop! So I get up. You could feel that energy. [It was] all on the jumbotrons. I just closed my eyes and said nothing for 10 seconds. Then I began with Aretha's "When your soul in the lost and found, who comes along to claim it?" I said, "My soul is in the lost and found. The question is: who will we allow to come along and claim it? Do we even know who we will let save it?" I'm just moving by the spirit. I hear Calvin say, "Yeah, yeah!" I ended by saying, "I want the God of your life and mine to come along and claim you." Afterwards people said, "It was not only what you were saying but that we could see what you were feeling and we tapped into that."

In an interview on Sunday, July 10, 2016, in the midst of recounting the joy and power of that moment of prayer, Smith paused, overcome by his emotions. A moment later, he collected himself and explained.

I'm surprised at my anger and disappointment. I was never afraid when I was in the civil rights movement. Even when that guy spat in my face. I'm afraid now. That's the difference. It is so toxic. Other friends say the same, "I don't know if someone will go off if they simply see me or hear me." I decided not to drive to Atlanta for the memorial [of Joann Nurss]. I don't want

to be a black man in a Mercedes driving down to the
south. Someone said he'd come with me, but then we'd
be *two* black guys in a Mercedes driving to Atlanta.
I was never afraid. Open-heart surgery—never afraid.
I'm afraid now. And when you're afraid, you're dangerous.

Smith has had to devise new ways to address the deep fear and
anger simmering in him and many others in the wake of these events.
Early in 2016, he was contacted by John Wygal, a congregant from
First Congregational Church (FCC) in Darien, Connecticut. Wygal
and his minister, Dale Rosenberger, had been talking about how to
create a context for discussing race issues at their essentially all-white
church. At first, Dr. Paul says, he felt tired. He did not want to take
up the challenge.

I said, "I don't want to help white people to do what
they know they need to do!" Wygal tried again. He said,
"At least talk to my pastor." So I went up to Darien and
met [Rev. Dale Rosenberger]. I had a beautiful time.
In July finally met John Wygal in the flesh. He said,
"You're everything that my pastor said you were." We
sat and planned the whole service.

The event was shaped by the fact that FCC's sanctuary needed
repairs and could not be used. Instead, Smith made some suggestions.

I said, when I used to go out to Ghost Ranch, I had
a program called "Under the Tent." [Rosenberger]
listened for a while and said, "You *are* good! And fur-
thermore, you'll have more people in the tent than in
the sanctuary!"

Smith and his friend and composer/musicologist Nolan Williams,
Jr. had been talking at length about how to use music to elicit deep

reflection and conversation on the topic of race. Rev. Williams had created a transcendent musical event on Martin Luther King, Jr. Day 2016 at the Kennedy Center in Washington that Smith had attended and found deeply moving. He invited Rev. Nolan to participate in the service in Darien. Williams suggested that teaching some new music to FCC's choir would be a powerful way to get the existing congregation involved in what would be a very different kind of service for them. Williams volunteered to drive up to Darien the Friday before the event to work with the choir and to bring musicians to support the performance.

On Sunday, September 18, 2016, Smith and friends convened for "Under the Sacred Canopy: A Racial Reconciliation Sunday," a special service at First Congregational Church in Darien. About 160 people joined Rev. Rosenberger and his associate ministers for an outdoor service built around the music of Rev. Williams, a sermon by Rev. Smith, a conversation facilitated by diversity expert Dr. Steven Jones and a panel discussion.

Many of the attendees had shared a meal at John Wygal's home the night before the event. Smith relates that,

> It reminded me of 30 years ago. We talked, celebrated, disagreed. A couple of Trump supporters felt they could speak their mind because I was there.
> What happened in that potluck dinner was so enriching. I want to be healthy enough to do more of that. Somebody said, "If you go with me, I'll try anything." It was like he was saying, "If you were working with us, I could change." It was almost confessional. He had been waiting for the opportune time to say that.[439]

The Sunday service opened with Williams leading the First Congregational choir singing "See Something, Say Something," an arrangement of the music he had used on a much larger scale in Washington. The upbeat refrain conveys the heart of his message:

Bad things happen when good people do nothing, say

nothing, just turn and walk away. Do something, say something, I say, hey … [440]

In the sermon, Rev. Smith used Dr. Thurman's metaphor of the deep-sea diver to ask people to make contact with the depths in themselves. He guided the congregation through a meditation, leading them inward toward what Thurman called "the luminous darkness." It is in that realm, Smith said, "where there is neither male, nor female, where you don't have to pretend. God asks us to be still – this is the level where God is. This is the level where it is all right to be me without making it hard for you to be you." It is from those depths, Dr. Paul suggested, that the courage to listen, change, and grow originates.

It was the lines, "Hands up, don't shoot" in Rev. William's lyrics that brought deeper matters into the open. Michael Brown was rumored to have said these words just before he was killed, and they subsequently became a chant used by protesters. One person at FCC said he didn't like hearing those words; another said he had no problem with them; a third said she thought it brought the media into the discussion in an unwelcome way. Several others expressed their concern for both innocent people getting shot and cops getting hurt in the line of duty. In concluding, one of the hired performers said that the term "reconciliation," has to be defined. She said that if someone's idea of reconciliation does not include taking account of harm done, it is not a useful concept for creating real change.

Rev. Smith spoke about the power of the music as well his own contributions:

> We can't have the anticipated conversation in Darien without something else. People won't remember what I say. I'm a good preacher but I pastor people. That's really what I do. Under the tent, we pastor. I embraced so many people; it was an opening for them. Someone said, "If you keep looking so deeply into me, I will want to cry."

Reverend Rosenberger told Smith afterward that he had never seen his congregation speaking the way they had under the tent. Clearly, Smith and his colleagues are developing a new and powerful kind of activism that has promise for the future.

> We want to ... create a paradigm that can be used, replicated ... the fears that keep you from talking— maybe, just maybe, a song that we sing together will loosen up your tongue. Open up your heart, touch your spirit. How can you be angry with that coming? ... Use music—it is a game changer.

Black intellectuals like Michael Eric Dyson have initiated another kind of public conversation with white Americans. A minister as well as a sociologist, Dyson has structured his searing new book, *Tears We Cannot Stop: A Sermon to White America*,[441] as a worship service. In it, he lays bare in plain and emotion-laden language, the devastating effects on non-white people of what has come to be called "white privilege."

In his Invocation, Dyson confronts head-on the devastating fear and sadness he faces as the father of black children who inevitably learn, as he did, that being black means that some people will be afraid of them or even hate them for no cause. He writes of his children learning that there are white people, fellow Americans, who will feel free to subject them to indignities, violence and even death – for simply being who they are. The book is a fervent plea to God for help finding a way to change this reality. In the Sermon section, Dyson asks white America to learn to recognize their freedom from this kind of rejection and to see how much suffering it inflicts on the lives of others – to see that they are born into a kind of privilege that may be invisible to them.

> Beloved, let me start by telling you an ugly secret; there is no such thing as white people ... You don't get whiteness from your genes. It is a social inheritance

that is passed on to you as a member of a particular group. And it's killing us, and, quiet as it's kept, it's killing you too.[442]

In the blunt language that is needed to cut through old ways of thinking, Dyson ultimately suggests,

> Beloved, to be white is to know that you have at your own hand, or by extension, through institutionalized means, the power to take black life with impunity. It's the power of life and death that gives whiteness its force, its imperative. White life is worth more than black life.
>
> This is why the cry "Black Lives Matter" angers you so greatly, why it is utterly offensive and effortlessly revolutionary. It takes aim at white innocence and insists on uncovering the lie of its neutrality, its naturalness, its normalcy, its normativity.
>
> The most radical action a white person can take is to acknowledge this denied privilege, to say, "Yes, you are right."[443]

In his Benediction, Dyson points the way forward:

> Empathy must be cultivated ... Do not tell us how we should act if we were you; imagine how you would act if you were us. Imagine living in a society where your white skin marks you for disgust, hate and fear. Imagine that for many moments. Only when you see black folks as we are, and imagine yourselves as we have to live our lives, only then will the suffering stop, the hurt cease, the pain go away.[444]

Dyson concludes by quoting "the great black prophet and mystic Howard Thurman."[445]

At the time when the slaves in America were without any excuse for hope and they could see nothing before them but the long interminable cotton rows and the fierce lash of the overseer, what did they do? They declared that God was not through …

Beloved, if the enslaved could endure, on the vine of their desperate deficiency of democracy, the spiritual and moral fruit that fed our civilization, then surely we can name and resist demagoguery; we can protest, and somehow defeat, the forces that threaten the soul of our nation. To not try, to give up on the possibility that we can make a difference, can make *the* difference, is to give up on our past, on our complicated, difficult but victorious past.[446]

14

*I am less fearful of death today thanks to Paul's writing. I now
know what I had hoped for all my life was possible, that I might
be able to face death without fear, with dignity, knowing that
closure is just a continuum of life itself.*
                Alton Waldon, Jr., 2000[447]

Look around you – this is what heaven should look like.
                Paul Smith to parishioners at First Church[448]

Soul-talking

Ever since the elderly German parishioner in Buffalo reached out to
him for succor in his final days of life, Dr. Smith has known that he
has a gift for supporting people coming to terms with death. It is one
of the most delicate responsibilities of any religious leader. Americans'
religious heterogeneity and our aversion to discussing or having contact with the dying and the dead pose additional challenges to clergy.
From that first improvised funeral in Athens, Georgia, in 1957 until
the present day, Dr. Smith's non-dogmatic flexibility has allowed him
to adapt to these vagaries. Over the years, he has developed many different ways of passing on wisdom and comfort to both the dying and
the bereaved. It has also been in this area of his professional life that
he has found his deepest resonances with Howard Thurman's thoughts.

As a leader of intentionally diverse congregations, Smith has long been disturbed by one peculiarity of American ideas about death—the notion, whether conscious or unconscious, that racial identity should shape even the treatment of a body after death. In Smith's experience, the absurdities of our belief in the reality of race are especially clear in our postmortem practices.

> You know racism goes even for burial! Blacks are buried in black cemeteries and whites in white cemeteries. Strange that white undertakers and black undertakers bury their own … I have never witnessed a black person being prepared at a white funeral home. It is rare indeed for a white person to be funeralized by a black undertaker. Unconsciously we go about our business as two separate societies. It is expected that when a black person dies, a black undertaker will be summoned. The same is true for a white person. There is something very wrong about this, yet it happens more than we care to acknowledge.

The same has been true of graveyards: "Until the 1950s, about 90 percent of all public cemeteries in the US employed a variety of racial restrictions."[449] As recently as ten years ago, white and black caretakers tended separate sections of one public cemetery in Waco, Texas. Though some town leaders considered it long overdue, it was only in 2016 that a chain-link fence dividing the two areas was finally removed.

Over the years, Smith has had opportunities to confound expectations on this score. In Atlanta in 1983, he broke with tradition when he stepped up to lead his white co-pastor, a white funeral home owner, and the gathered mourners of a white parishioner.

> At Hillside we have an opportunity to break yet another barrier and we have. At Turner's Mortuary on N. Decatur Rd. a few weeks ago the test was given. I was the only black person there and of course it was never

assumed that I could actually be the minister—just a friend of the family. Mr. Turner's face said it all when I watched him enter the chapel where the family had gathered. George [McMaster], the other pastor was equally observant and was sensitive to the situation. I asked the service to begin by making an announcement and then asking George to pray. The ice was broken, however the stares were there; amazement resided with most of the family friends. The family has long since dealt with the issue and have been supportive and open from the first day of my pastorate at Hillside.[450]

Even in the final years of the twentieth century, a black pastor serving white congregants in their final days was not necessarily expected or acceptable to everyone. At First Church in Brooklyn, a strong-willed Southern parishioner went with Rev. Smith to a local funeral home to ensure that he would be permitted to fulfill his pastoral duties for a white parishioner who had died.

When white people [died] at FPC, I started doing their funerals. There were black and white undertakers; there still are! So I went to the white undertakers with a friend from the church … She would say, "This is Paul and he's going to do the service." And they couldn't refuse … Even in Brooklyn Heights, I had to win people over.

There is some evidence that attitudes are slowly changing. Local heritage groups are beginning to attend to forgotten burial grounds.[451] The mortuary business is beginning to see some overlap between the white and black use of funeral homes.[452] In 2011, the black and white proprietors of a combined black and white funeral services business in Tennessee said, "the expected racial tension arising from having a white service next to a black one has failed to materialize."[453] Some have pointed out that there is a loss of historical and cultural tradition when black families fail to use black mortuary services.[454] However, without a conscious effort to change things, it appears likely that the segregation of the dead in America will continue, reinforcing the odious untruth that black bodies and white bodies—even black and white souls?—are fundamentally different.

Rev. Smith knows otherwise. In his book *Facing Death*, published in 1998, Smith shares from his decades of pastoral experience. In the introduction, he reveals that helping people face death is an aspect of ministry that "for me has been exceptionally rewarding and has shed a light on all the other parts of my work."[455] He believes there is much to learn from the terminally ill that "can make our living richer and our dying more peaceful."[456]

Over the years, Smith has come to see that there is something extraordinary about the final days and hours of people's lives. He writes,

> There is a clarity of thought and a stark honesty that tends to take over when a person is dying—as if, as the person loses strength and energy he saves all his resources for that which is essential. This is the deep speaking to the deep. Put another way, it can be defined as "soul-talking." When we speak from the deep in our souls, there is no need for pretense or denial. The soul is laid bare before our Creator and before ourselves.[457] … those who are facing death acquire a wisdom that is uniquely their own as they begin speaking and responding to the deep inside of themselves. It is available to those who are aware they are dying and who respond by answering the call of the deep, or soul-talking. "Such knowledge is too wonderful for me; it is high, I cannot attain unto it," the psalmist says in Psalms 139.[458]

Smith's familiarity with this liminal phase of life has come through pastoring hundreds of people. In his book, he has chosen six cases that help illuminate some of his discoveries. Of his long-time friend, physician, and colleague from Long Island College Hospital, Dr. John Edson, he writes,

Once at lunchtime, I asked the nurse if I could feed John. I still don't quite know why I made this request, except that at the time it seemed the natural thing to do. It was something very special and deeply moving about the experience. I still remember the quietness in the room as I got into the rhythm of lifting the spoon to his mouth just as he opened it. This became a sacramental moment for me, symbolizing the Lord's Supper or the Holy Communion of the Christian tradition … there are few moments more sanctified than those spent lifting a spoon to another human being's mouth.[459]

In pastoring Jean Young, the wife of his lifelong friend Ambassador Young, Smith suggested her family keep a notebook handy in the hospital so they could write down her thoughts and instructions. They learned to "adjust to the timeframe" of a person near the end—to slow down and listen when she spoke from the depths of her being. He finds,

… people who are dying speak slowly and purposefully in a particular and characteristic cadence and rhythm. Listening to them requires great focus and attention— the things they have to say tend to be profound, yet they are often somewhat concealed by the symbolism and poetic brevity with which they are expressed … [460]

Smith finds Howard Thurman's concept of becoming "centered" to be profoundly useful for both the dying person and those attending to them. Speaking again of his friend John Edson, he explains what this entails.

… opening myself up to hear what God is saying to me and thereby enabling me to hear what John was saying to me too. Each time I took John's hand, he and I immediately entered spiritual ground … His experience of the agony seem[ed] to become more bearable as he and I centered. In centering, we opened ourselves to

each other. There were no pretenses. We [laid] ourselves
bare before each other and before God.[461]

Smith relates that for Arthur Ashe, Dr. Thurman's writing became
a "touchstone," a grounding focus for centering.[462] At fireside meetings
in Smith's wood-paneled study at First Church, Ashe and Smith read
and discussed Thurman's writing and listened to audiotapes of the
revered minister speaking. In his memoir, Ashe wrote warmly: "In the
past months, I have spent some happy hours talking with Paul about
Thurman and his work."[463] He mentions an occasion when he, his wife
Jeanne, Andrew Young, and Paul joined hands and prayed together.[464]
Smith remembers it well, calling it a "sacramental moment."

> … the tightening of Arthur's hand in mine, the qui-
> etness in the room, and most of all the depth and
> breadth of Andy's prayer, which seemed to light up
> the air around us.[465]

In the years since his book was published, Dr. Paul's pastoring has
become even more quiet, precise, and practical. His physical presence
is sometimes all he can offer and all that is needed. He is unafraid to
reach out to the dying person or to those who grieve, knowing how
powerful simple touch can be. He advises the dying and their families
to speak while there is time, to ask their questions and make their
peace. He can often tell a family when it appears the end is near, so
familiar has he become with the way approaching death affects the
body. He sometimes anoints the body of the deceased person with oil
while praying with the family.

Reverend Smith has learned that at some point, he must explain
to people in plain language what will happen after their loved one's
death. He makes sure people understand that the undertaker's employees will arrive and without any ceremony, load the body of the
deceased into a zippered bag. He warns the family that this process is
entirely impersonal; the workers are simply doing a job they perform
multiple times in the course of a day. Smith has found that knowing

such simple details makes it easier for people get through the first hours and days of bereavement.

After the death of Prince Rivers, Smith's dear friend and colleague from Hillside Church in Atlanta, Rivers's son posted on a Duke Divinity School blog about the distinctive kind of care he was given by Smith. Prince Raney Rivers is himself a minister who writes that he has "preached more funerals than I care to remember."[466] Having been informed that his father had acute kidney failure, Rev. Rivers knew he had to call his father's old friend (emphasis in the original).

> By his patient listening and thoughtful reflection, Paul reminded me that we make a mistake when we equate caring with fixing. He never told me how I *should* feel. He gave me the room to rattle off a litany of contradictory emotions. His priestly presence helped me find the source of my strength and gave me permission to be weak.
>
> Interestingly, Paul had more questions than answers. After a few particularly insightful questions, he said he was "taking my temperature." We enjoyed a good laugh about that. I had not ever heard this metaphor related to pastoral care, but I loved it. It meant he was listening not only to what I said, but how I said it, to how I breathed, paused, and sighed. Years of walking beside people in their pain equipped him to listen from many different angles.[467]

Rev. Smith's pastoral approach surprised Rev. Rivers in other ways. Smith asked him,

> "What hard questions do you want to ask your dad?" That was such a blessing to hear. It sobered me to the urgency of the moment long enough to think clearly about anything unsaid or unasked …
>
> Paul drove here to Winston-Salem and arrived a few

days before Dad died. He invited everyone to sit around my dad's bed and tell stories about him. Now, when I think about those difficult days and smell the unmistakable aroma of a hospital room, I can think about the stories we told and the laughter we shared …

I really didn't want Paul to leave, but his departure was also a gift. He knew that he had gone as far with us as he could. He helped us know that death was not the worst thing that could happen to Dad. Paul interceded for us, blessed my father, and stepped aside. He prayed a prayer that afternoon that can only be described as "deep calling unto deep" (Psalm 42:7). From that moment forward I stopped waiting for death and began to anticipate life. Thank God for good pastors.[468]

A natural extension of Smith's deeply compassionate pastoral work is his concern for end-of life management of pain and suffering. Rev. Smith has written and spoken about the underuse of palliative care and hospice by African Americans.[469] In his view, people should not deny themselves the comforts of hospice because they believe it is somehow inimical to their faith. As chair of the Ethics Committee of the Board at Long Island College Hospital, Smith helped create policies for families deciding whether to remove someone from life support.

Responding especially to his brother Willie's difficult death, Smith has become an advocate for end-of-life rights. In a recent article in a Brooklyn newspaper Rev. Smith explains.

For some, death comes suddenly and unexpected. For others, like the terminally ill, death comes slowly—as if approaching over the horizon. It can be seen coming and even be predictable.

Such was the case for my youngest brother, William Rollie Smith, who died of AIDS many years ago. I've been bedside for many deaths, and my brother's was among the worst I've seen. So agonizing was his pain that he begged his doctors to amputate his aching limbs. Time and again he asked our mother and me to help him die, but we told him it just wasn't an option. But it should have been.[470]

Smith has served for some years on the Board of Advisors for Compassion & Choices, a national nonprofit organization dedicated to advocating for end-of-life options.[471] Through the efforts of such advocacy groups, "Death With Dignity" legislation has become law in five states (California, Colorado, Oregon, Vermont, and Washington) and the District of Columbia. The idea appears to be gaining general acceptance. As of January 2017, some 20 percent of Americans live in a state that permits some form of physician-assisted aid-in-dying.[472] While the Catholic Church and other religious institutions have strongly held objections to this, Smith's support for such options emerges out of his lifetime's work supporting the dying in their final days.

Particularly with those whose loved ones have met an untimely death, Smith has developed his own forms of solace. He reminds the grieving that memory is to be treasured, not avoided. As he wrote recently in an email to a man who had lost his daughter to multiple sclerosis,

> Please know that you and your family are in my prayers as you grieve for your beloved daughter and her family … I often say to my congregation that God's gift to the human spirit in times of loss is the gift of memory. With memory you will recall the date of [the daughter's] birth and the joy you felt as you held her for the very first time. With memory you can recall her own joy with the birth of her children (your grandchildren). With memory you can recall those very special moments that only a father can feel being with their daughters … Thank God for the gift of memory … [473]

With Rev. Smith's support toward the end of his life, Arthur Ashe was particularly comforted by the insights in Thurman's *Deep River: The Negro Spiritual Speaks of Life and Death.* Published in 1975, this volume brings together the texts of public lectures Dr. Thurman gave in the 1940s. In these talks, Thurman was reclaiming and celebrating the wisdom enshrined in the songs of the enslaved Africans in this country. In the introduction to *Deep River*, Thurman notes that this music was appreciated anew by those involved with the Civil Rights movement, who "found sources of inspiration and courage in the spiritual insights that had provided a windbreak for our forefathers against the brutalities of slavery … "[474]

Thurman grandmother Nancy Ambrose had herself been a slave, and she is credited with being one of the major intellectual influences in his life.[475] It was through her example that Thurman learned about the "spiritual and experiential essence of the faith.[476]

In the essay entitled "The Negro Spiritual Speaks of Life and Death," Thurman brings discerning erudition to his study of Spirituals. In plumbing the depths of their theology, Thurman first reminds the reader that for the enslaved, death was

> … a fact, inescapable, persistent. For the slave, it was extremely compelling because of the cheapness with which his life was regarded. The slave was a tool, a thing, a utility, a commodity, but he [or she] was not a person … If a slave were killed, it was merely a property loss, a matter of bookkeeping. The notion of personality … had no authentic application in the relationship between slave and master.[477]

In his inimitable prose, Thurman lays bare what today would be called the trauma inherent in this extreme imbalance of power.

> Death by violence at the hand of nature may stun the mind and shock the spirit, but death at the hands of another human being makes for panic in the mind and outrages the spirit. To live constantly in such a

climate makes the struggle for essential human dignity unbearably desperate. The human spirit is stripped to the literal substance of itself.[478]

Thurman then asks what the Spirituals suggest about the attitude of the enslaved toward death. Historically, he notes, everyone was much more familiar with death one hundred years ago than we are today. Perhaps even more so in twenty-first century America, workers in hospitals, morgues, and funeral homes are among the few who have contact with the dead on a regular basis. Thurman contends that "the result is that death has been largely alienated from the normal compass of daily experience."[479] He finds that our antipathy toward anything associated with death in fact deprives us of knowledge that could help us deal with its occurrence. He says "therapeutic effects are missed"[480] when we avoid encountering the dying or the dead. Tellingly, Thurman writes,

> This was not the situation with the creators of the Spirituals. Their contact with the dead was immediate, inescapable, dramatic. The family or friends washed the body of the dead, the grave clothes were carefully and personally selected or especially made. The coffin itself was built by a familiar hand ... During all these processes, the body remained in the home—first wrapped in cooling sheets and then "laid out" for the time interval before burial. In the case of death from illness all the final aspects of the experience were shared by those who had taken their turn "keeping watch" ... [481]

Thurman's meditations on the experience of death still have profound power. Quoting the text of one of the Spirituals, Thurman asks,

> How significant is death? Is it the worst of all possible things that can happen to an individual? ...
> Obvious indeed is it here that death is not regarded as

life's worst offering. There are some things in life that are worse than death. A man is not compelled to accept life without reference to the conditions upon which the offering is made. Here is something more than a mere counsel of suicide … A radical conception of the immortality of man is apparent because the human spirit has a final word over the effect of circumstances. It is the guarantee of the sense of alternative in human experience, upon which, in the last analysis, all notions of freedom finally rest. Here is a recognition of death as the one fixed option which can never be taken from man by any power, however great, or by any circumstance, however fateful.[482]

Thurman believes that the music of the enslaved expressed a transcendent view of God's plan for them.

… the profound conviction that God was not done with them, that God was not done with life. The consciousness that God had not exhausted His resources or better still that the vicissitudes of life could not exhaust God's resources, did not ever leave them. This is the secret of their ascendancy over circumstances and the basis of their assurances concerning life and death. The awareness of the presence of a God who was personal, intimate and active was the central fact of life and around it all the details of life and destiny were integrated. [483]

With great delicacy, Thurman illuminates the reality that *anyone* can make choices about how they perceive and respond to the circumstances of death (emphasis in the original).

The fact that death can be reduced to a manageable unit in any sense, whatsoever, reveals something that is profoundly significant concerning its character. The significant revelation is in the fact that death, as an event, is spatial, time encompassed, if not actually time bound, and therefore partakes of the character of the episodic ... There is, therefore, an element of detachment for the human spirit, even in so crucial an experience. Death is an experience *in* life and a man, under some circumstances, may be regarded as a spectator *of*, as well as a participant *in*, the moment of his own death.[484]

Though Smith's own professional life has differed from his mentor's in significant ways, Smith shares an unusual number of critical characteristics with his teacher. Like Thurman, Smith was instructed by a strong and seasoned Christian grandmother with a rock-solid faith. Like Thurman, Smith believes "God is the 'ground of being.' God is not only the Creator of animate and inanimate objects but also of life itself." [485]As Dr. Paul's dear friend Rev. Marvin Chandler puts it,

> Dr. Thurman saw God in everything and Paul sees that as well. Not in the sense that a lot of people mean when they say that they see God. More in the sense of there is a presence in life that nothing in life can snuff out. Paul sees that energy, that life is dynamic.[486]

Paul Smith's lifelong ministry has manifested the belief he shares with Thurman, that

> ... the Church should not limit its sources of religious insight to Jesus and the Bible. Other religions' faith claims, materials from the arts, and any discovery which opens a door to knowing God are useful to Christian nurture ... The Christian Church should discover that it is including more and more people and concerns, which are outside its fellowship, within its loving circle.

This means that the Church confronts all barriers to community.[487]

With distinctive persistence, person-to-person commitment, and self-revelatory capacity, Smith has reached out to all his parishioners while keeping his preaching fully grounded in his experience as a black man in America. Following the example of Thurman's Church for the Fellowship of All Peoples in San Francisco in the 1940s, Smith recognizes that

> ... opportunities must be established for people to be in primary fellowship in order to express love and to be loved ... This is where ... the Christian Church has such a great opportunity and responsibility. It has the ethic, the informing beliefs, and the calling to establish a loving, inclusive, inter-racial environment.[488]

Smith agrees with Thurman that

> ... racism is inimical to the formation of identity. Neither blacks nor whites can attain a proper sense of self and give full expression to their potential in an environment of prejudice, segregation, and violence.[489] In ignoring and oppressing blacks, American religionists have ignored and oppressed the group of people who reveal in distinctive ways the truth of Jesus ... Whites can learn from and be evangelized by the spirituality which is found in the black religious experience.[490]

Rev. Smith knows that there is healing for *all* people—not simply people of color—in recognizing and embracing the profound wisdom of the African American experience in this country.

Perhaps most penetratingly, Luther Smith's insights about Thurman help give voice to Rev. Smith's special effect on people. These qualities seem to have developed naturally in Smith long before making Thurman's acquaintance.

> His charisma is the result of persons feeling related to him … The sensation of intimacy is not only because [he] addresses the concerns of others, but also because he lays bare his inner life. In speaking and writing he discloses the struggles, pain, humor, embarrassments, despair and hope of his life. The listener or reader feels entrusted with a viewing of [Smith's] self. He allows his audience to know how he has wrestled with God and the hard questions of life, and how this process has not only brought answers and resolution, but more questions and tension. [491]

Luther Smith writes incisively about the impact of such relationships.

> The naked exposure to someone's self is a privilege reserved for intimate relationships. It involves trust on the part of the giver, and assumes care from the receiver. The willingness to share one's self is an invitation to intimacy—an intimacy that invites one to the holy ground of the heart (the indwelling abode of God) … [Smith] seems to speak from the center of his being. [492] [Smith's] life is exemplary of his convictions … He is what he expounds … This genuineness means convictions are integral to one's very being. [493]

Perhaps even more so than Thurman, Smith "is not just an example, but an inspirer; not just a leader, but a maker of leaders; not the authority but a revealer of authority." [494]

Intentionally and unintentionally, Dr. Paul has carried the wisdom of his mentor forward into the present day. The story of Smith's life is uplifting because, like Thurman's, it has been grounded in

... optimism and hope. His optimism hinges on the belief that God is in creation working toward harmony completion and the highest good ... More profound is [his] sense of hope. His hope is derived from the feeling of security, power and meaning received through religious experience. [Smith's] mysticism, his reliance upon the God-encounter, assure[s] him that love can be experienced in the midst of hate, meaning in chaos, peace in the midst of turmoil, fulfillment in non-supportive circumstances, and unity and wholeness within separateness and fragmentation.[495]

Dr. Luther Smith recently summed up about the relation between Dr. Smith and Dr. Thurman.

One would be hard pressed to find many whose lives and sense of vocation have been [affected more] than Paul by Thurman's witness. Paul's work is a testimony to Thurman's significance and influence as well as testimony to Paul's character.[496]

Rev. Smith believes it is significant that Dr. Thurman himself had a mystical end-of-life experience. On April 9 of 1981, Rev. Smith received a frightened middle-of-the-night phone call from Anna Lee Scott in St. Louis saying Dr. Thurman's daughter, Anne, had called her, in great distress. Rev. Smith called Anne and learned that she had been called to the hospital and was present when her father had had a kind of dream or vision during which he seemed completely out of touch with reality. He seemed so unlike himself and unreachable that his daughter was deeply afraid. The doctors later said he had had two close encounters with death that night. Smith recorded some of what Thurman's daughter told him her father had said out loud.

[Thurman said] I know my redeemer lives; he lives in my soul. He kept repeating that phrase during intervals.

Over and over again he spoke to his creator. He kept
pointing to something. His eyes became yellow and
fixed. He did not know me; he cried like a baby and I
kept saying " I know, I know" and I hugged him. What
he had believed all of his life seemed to be of no avail …

Smith went on in his journal,

I have heard experiences similar to this one, yet there
was something quite different and special about it.
Perhaps some of it is due to the particular relationships
I share with the Thurmans. Whatever, it has reaffirmed
my belief and interest in "walks through death."[497]

In early April 1981, about a week before his death, Thurman
talked to his assistant Joyce Sloan about his experience in the hospital.
Fortunately, she recorded the conversation. Smith says he played that
tape over and over for Arthur Ashe. They strained to understand what
was said, because the cassette tape was of such poor quality. It was not
until after Ashe died that Smith learned from Thurman's wife Sue that
a transcript of the tape existed. Smith says of these facts,

I felt badly that I had not known about the transcript
in time for Arthur to read it, but I am convinced that
even in that poor quality audiotape he heard something important … His reading of Thurman's work,
sometimes by himself, sometimes aloud with his wife,
and his discussions with me all helped Arthur find the
courage to face his death.[498]

The transcript of the tape appears to have been hastily typed, but
it shows how Thurman came to interpret what had happened at the
hospital. His exegesis did not touch on sadness or fear. He stated firmly
that he had not had an out-of-body experience. Rather, his explanation
of what had occurred in his hallucinatory state was more forthright.

This is an account of something that may not ever have happened or could not happen but did happen. It has to do with an experience, one experience of illness that took me where, I am not sure …

The problem there was the fight that I was having with death. I did not understand what death was about and I wanted to know who or what was ultimately responsible. I wanted to know, for instance, whether there was any difference between that which determined the death of a male as over against that of a female. And I wanted to know further who called the shots? Who said this person lives and that person dies? I went all through the evening asking that question and trying to get an answer because I wanted to face the person who had ultimate responsibility for life or death over all living things …

… I wanted to know from him, "was there ultimately any difference between the colors of people?" Because this is my concern of how you deal with the question of a black person as over against a white person? Are there elements known only to you by which you judge? And if that's the case the whole scheme of creation is evil …

And when I found I could not have much discussion then I said, "Who are you? Are you God? Are you a Creator of things or are you the Creator of existence itself? And if so, ultimately what is the difference between black and white? Now if there's no answer then why perpetuate the sense of ultimate separation—separateness? If there is an answer give us the secret so that when we observe your behavior pattern we can do it without judgment and know that it is not an evil thing … I feel there is something evil about a distinction, ultimate distinction between human beings if its just a capricious thing. Is there some valid hidden secret that makes differences between black and white, because that's what I'm concerned about. And ultimately what does it mean? And by what right did you make a choice of which would be which and how can you make it hold? Now, I said, I'm going to follow you to the ends of existence until you give me an answer to these questions."

… I was wrestling with that thing all night long because I couldn't find any ultimate authority that would take responsibility of making the difference between black and white. And I felt there was some hidden reason why I couldn't do it. And I was determined to bird dog it throughout all the universe.[499]

It is unclear who the great theologian believed he was talking to—God or Death or some other entity. Whomever he was addressing, it is entirely in keeping with Thurman's lifelong pursuit of justice and equality that he seized the opportunity to ask whether Spirit intended for people's differences to separate them—to ask whether inequality was built into the order of creation. For him, at the end of a long life of intellectual and spiritual rigor, an affirmative answer was unthinkable. Nonetheless, though he would have been shattered to learn that racism was in God's plan for humanity, Thurman had the fortitude within him to demand an explanation of it when he saw the chance.

Paul Smith sees this testimony as deeply evocative of Dr. Thurman's character and worldview. To him, it is a final assertion of Dr. Thurman's belief in the essential oneness of all people. Smith hears in it the cadence of a passage in Galatians 3:28 about the equality of Jesus' followers.

> There can be neither Jew nor Greek, there can be neither bond nor free, there can be no male and female; for ye all are one man in Christ Jesus.

Smith's own work and character have been profoundly shaped by the same questions. From his earliest journal writing to the present day, he has been probing the meaning and nature of death. And like his mentor before him, Smith's instinct is that evil is *not* at the heart of the cosmos. His experience shows that in life and in death, the only real differences between people are those we ourselves create. He has seen through the myths and knows that it is human fear, anger, greed, and hatred as well as social ideologies that have so destructively separated people.

Further, Rev. Smith knows that it is not God who must rid us of this scourge. Over several centuries, Americans have invented and passed down complex and virulent racial attitudes with staggering consequences for human suffering. Only we can do the reflective work, gain the experiences, have the discussions that are essential if we are to unlearn and redefine our beliefs about each other. Only we can reach out and identify our common humanity for the common good.

Postlude: June–November 2016

"I think the sound of the 'genuine' is how he'd describe God."
Mike Trautman, 2016[500]

It took ten years for First Presbyterian Church of Brooklyn to find strong new leadership; it has also taken that long for Dr. Smith to fully let go of First Church. Driving from Maryland on a frequent basis or talking on the phone, his pastoring has still tied him closely to his Brooklyn parishioners. He regularly visited two of his closest FPC associates, Dorothy Turmail and Dorothy Gill, until their deaths in 2012 and 2014, respectively, and then presided over their funerals.

In early 2016, his even older friend and colleague from Atlanta, Dr. Joanne Nurss, was diagnosed with a fast-progressing cancer. Her case was perhaps hardest of all on Smith. Dr. Nurss had seen his daughters grow up, been a stalwart member of the Session in Atlanta, and had helped edit Smith's book. The irony was not lost on either of them that she now needed the end-of-life care she had assisted him in dispensing to many. Smith kept a special journal throughout the months he ministered to her. At the end, they had two final days of conversation and contemplation. He says now, "We covered everything that two human beings could talk about before someone dies."

At Dr. Nurss's instigation, Rev. Smith took what was for him, an unusually active role in her care. When the physical therapy she was getting in preparation for chemotherapy became too painful, Smith asked the hospital administration to change the treatment plan. Following his friend's wishes, he helped her review and finalize her affairs. He located her notes on how her funeral should be celebrated. While Joanne was in hospice, she insisted he stay at her home. Nurss's spacious apartment had been a key site in his Atlanta ministry and was thick with memories. He says, "That was like a second home for me … We had discussions there; it shaped my ministry. There were intellectual battles, teas, gatherings, all kinds of things."

In pastoring Dr. Nurss, Smith invited Rev. Beth Waltemath, who leads the church Nurss attended outside Atlanta, to join him. Dr. Nurss knew that by including Rev. Waltemath, Smith was passing on some of his knowledge to the next generation, and this served them all.

> When I left, Joanne could see me through Beth. Beth learned how to ask the hard questions—questions like—"When you see your body deteriorating, what does that say to you?" She could see herself wasting away. Beth said, "You can ask that?" … What I was able to do was to get [Joanne] to understand that everything I had taught her about God would be coming into play right now. I read to her from my journal about her. I was keeping notes and prayers, every day.

Rev. Waltemath was due to have a child six weeks later, and Smith intuitively knew he could acknowledge to both of them that the child was the future. Quoting Thurman, he recalls,

> I put my hand on Beth's belly and said, "The birth of a child is life's dramatic answer to death. Here's the new light. Your light is about to go out." Joanne knew but knew it even better after I came.

Dr. Nurss died in May 2016, and her memorial was held in July. Overwhelmed with the news about the deaths in the black community that month and for a time afraid to even drive his car for fear of being harassed by police, Rev. Smith made the decision not to officiate. He had seen all their friends and colleagues on his visits to Dr. Nurss's hospital room and felt he had done all he was needed to do.

A few short months later, a remarkable confluence of events convinced him that he had made the right choice in stepping back. Rev. Smith had been invited to return to Brooklyn on November 17 to receive a lifetime achievement award from his colleagues in the Brooklyn hospital and health-care community. A few days before the event, he received word that Dorothy Turmail's husband, one of the original group that had called him to First Church, had died. Richard Turmail had been playing tennis when he was struck by a heart attack. Smith was asked to participate in the memorial service but declined, although he was unsure about his decision.

Significantly, Rev. Adriene Thorne, Smith's successor at First Church, had just been installed at First Presbyterian on November 13. Looking for clues as to his proper path forward, Smith took the opportunity to walk alone through First Church. There, he was surprised to find cloth bags hanging on each pew. Upon further investigation, they proved to be "gratitude bags." Suddenly he had the insight he had come there seeking.

> I realized this was her imprimatur. That's who she is. That's why I walked through. It confirmed for me that it's about Adriene now. It was about Paul—now it is about Adriene. I was not at the installation because I had had my time. Now it was her time.

Smith also realized clearly that he had been right to not preside at the memorial service for Dick Turmail since Rev. Thorne had been the man's pastor in his final days. Together, these critical insights allowed Smith to let go of feeling responsible for all the funerals, weddings, or other ceremonies for First Church; he was finally certain that his congregation had moved on.

The gala event at which Smith was celebrated was held in a beautifully restored warehouse on the Brooklyn side of New York Harbor. The soirée and fundraiser brought together people who had worked hard to bring high-quality health care to the people of Brooklyn.[501] In addition to Dr. Paul, two others with long records providing health care to the community were honored. Hosting the event was the former CEO of Cobble Hill LifeCare and Holocaust survivor Olga Lipschitz. Guests included Smith supporters who had not seen each other in years—Honda executives, First Church Board members, doctors who had worked at LICH, and many of Smith's own family members. Dear friends like NBA player and celebrated coach Lenny Wilkins and his wife Marilyn were among those who bought a page in the dinner's souvenir book. Letters conveying the best wishes of New York State politicians including Governor Cuomo, Mayor de Blasio, Congressman Hakeem Jeffries, and others were also printed there. About forty of Smith's family and friends expressed their love and respect for him at a very long and boisterous table.

Compounding the emotion that evening was the fact that Donald Trump had been elected president ten days earlier. Having Trump succeed the president in whom Smith has taken such pride has seemed the ultimate insult to Smith. The level of his dismay rivals what he felt about the appointment of Clarence Thomas to Thurgood Marshall's seat on the Supreme Court in 1991. In both cases, the contrast between a departing giant of the black community and the man chosen to replace him could not be more stark. Smith expressed fury over the Clarence Thomas decision in his journal. The ascension of an overtly bigoted candidate to the nation's highest office has been even more devastating.

After presenting the other awards and quieting the hundred or so guests, Mrs. Lipschitz brought gravity to the occasion by speaking from her personal experience of the Holocaust. Her words made clear her great regard for Dr. Paul.

> ... believe me, in my life, I have seen evil. I have looked at the face of [Adolf] Eichmann and he looked at me ... this was in Auschwitz. And because of that, I have seen his face, even though I was a child, for that was the face of evil.

And here, my friend Dr. Smith is a face of goodness
and when he opens his mouth, all the good things come
out … So ladies and gentlemen, here is a man who is
a pastor, who is a friend, who has done more kindness
for human beings than anyone that I know.[502]

As Smith rose to speak amidst applause, a woman at his table
called out, "You go, Paul!" and there was laughter. An inscription on
the plaque presented to Smith was read.

In tribute to you for many years for bringing joy, peace
and love to communities in service; for compassion
and respect for every person who crosses your path …
we salute you for decades of significant achievements
and wish you good health, strength and happiness for
many years to come.[503]

Then Rev. Smith took his place at the microphone, full of gratitude
but also aware of the heaviness of the mood.

Well, thank you so very much. To my co-honorees, I
thank you for all of the contributions you have made to
the community that we all love so much. I also want to
thank Olga, who in the midst of so many battles that
we took on, she was always there supporting, putting
together contacts that made it possible for us to do the
things we were able to do.
Three months ago one of my former students asked
me—how did I make my ministry so successful? That
is easy—you get a whole lot of people who are a lot
smarter than you, [and then] you can do anything that
you want to do! And I mean that. So I am surrounded
by a host of witnesses who have come to join me in
this award this evening.
One of the beautiful things about being pastor is that

you have a lot of surrogate sons and daughters, and many of them are here this evening. But I do want to give thanks for [two] of my four grandchildren are here, my son-in-law is here, my daughter is here. But most of all my wife of fifty-six years this year (applause) … she keeps saying that if you want to make fifty-seven, there are some conditions (laughter). So I honor that and make sure that I make number fifty-seven.

… So let me cut to the chase … I've been gone ten years. I retired ten years ago. And just about a year ago I had open-heart surgery—bypass … I wake up [and] other than my wife and my daughter, I see John Utendahl, one of my surrogates standing there … I'm all chewed up, chest cut open, and he's making these faces at me! And I think it is payback for the many times I kicked his butt on the tennis court! (laughter]).[504]

Speaking more slowly and with greater emphasis and emotion, Rev. Smith began to pray. He chose words that would resonate with a markedly heterogeneous crowd in terms of age, religion, profession, ethnicity, and cultural background.

So let me just say this, we need to understand that what's in this room tonight is what our purpose is—our God. In Thee, we are more loving, we're stronger, we're more likable. We're more reflective when we can be together like we are in this room right now. And there are times when the water in the well is low, there are times when we wonder what role, what voice we are going to take, and yes, there are times when you just want to wring your hands and say, "I've had it." I'm here to tell you that all that is part of life; we all experience that.[505]

Looking out at the now-hushed crowd, Smith was aware of the

profound sadness, anger, and fear the election results had engendered in people so dear to him. He searched his heart for the words with which to entreat them to not lose hope (his emphasis).

> … if there has been any kind of success that we've all had, and we've seen it in this community, it is that we all come together to make our community great. To make the institutions we work for great. For the people in our lives who give us *meaning*, that's why we are here and that's what's in common with us.
>
> So I'm going to leave you with a quote—this one really speaks to me—so listen to that and give yourselves not only a pat on the back, but the courage, the wisdom, the love, the determination to go forward.
>
> Listen to this quote: "I am no longer accepting the things I cannot change; I am changing the things I cannot accept." Got it? I am no longer accepting the things I cannot change, I am changing the things I cannot accept. What this really says to us is that we are always, always, on the path to somewhere, to somewhere, and if we lose sight of that, who are we? What are we? And who we are—we are Cobble Hill Health Center. We are Cobble Hill and Brooklyn Heights and Boerum Hill. We are those people and we believe that it is always possible to accomplish anything we wish to accomplish so long as we recognize our oneness—*our oneness*.
>
> I haven't preached for a long time [laughter], so let me just—one of the things that really holds me together other than daughters, wife and grandchildren and the love of friends, is the awareness that the God of my life and yours makes all things *new*.
>
> Walk tall Cobble Hill! Walk tall Brooklyn Heights! Walk tall all of you who are in the room, because *I have not come this far for God to leave me!*[506]

Buoyed by cheers and applause, Smith found his seat at the long table once again.

Writing in his journal about the event afterwards helped him articulate what had filled his heart at the Cobble Hill event and what he believes had moved others.

> I've been thinking of ... how the room got quiet at the gala, after so much talking at the table. It really started with Olga's introduction, the applause ... I don't think I ever had applause when walking up to speak. That was the signal to me that something was going to come through me to those who were waiting to hear what I had to say. So the fact that you, my daughters, my surrogates, Fran, everybody was there at that long table—you all were empowering me. I think Martin Luther King probably had people there who affirmed him. He was able to take tragedy and turn it into triumph, turn disappointment into discernment. I think because you were all there, who make me who I am, it made me able to tap into what those who were waiting wanted me to say.
>
> ... I touched what the people were thinking and feeling. [It felt like] now we are all on the same page—open to what God has to say to us—Thurman's "the waiting moment."

Cutting through all the bittersweet emotions that night, Smith followed his heart to say,

> We are not called necessarily to believe in Trump or Obama—we are called to believe in the sound of the genuine. So when we hear it, we recognize that which keeps us grounded. I don't need to be right; I just need to be heard ... We must find ways to listen for voices that are genuine, sensitive, ready to move.

—ɯ—

When Dr. Paul makes his own journey into the unknowable, the choices he has made over his long life will ensure that he goes with more experience and awareness than most. His work helping others through "the transition" has prepared him to go with his eyes and his heart open. There will be joy in going "wherever Jesus is" but also sadness about those he leaves behind. As he wrote a few years ago,

> What makes me cry and tear up is the fact that death takes me down from the mountain called life. It is here that I have enjoyed all of God's many blessings to me. I don't want to leave my daughters or my wife or my beautiful grandkids. I thoroughly enjoy life even with its challenges …
>
> I know I cannot stay here forever. I know my days on the planet will soon be over. That is what makes me cry—knowing it all must come to an end some day. The second chance I have been given to help raise our grandkids fills my soul. Growing older with Fran and enjoying each other as we age brings untold happiness to me. I want to be the first to go before Fran or any of our grandkids and our daughters. I don't think I could stand living without Fran. I feel she would handle my death better than I would handle hers.
>
> As I write, I continue to be more and more curious about what is on the other side of life as I know it. If anything, I am being drawn to the edge and I want to be pushed over that edge so I can begin to fly … O God, I pray that I may die easy when I die. May I soar about the clouds and discover Your Presence as I learn how to fly in that other place—the place on the other side of life. And so it is![507]

Sources

Aplin, Beth
  2006 "Rev. Dr. Paul Smith, Pioneering B'klyn Heights Pastor, To Retire." *Brooklyn Daily Eagle*. June 27.
Ashe, Arthur and Rampersad, Arnold
  1993 *Days of Grace: A Memoir.* Ballantine Books, NY.
Auchmutey, Jim
  1980. "Guess Who's Coming to Worship?" *Presbyterian Survey* Vol. 7, pp. 24–25.
Austin, Charles
  1983 "North-South Rift of Presbyterians Healed by Merger." *New York Times*, June 10.
Bailey, Sharon
  1979 "White Church Takes Itself a Black Pastor. *Atlanta Constitution*, Nov. 5.
Belafonte, Harry, with Michael Shnayerson
  2011 *My Song: A Memoir of Art, Race, and Defiance.* Vintage Books, NY.
Bird, David
  1986 "Amid Some Unease, Brooklyn Church Takes a Black Pastor." *New York Times*. January 29.
Bogan, Jesse, Hollinshed, Denise, and Deere, Stephen
  2014 "Why Did the Michael Brown Shooting Happen Here?" *St. Louis Post Dispatch,* August 17.
Bogan, Jesse and Moskop, Walker
  2014 "As Low-income Housing Boomed, Ferguson Pushed Back." *St. Louis Post Dispatch,* October 19.
Botelho, Greg and Jones, Sheena.
  2004 "Man Gets 4 Years For Hazing Death of FAMU Drum Major." www.cnn.com/2015/09/04/us/famu-hazing-sentencing/index.html
Branch, Taylor
  1988 *Parting the Waters: America in the King Years 1954–63.* Simon and Schuster Paperbacks, NY.

1998 *Pillar of Fire: America in the King Years 1963–65.* Simon and Schuster Paperbacks, NY.

2006 *At Canaan's Edge: America in the King Years 1965–68.* Simon and Schuster Paperbacks, NY. Pp. 60, 73, 78, 80–81.

2013. *The King Years: Historic Moments in the Civil Rights Movement.* Simon and Schuster Paperbacks, NY.

Brown, Barbara

1980–81 "Pastor in Transitional Church Must Be Creative, Courageous, Compassionate." *Ministry & Mission.* Undated article.

Brown, Necole et al.

2010 "Healthy Families Brooklyn: Working with Health Advocates to Develop a Health Promotion Program for Residents Living in NYC Housing Authority Developments." *Journal of Community Health,* Vol. 36, Issue 5, pp. 864–873.

Christman, Steven M. and Mark, Jillian M.

2104 "Guidelines on Dealing With Suspected Shoplifters." *New York Law Journal,* May 19.

Chu, Jeff.

2014 "We Don't Need Peace—We Need Unrest." *Beaconreader. com,* August 20.

Cone, James H.

1997 [1969] *Black Theology & Black Power.* Harper & Row, NY.

Demer, Lisa

1982 "More Than Surviving: Hillside Stands Out With Whites, Blacks, Together." *Dekalb News/Sun,* June 2.

Downey, Clifford J.

2010 *Images of Rail: Kentucky and the Illinois Central Railroad.* Arcadia Publishing, Charleston, SC.

Dudley, Carl S.

2006 "My Experience with Dr. Martin Luther King Jr." Email circulated to Dudley family members and others. Used with permission.

2007 "The Second American Revolution: As seen through

the Window of Berea Church 1962–1973. Stories for our grandchildren." Essay circulated to Dudley family members and others. Used with permission.

Dudley, Nathan
1979 "Laclede Town: The Life of a Great American Urban Renewal Project." Unpublished undergraduate paper submitted, January 11, 1979, Yale University. Used with permission.

Dyson, Michael Eric
2017 *Tears We Cannot Stop: A Sermon to White America.* St. Martin's Press, NY.

Elliott, Andrea
2005 "Macy's Settles Complaint of Racial Profiling for $600,000." *New York Times*, January 14.

Elliott, Eileen
2007 "New 'Healthy Families' Program in Brooklyn." *NYC Housing Authority Journal*, Vol. 37, No. 2.

Fields, Karen E. and Barbara J. Fields
2012 *Racecraft: The Soul of Inequality in American Life.* Verso, NY.

Francis, Leah Gunning
2015 *Ferguson & Faith: Sparking Leadership & Awakening Community.* Chalice Press, St. Louis.

Feuer, Alan
2014 "Macy's To Pay $650,000 to Resolve Bias Inquiry." *New York Times*, August 8.

Frost, Mary
2014 "SUNY board official approves sale of Long Island College Hospital to Fortis." *Brooklyn Daily Eagle*, June 25.

Goodman, J. David.
2013 "Macy's and Barneys Among Stores to Post Shoppers' 'Bill of Rights.'" *New York Times,* December 9.

Gordon, Buford F.
2009 [1922] *The Negro in South Bend: A Social Study.* Wolfson Press, Indiana University, South Bend.

Graham, Lawrence Otis
   2000 *Our Kind of People: Inside American's Black Upper Class.*
   Harper Perennial, NY.
Halla, Frederick A.
   1998 "Macy's Donates to First Presbyterian." *Brooklyn Daily
   Eagle,* November (exact date not noted on news clipping).
Harding, Vincent.
   1968 "The Religion of Black Power." In *The Religious Situation:
   1968,* ed. D.R. Cutler. Beacon Press, Boston, MA.
Harrison, Lowell H. and Klotter, James C.
   1997 *A New History of Kentucky.* University of Kentucky Press,
   Lexington.
Hartocollis, Anemona
   2013 "Nurses Roam Empty Halls as Long Island College
   Hospital Is Prepared to Close." *New York Times,* July 18.
Healy, David H.
   2009 "We Stand on his Shoulders: Rev. Buford F. Gordon in
   South Bend, Indiana." In Gordon, Buford F. [1922] *The Negro
   in South Bend: A Social Study,* pp. 1–14. Wolfson Press, Indiana
   University, South Bend.
Heuser, F. J.
   2012 "Presbyterians and the Struggle for Civil Rights." *Journal
   of Presbyterian History* 90(1): 4–15.
Hill, Marc Lamont
   2016 *Nobody: Casualties of America's War on the Vulnerable, from
   Ferguson to Flint and Beyond.* Atria Books, NY.
Holley, Peter.
   2016 "A Segregated Cemetery Divides a Texas Town."
   Washington Post, June 7.
Katz, Andy
   2016 "Cobble Hill Health Center 40th Anniversary rocks
   aging." *Brooklyn Eagle.* November 18.
Johnson, Lyndon B.
   1965, March 15. *Voting Rights Act Address,* Washington, DC.
Kraus, Neil

2000 *Race, Neighborhoods and Community Power: Buffalo Politics 1934–1997.* SUNY Press, Albany, NY.

Lewis, John, with Michael D'Orso
1998. *Walking with the Wind: A Memoir of the Movement.* Harcourt Brace and Co., NY.

Looker, Benjamin
2004 *BAG: "Point from which creation begins"; The Black Artists' Group of St. Louis.* Missouri Historical Society Press, St. Louis.

May, Gary
2015 *Bending Toward Justice: The Voting Rights Act and the Transformation of American Democracy.* Duke University Press, Durham.

McInnish, Sue
1982 "Ministers Relate Williams Case to Parable of Good Samaritan." *Montgomery Advertiser*, March 1.

Murumba, Sam
2006 "Brooklyn Law School Professor Comments on the Rev. Paul Smith." *Brooklyn Daily Eagle,* July.

Norsen, Francesca
2000 "Seminar Explores Islamic Connection to Judeo-Christian Traditions." *Brooklyn Daily Eagle*, February 17–27.
2005 "Dr. Paul Smith's Church Welcomes Amb. Andrew Young to Preach." *Brooklyn Daily Eagle*, March 31. Published online. Retrieved May 12, 2016.

Pearl, Andrea
1986 "Paul Smith Takes Over As New Reverend Of 1st Presbyterian." *Heights Press.* September 25.

Powers, Ann.
2000 "A Two-fold Mission of Piety and Pop." *New York Times,* October 27.

Rector, Kevin
2016 "Charges Dropped: Freddie Gray Case Concludes with Zero Convictions Against Officers." *Baltimore Sun,* July 27.

Pratt, Robert
2017 *Selma's Bloody Sunday: Protest, Voting Rights and the*

Struggle for Racial Equality. Johns Hopkins University Press, Baltimore, MD.

Prugh, Jeff
1979 "White Church in South Picks Black Pastor." *Los Angeles Times,* December 8.

Rivers, Prince Raney
2010 "Call and Response Blog: A Good Pastor at the Hour of Death." June 7. www.faithandleadership.com/prince-raney-rivers-good-pastor-hour-death.

Robinson, Gabrielle
2015 *Better Homes of South Bend: An American Story of Courage.* History Press, Charleston, SC.

Robles, Frances
2016 "New Ferguson Chief Sees Challenge and Vows Change." *New York Times*, May 9.

Rothstein, Richard
2014 "The Making of Ferguson: How Decades of Hostile Policy Created a Powder Keg." www. prospect.org/article/making-ferguson-how-decades-hostile-policy-created-powder-keg.

Scanlon, Leslie
2014 "Unrest in Ferguson: A Conversation with Mike Trautman." *Presbyterian Outlook.* pres-outlook.org., October 6. Retrieved 2–8-16.

Schaeffer, Dominic
2003 "Laclede Town: Impressions of a Native Son." The Commonspace: Grassroots Civics and Culture in St. Louis website. www.thecommonspace.org/2003/10/communities.php. Retrieved 3–15–16.

Severson, Kim
2012 "Helpful Hands on Life's Last Segregated Journey." *New York Times*, June 23.

Singer, Natasha
2014 "For Macy's, a Makeover." *New York Times,* November 1.

Smith, Ellis

2016 "Funeral Home Offers Itself as Crossing Racial Lines."
Times Free Press, Chattanooga, TN, Oct. 22. Retrieved June 4,
2016.

Smith, Greg B. and Bill Hutchinson
1999 "Gristedes Says 'Sorry' to Reverend." *New York Daily
News*, March 22.

Smith, Jr., Luther E.
1979 "Black Pastor Tackles Job: A Declining White Church."
Miami Herald, December 27. (No byline.)
2006. *Howard Thurman: The Mystic as Prophet.* Friends United
Press, Richmond, IN.

Smith, Paul
Hartford journal "No. 5" (1957–65).
Federal Supply Service Record journal (1959–68).
Atlanta journal "No. 1" (1982–1987).
Atlanta journal "No. 3" (1979–1989).
Ghost Ranch journal (June 15—September 24, 1991).
First Church journal "#15" (March 6—November 30, 1989).
Large First Church journal (1991—2006).
New York Urban League journal (May 29-September 26,
2013).

1957 *A Comparison of the Baptist and Congregationalist
Denominations.* Unpublished senior thesis submitted in partial
fulfillment of the requirements for the degree of Bachelor of
Arts. (Courtesy of Savery Library, Talladega College).
1976 "The Black Church: Our Heritage of Faith." *Proud,* Vol.
7(2): 4–8.
1977 *The Relation of Black and Jewish Students Living in
the Residence Halls of a Multi-Racial Midwestern University.*
Unpublished PhD thesis, Eden Theological Seminary, St. Louis,
Missouri.
1998 *The Deep Calling to the Deep: Facing Death.* Coat of Many
Colors, Brooklyn Heights, NY.
2016 "OPINION: In support of end-of-life options. *Brooklyn*

Daily Eagle, May 24.

2014 Blog post. "Something to Think About," March 4.
2014 Blog post. "I'm Back and What a Mess," August 1.
2014 Blog post. "In Search of Common Ground," August 23.
2014 Blog post. "The Need for Constancy, Not Consistency," September 27.
2015 Blog post. "When Your Cup Runneth Over … " June 25.

Smith, Paul, Malik, Shaykh Ibrahim Abdul and Wright, Jeremiah
2007 "Theological Perspectives on Death and Dying for African Americans: Christian & Islamic Perspectives." In *Key Topics on End-of-Life Care for African Americans*, electronic book posted on the website of the Duke Institute on Care at the End of Life at Duke University Divinity School, Durham NC. http://www.rwjf.org/en/library/research/2007/09/duke-institute-publishes-electronic-guide-on-end-of-life-issues-.html

Span, Paula
2017 "Physician Aid in Dying Gains Acceptance in the US." *New York Times,* January 16.

Sweets, Ellen
1997 "Laclede: An Experiment in Ethnic Harmony." *Seattle Times,* November 9. Retrieved January 26, 2016.

Thurman, Howard
1975 *Deep River: The Negro Spiritual Speaks of Life and Death.* Friends United Press, Richmond, IN.
1980 "The Sound of the Genuine." Baccalaureate Address, Spelman College. Jo Moore Stewart, ed. *Spelman Messenger* Summer Vol. 96 (4): 14–15.

Young, Andrew
2008 *An Easy Burden: The Civil Rights Movement and the Transformation of America.* Baylor University Press, Waco, TX.

Young, Jennifer
2016 "The Persistent Racism of American's Cemeteries." *Atlas Obscura www.atlastobscura.com,* September 7.

US Dept .of Justice, Civil Rights Division
2015 *Investigation of the Ferguson Police Department.* https://
assets.documentcloud.org/documents/1681213/ferguson-
police-department-report.pdf
Waldon, Jr., Alton R.
2000 "Deep Like A River." *Boulé Journal.* Spring.
Watkins, Tom
2011 "FAMU Band Leader Drummed Out in Wake of Death
Linked to Hazing." www.cnn.com/2011/11/23/us/florida-
hazing-death/index.html
Wilkerson, Isabel
2010 *The Warmth of Other Suns: The Epic Story of American's
Great Migration.* Vintage Books, NY.

Interviews with Rev. Dr. Paul Smith:

7-31–13
7-29-14
7-29-14(b)
7-30-14
10-11–14
1-16–15
1-17–15
1-18–15
1-19–15
3-10–15 (phone)
3-27–15
5-28–15
6-5-15 (phone)
10-5–15
1-23–16 (phone)
2-9–16
2-10–16
2-11–16

2-12–16
7-10–16
8-2–16
8-3–16
12-10–16
3-2–17
3-3–17
3-9–17
7-30–17

Interviews and correspondence with others:

Necole Brown, 8-4–16
Marc Burt, 1-25–15
Sue Carlson, 1-20–15, 7-30–15, 7-6–16 (phone)
Pam Champion 1-15 (email)
Marvin Chandler, 8-17–14 (phone)
Marvin and Portia Chandler, 3-31–16, 2-23–17
Krista Smith Clapp, 3-20–16
Charles Clayman, 1-29–16
Fred Davie, 5-20–15, 6-2–15
Nathan Dudley, 3-11–15 (phone), 1-26–16
Paula Francis, 12-22-16
Ed Goldberg, 9-16–15, 6-16–16
Howie Hodges II, 4-14–16
Jim Johnson, 11-23–15
Marsha Larner, 2-2–16
David Lewicki, 2-3-15 (email)
Sam Murumba, 6-22–16
Amy Neuner 6-21–16 (email)
Joanne Nurss 1–25–15a, b., 4-30–16
Ellen Oler, 5-23–16
Kathleen Smith Randolph, 4-2–16
Frances Smith, 1-17–15, 1-18–15, 2-9–16, 2-10–16

Jeffrey Smith, 6-14–16 (email)

Luther Smith, Jr., 6-22–15 (phone)

Marcia Smith, 6-22–16

Bernard Streets, May 31, June 7, June 15, July 23, August 8, 2016 (email)

Marlene Smith Wright, 8-15–14, 2-10–16 (phone), 3-30–16

Rev. Mike Trautman, 2-17–16 (phone), 4-3–16

John Utendahl, 8-3–16 (phone)

Mercia Weyand, 6-10–16 (phone)

Leonard Wilkens, 9-11-17 (phone)

Andrew Young, 6-10–16 (phone)

Endnotes

1   Fields and Fields 2012, 146–147.
2   Thurman 1980.
3   Cone 1997, 53.
4   Branch 2006, 60.
5   Ibid., 73.
6   May 2015.
7   Pratt 2017, 50.
8   Lewis 1998, 343.
9   Ibid., 78.
10 Quoted in Pratt 2017, 74.
11 Dudley 2007.
12 Ibid.
13 Branch 2006, 80–81.
14 Johnson 1965.
15 Lewis 1998, 361–2.
16 Ibid., 363.
17 Shelby County v. Holder, 570 US. 2 (2013).
18 May 2015.
19 Pratt 2017, 4.
20 Smith, P. 1998, 2–3.
21 Downey 2010, 7.
22 See www.gravescountyky.com/relocation/communities.php.
23 This information was discovered by Ramin Streets.
24 Spelling and grammar here follow the original as closely as possible. Odie's sentences frequently flow together with only a small extra space to indicate the beginning of a new sentence. Punctuation or capital letters have been added where necessary to allow the diary to be more easily read.
25 Spelling and grammar here follow the original as closely as possible. Odie's sentences frequently flow together with only a

small extra space to indicate the beginning of a new sentence. Punctuation or capital letters have been added where necessary to allow the diary to be more easily read.

26 Harrison and Klotter 1997, 216.
27 Ibid., 235.
28 Ibid., 180.
29 Ibid., 247.
30 Ibid., 22ff.
31 Ibid., 229.
32 *New York Times*, December 23, 1896. No byline.
33 *New York Times*, December 24, 1896. No byline.
34 Undated newspaper clipping.
35 "Overby." Obituary, *South Bend Tribune*.
36 Robinson 2015, 24.
37 Healy 2009, 6.
38 Robinson 2015, 27ff.
39 Ibid, pp. 44-45.
40 Email correspondence with Bernard Streets, 8–30–17.
41 Ibid.
42 Dated June 1, 1947; signed by Instructor Richard Vander Hagen.
43 Lewis 1998, 27.
44 P. Smith, 1957, 80.
45 Auchmutey 1980, 25.
46 See www.talladega.edu.
47 Obituary, *Chicago Tribune*, June 25, 1979.
48 Young 2008, 97.
49 See www.apa1906.net.
50 Graham 2000, 85.
51 Ibid., 86.
52 Young 2008, 97.
53 Branch 1988, 217.
54 Interview with Fran Smith, 1-17-15.
55 Ibid.
56 P. Smith, 1957, 33.

57 Ibid.
58 Ibid., 58.
59 Ibid., 62–3.
60 Ibid., 71–2.
61 Ibid., 47, 56.
62 Letter from Dr. Raymond Pitts to Paul Smith, February 1958.
63 Branch 1988, 417–18.
64 See www.hartsem.edu.
65 In those days, Hartford Theological Seminary was one of four Schools in the Hartford Seminary Foundation including the Kennedy School of Missions. These have since merged.
66 Newspaper clipping; possibly from the *Hartford Courant.*
67 A holiday said to have been started by the Federal Council of Churches in 1922 and perpetuated by the National Council of Churches into the 1950s. See kingencyclopedia.stanford. edu/encyclopedia/encyclopedia/enc_national_council_of_the_ churches_of_christ_in_america_ncc/
68 New York Urban League journal.
69 Kraus 2000.
70 Probably *South Bend Tribune*, 1960.
71 Auchmutey 1980, 25.
72 Ibid.
73 Branch 1988, 418.
74 Interview with Andrew Young 8–31–16.
75 Ibid.
76 "Ex-Resident Gets Urban League Post," newspaper clipping— probably *South Bend Tribune*, October 1963.
77 Kraus 2000, 24ff.
78 See nul.iamempowered.com/who-we-are/mission-and-history.
79 Interview of Rev. Marvin Chandler by historian Laura Hill, 2009. See www.library.rochester.edu Rochester Black Freedom Struggle Online Project—Marvin Chandler.
80 Interview with Rev. and Mrs. Marvin Chandler, 3–31–16.
81 See http://hirr.hartsem.edu/about/dudley_vitae.htm.
82 Interview with Frances Smith, 2-9-16.

83   Interview with Luther Smith, Jr., 6–22–15.

84   Sweets 1997.

85   Looker 2004.

86   Sweets 1997.

87   Looker 2004, 25.

88   Sweets 1997.

89   N. Dudley, 1979, 17.

90   Ibid.

91   Interview with Kathy Smith Randolph, 4-2-16.

92   N. Dudley, 1979, 15.

93   Interview with Dr. Joanne Nurss, 1–15–15.

94   Looker 2004, 22–23.

95   C. Dudley, 2007.

96   Interview with Nathan Dudley, 1–26–16.

97   Ibid.

98   "The Christian Response to Death." Berea Church Booklet dated Easter 1965.

99   Federal Supply Service Record journal, 4–67.

101 Interview with Rev. Dr. Luther Smith, 6–22–15.

102 1976. "Proud's Platform." Proud, Vol. 7(2): 3.

103 Smith 1976, pp.8.

104 Federal Supply Service Record journal, 4-2-67.

105 Ibid.

106 Sweets 1997.

107 Interview with Rev. Dr. Luther Smith, 6–22–15.

108 Letter from Leonard Smith, Sr. to Paul Smith, 1977.

109 Interview with Kathleen Smith Randolph, 4–2-16.

110 Ibid.

111 Interview with Leonard Wilkens, 9-11-17.

112 Harper & Row, New York.

113 Ibid., 53–4.

114 Ibid., 65.

115 Ibid., 68. Emphasis in the original.

116 Ibid., 69.

117 Ibid., 74.

118 Ibid., 148–149.
119 See www.ilasting.com/johnhoad.php.
120 See www. secondchurch.net/history/history-and-architecture. php.
121 Auchmutey 1980, 25.
122 See www.ulstl.com. 2014 Roadmap To Empowerment. ULStL Annual Report, "Timeline and Milestones."
123 See http://www.presidency.ucsb.edu/index.php Richard Nixon: Eulogy delivered in Lexington Kentucky, March 17, 1971.
124 Graham 2000, 130. Emphasis in the original.
125 "Washington U. Post For the Rev. Paul Smith." Newspaper clipping, possibly from the *St. Louis American.*
126 Ibid.
127 "Overby." Obituary, *South Bend Tribune* (undated newspaper clipping; almost certainly 1975).
128 Atlanta journal "No. 3," 4–9-83.
129 Letter from Rev. Dr. Howard Thurman to Paul Smith, Feb. 18, 1975.
130 L.E. Smith, 2007, 13.
131 L.E. Smith, 2007.
132 Ibid.
133 Luther Smith relates that it may have been seen in his house rather than his briefcase.
134 Thurman 1976, Preface.
135 Thurman 1976, 13.
136 Ibid., 34.
137 Ibid., 41.
138 Ibid.
139 Thurman, 65. Emphasis in the original.
140 Ibid., 72.
141 Ibid., 73.
142 Ibid., 75–76.
143 Ibid., 76.
144 Ibid., 82-83.

145   Ibid., 100–101.

146   Ibid.

147   Thurman, 98.

148   Ibid., 106.

149   L.E. Smith, 2007

150   Ibid., 164, 213.

151   Ibid., 105.

152   Ibid., 85.

153   Ibid., 194.

154   Letter from Dr. Thurman to Rev. Smith, date unreadable.

155   P. Smith, 1977, 29.

156   Smith, P. 1977.

157   Ibid., 49.

158   Ibid., 51.

159   Ibid., 52, Emphasis in the original.

160   Ibid., 31.

161   Ibid., 29.

162   P. Smith, 1977, 70–71.

163   P. Smith, Addendum, 1.

164   Ibid., 2–3.

165   Ibid., 2.

166   Ibid., 1.

167   Ibid., 4.

168   Ibid., 5.

169   Ibid., 5.

170   Ibid., 10–11.

171   Ibid., 7–8.

172   Ibid., 15.

173   "We're Tellin" by Mel and Thel. *St. Louis American,* May 1978.

174   L.E. Smith, 2007, 6.

175   See www.morehouse.edu/about/legacy.html.

176   Ibid.

177   Interview with Howie Hodges II, 4–14–16.

178   Ibid.

179 Ibid.
180 Ibid.
181 Ibid.
182 Ibid.
183 Ibid.
184 Ibid.
185 Ibid.
186 Ibid.
187 Atlanta journal "No. 3," 8–20–79.
188 Demer 1982.
189 Prugh 1979.
190 McInnish 1982.
191 Atlanta journal "No. 3," 8–13–80.
192 Bailey 1979.
193 Atlanta journal "No. 3," 8–13–80.
194 S. Bailey, 1979.
195 (No byline) 1979.
196 Prugh 1979.
197 Auchmutey 1980, 24.
198 Prugh 1979.
199 Ibid.
200 Ibid.
201 Demer 1982.
202 Interview with Joanne Nurss, 1–25–15.
203 Ibid.
204 Ibid.
205 Ibid.
206 https://www.agnesscott.edu.
207 Atlanta journal "No. 3," 3/31/83.
208 Ibid.
209 http://www.nytimes.com/1983/06/11/us/north-south-rift-of-presbyterians-healed-by-merger.html
210 Atlanta journal "No. 1," 6–10–83.
211 Atlanta journal "No. 3,"10–23–83.
212 Ibid., 3–31–83.

213 Atlanta journal "No. 1," 2–1-82.
214 Interview with Mike Trautman, 2–17–16.
215 Interview with Mike Trautman, 4–3-16.
216 Email correspondence with Mike Trautman, 2–9-16.
217 Interview with Mike Trautman, 2–17–16.
218 Ibid.
219 Interview with Mike Trautman, 4–3-16.
220 Interview with Mike Trautman, 4–3-16.
221 Interview with Mike Trautman, 2–17–16.
222 Ibid.
223 Thurman 1980.
224 Thurman 1980.
225 Flyer and invitations of the Howard Thurman Enrichment Circle, Atlanta, Georgia.
226 Letter from Mrs. Leon B. Smith, April 5, 1986.
227 Letter from Doris and Walter Jones, March 25, 1986.
228 Letter from Dan and Dale, April 5, 1986.
229 Atlanta journal "No. 3," 4–10–81.
230 Interview with Andrew Young, 8–13–16.
231 See www.fpcbrooklyn.org/about-us/history.
232 Ibid.
233 Bird 1986.
234 Atlanta journal "No. 3," 10–27–85.
235 Ibid.
236 Bird 1986.
237 Ibid.
238 Ibid.
239 Ibid.
240 Pearl 1986.
241 Installation program, Sunday, Sept. 21, 1986.
242 Ibid.
243 Ibid.
244 Ibid.
245 Interview with Marcia Smith, 6–22–16.
246 Metro Datelines (no byline). "Dalai Lama Receives

Humanitarian Award." *New York Times*. September 30, 1987.
247 Interview with Ellen Oler, 5–23–16.
248 Interview with Mercia Weyand, 6–10–16.
249 Interview with Sam Murumba, 6–22–16.
250 Interview with Marcia Smith, 6–22–16.
251 Interview with Sam Murumba, 6–22–16.
252 Interview with Mercia Weyand, 6–10–16.
253 Solarz and Owens were long-time Congressmen from Brooklyn; Rev. Sherrill and Rabbi Brinker led congregations in the neighborhood. The National Committee for a Sane Nuclear Policy (SANE) was an organization that lobbied for nuclear disarmament.
254 Ibid.
255 Interview with Charles Clayman, 1–29–16.
256 Ibid.
257 Ibid.
258 Ibid.
259 Ibid.
260 Ibid.
261 Interview with Nathan Dudley, 1–26–16.
262 Ibid.
263 Interview with Jim Johnson, 11–23–15.
264 Ibid.
265 Interview with Fred Davie, 5–20–15.
266 Ibid.
267 Ibid.
268 Ibid.
269 Ibid.
270 https://www.pcusa.org/news/2015/3/20/what-same-sex-marriage-means-presbyterians/
271 Murumba 2006.
272 Interview with Sam Murumba, 6–22–16.
273 Large First Church journal.
274 Interview with Marcia Smith, 6–22–16.
275 Ibid.

276   Interview with Amy Neuner, 6–21–16.
277   Transcript of address to First Church by Janet Dewart Bell, 2006. Used with permission.
278   Ibid.
279   Ibid.
280   Ibid.
281   Interview with Sam Murumba, 6–22–16.
282   Ibid.
283   Interview with Andrew Young, 8–31–16.
284   Ghost Ranch journal, 8-7-91.
285   Interview with Krista Clapp, 3–20–16.
286   Interview with Sam Murumba, 6–22–16.
287   Ibid.
288   Powers 2000.
289   Interview with Amy Neuner, 6–21–16.
290   Email correspondence with Amy Neuner, 6–28–16.
291   Interview with Amy Neuner, 6–21–16.
292   Ibid.
293   Ibid.
294   Ibid.
295   Interview with Sam Murumba, 6–22–16.
296   Ibid. Jim Johnson was the quiet benefactor who made it possible for First Church to purchase its African American hymnals.
297   Interview with Jim Johnson, 11–23–15.
298   See www.professorderrickbell.com.
299   Interview with Sue Carlson, 7-5-16.
300   Interview with Ellen Oler, 5–23–16.
301   Interview with Sam Murumba, 6–22–16.
302   Interview with Mercia Weyand, 6–10–16.
303   Interview with Ellen Oler, 5–23–16.
304   Interview with Sam Murumba, 6–22–16.
305   Norsen 2000.
306   Ibid., 17.
307   E.g., Catholic cable channel TV show called "In

Conversation: Tolerance Plus." Telecare—Channel 25
program #011.
308 Letter from Mike and Maria Avram, Jan. 19, 1999.
309 Interview with Mercia Weyand, 6–10–16.
310 Ibid.
311 Interview with Sue Carlson, 7-5-16.
312 Ibid.
313 Ghost Ranch journal, 6–25–91.
314 Ibid.
315 Ibid.
316 Interview with Marvin Chandler, 3–31–16.
317 Interview with Marvin Chandler, 8–17–14.
318 Ibid.
319 Ibid.
320 Ibid.
321 Ibid.

322 Interview with Paul Smith, 2–11–16.
323 Smith and Hutchinson 1999.
324 Ibid.
325 Email correspondence with David Lewicki, 2–3-15.
326 See http://investors.macysinc.com/phoenix.
       zhtml?c=84477&p=irol-reportsannual
327 Singer 2014.
328 Email correspondence with Edward Goldberg, 8–1-16.
329 Interview with Edward Goldberg, 6–15–16.
330 Email correspondence with Ed Goldberg, 8–1-16.
331 Interview with Edward Goldberg, 9–16–15.
332 Email correspondence with Edward Goldberg, 8–1-16.
333 Interview with Edward Goldberg, 9–16–15
334 Email correspondence with Edward Goldberg, 8–1-16.
335 Interview with Edward Goldberg, 9–16–15.
336 Halla 1998.
337 See www.talladega.edu/amistadmurals/
338 Elliott 2005; Feuer 2014.

339   Singer 2014.
340   Interview with Edward Goldberg, 6–15–16.
341   Christman and Mark 2104.
342   Elliott 2005.
343   Ibid.
344   Ibid.
345   Email correspondence with Ed Goldberg, 8-1-16.
346   Ibid.
347   Interview with Jeffrey Smith, 6–14–16.
348   Ibid.
349   Ibid.
350   Ibid.
351   Ibid.
352   Ibid.
353   Interview with Jeffrey Smith, 6–14–16.
354   Interview with Marc Burt, 1–25–15.
355   Ibid.
356   Ibid.
357   Ibid.
358   See www.hcasc.com/index.asp
359   See www.hondabattleofthebands.com/invitational-showcase
360   Email correspondence with Pamela Champion, February 2015.
361   See www.arthurashe.or www.arthurashe.org/life-story.html.
362   Ashe and Rampersad 1993, 321.
363   Ibid., 320.
364   First Church journal "#15," 4–16–89.
365   Ibid., 4–17–89.
366   Ibid., 311.
367   Ibid., pp. 302. Photo of Dr. Smith, Dr. Luther Clark and Jeanne Moutoussamy at an Institute fundraiser in *Jet*, 85(8): 39. December. 20, 1993.
368   See www.arthurasheinstitute.org
369   See www.brooklynbridgepark.org/pages/history
370   Hartocollis 2013.

371 Frost 2014.

372 Interview with Charles Clayman, 1–29–16.

373 Ibid.

374 Ibid.

375 Norsen 2005.

376 "Celebrating the Ministry of Rev. Dr. Paul Smith." First Presbyterian Church of Brooklyn program.

377 Letter from Rev. David Dyson to Paul Smith, May 31, 2006.

378 Elliott 2007.

379 Interview with Necole Brown, 8-4-16.

380 Elliott 2007.

381 Brown et al. 2010.

382 Interview with Necole Brown, 8-4-16.

383 http://kff.org/hivaids/fact-sheet/black-americans-and-hiv-aids/

384 Interview with Necole Brown, 8-4-16.

385 www.usda.gov/wps/portal/usda/usdahome?contentidonly=true&contentid=bio-mensah.xml Retrieved Sept. 17, 2016.

386 Interview with Jim Johnson 11–23–15.

387 Ibid.

388 Ibid.

389 Ibid.

390 Ibid.

391 Ibid.

392 Ibid.

393 Ibid.

394 Interview with John Utendahl, 8–3-16.

395 Ibid.

396 Ibid.

397 Interview with Marsha Larner, 2–2-16.

398 First Church journal "#15," 3–17–89.

399 First Church journal "#15," 5-3-89.

400 New York Urban League journal, 6–28–13.

401 Smith 2014, "Something … "

402 Smith 2014, "I'm Back … "

403   www.nytimes.com/interactive/2014/08/13/us/ferguson-missouri-town-under-siege-after-police-shooting.html Updated Aug. 10, 2015. Retrieved July 11, 2016.

404   Ibid.

405   Ibid.

406   Francis 2015.

407   Ibid.

408   Ibid.

409   Smith 2014, "In Search …"

410   Ibid.

411   Interview with Mike Trautman, 2–17–16.

412   Smith 2014, "The Need … "

413   Email correspondence from Mike Trautman to Paul Smith, September 28, 2014.

414   Email correspondence from Paul Smith to Mike Trautman, September 29, 2014.

415   Francis 2015.

416   Interview with Mike Trautman, 2–17–16.

417   Quoted in Chu 2014.

418   Interview with Mike Trautman, 4–3-16.

419   Leslie Scanlon, 2014.

420   Ibid.

421   Ibid.

422   Francis 2015, 94.

423   DOJ Report 2015, 6.

424   Ibid.

425   Robles 2016.

426   Interview with Mike Trautman, 2–17–16.

427   Bogan, Hollinshed and Deere 2014.

428   Ibid.

429   Ibid.

430   Bogan and Moskop 2014.

431   Hill 2016.

432   Ibid., pp. 28.

433   Rector 2016.

434 Smith 2015, "When Your Cup … "
435 Ibid.
436 Ibid.
437 Ibid.
438 Rev. Dr. Calvin Butts of the Abyssinian Baptist Church in
     New York City.
439 Ibid.
440 Song by Rev. Nolan Williams, 2016.
441 Dyson 2017.
442 Ibid., 44.
443 Ibid., 104.
444 Ibid., 212.
445 Ibid., 222.
446 Ibid., 223.
447 Waldon, Jr. 2000, 64.
448 Paul Smith at First Presbyterian Church in Brooklyn. Quoted
     by parishioner Reeves Carter in Aplin 2006.
449 Young 2016.
450 Atlanta journal "No. 3," 2–6-83.
451 Holley 2016.
452 Sapong 2016.
453 E. Smith, 2011.
454 Sapong 2016.
455 P. Smith, 1998, 1.
456 Ibid., 33.
457 Ibid., 8.
458 Ibid.
459 Ibid., 2–3.
460 Ibid., 33.
461 Ibid., 52.
462 Ibid., 133–4.
463 Ashe and Rampersad 1993, 320.
464 Ibid., 311.
465 P. Smith, 1998, 138.
466 Rivers 2010.

467 Ibid.

468 Ibid.

469 Symposium held at Riverside Church in 2005; Smith, P. Malik and Wright 2007.

470 P. Smith, 2016.

471 See www.compassionandchoices.org

472 Span 2017.

473 Email correspondence, Paul Smith with a fraternity brother, August 1, 2014.

474 Thurman 1975, 3.

475 L. Smith, Jr., 2006.

476 Ibid.

477 Thurman 1975. Second Essay, "The Negro Spiritual Speaks of Life and Death," 13–14.

478 Ibid., 14–15.

479 Ibid., 18.

480 Ibid., 19.

481 Ibid., 19–20.

482 Ibid., 15–16.

483 Ibid., 37–8.

484 Ibid., 17.

485 L. Smith, Jr. 1991, 73.

486 Interview with Marvin Chandler, 8–17–14.

487 L. Smith, Jr. 1991, 87.

488 Ibid., 122.

489 Ibid., 107.

490 Ibid., 113–14.

491 Ibid., 188, 190.

492 Ibid., 190.

493 Ibid., 193.

494 Ibid., 194.

495 Ibid., 213–14.

496 Interview with Luther Smith, Jr., 6–22–15.

497 Atlanta journal "No. 3," 4/9/81.

498 P. Smith, 1998, 136–7.

499 Transcription by Joyce Sloan.

500 Interview with Mike Trautman, 2–17–16.

501 Katz 2016.

502 Transcription of recording made at Cobble Hill Health Center gala, Nov. 17, 2016.

503 Ibid.

504 Ibid.

505 Ibid.

506 Ibid.

507 New York Urban League journal, 6–4-13.

54915707R00197

Made in the USA
Middletown, DE
07 December 2017